Singapore

Singapore is a paradox. On the surface it is a free-trade capitalist economy, yet for its citizens and some visitors it is one of the most intensely policed and closely controlled countries in the world. This book examines Singapore's culture of control, exploring the city-state's colonial heritage as well as the forces that have helped to mould its current social landscape.

Singapore is a country that has, in 40 years, progressed from colonial status to become one of Asia's economic powerhouses. Taking a comparative approach, Carl Trocki demonstrates the links between Singapore's colonial past and independent present, focusing on the development of indigenous social and political movements. In particular, the book examines the efforts of Lee Kuan Yew, leader of the People's Action Party from 1959 until 1990, to produce major economic and social transformation. Trocki discusses how Singapore became a workers' paradise, but what the city gained in material advancement it paid for in intellectual and cultural sterility.

Based on the latest research, the book addresses the question of control in one of the most prosperous and dynamic economies in the world. *Singapore: wealth, power and the culture of control* provides a compelling history of post-colonial Singapore and will appeal to those interested in Asian political culture, Asian history and economic development.

Carl A. Trocki is Professor of Asian Studies in the School of Humanities and Human Services at the Queensland University of Technology in Brisbane, Australia. He has published on Singapore, Malaysia, Thailand, the Chinese diaspora and the drug trade in Asia.

Asia's Transformations

Edited by Mark Selden

Binghamton and Cornell Universities, USA

The books in this series explore the political, social, economic, and cultural consequences of Asia's transformations in the twentieth and twenty-first centuries. The series emphasizes the tumultuous interplay of local, national, regional, and global forces as Asia bids to become the hub of the world economy. While focusing on the contemporary, it also looks back to analyse the antecedents of Asia's contested rise. This series comprises several strands:

Asia's Transformations aims to address the needs of students and teachers, and the titles will be published in hardback and paperback. Titles include:

Debating Human Rights
Critical essays from the United States and Asia
Edited by Peter Van Ness

Hong Kong's History
State and society under colonial rule
Edited by Tak-Wing Ngo

Japan's Comfort Women
Sexual slavery and prostitution during World War II and the US occupation
Yuki Tanaka

Opium, Empire and the Global Political Economy
Carl A Trocki

Chinese Society
Change, conflict and resistance
Edited by Elizabeth J Perry and Mark Selden

Mao's Children in the New China
Voices from the Red Guard generation
Yarong Jiang and David Ashley

Remaking the Chinese State
Strategies, society and security
Edited by Chien-min Chao and Bruce J Dickson

Korean Society
Civil society, democracy and the state
Edited by Charles K Armstrong

The Making of Modern Korea
Adrian Buzo

The Resurgence of East Asia
500, 150 and 50 year perspectives
Edited by Giovanni Arrighi, Takeshi Hamashita and Mark Selden

Chinese Society, 2nd edition
Change, conflict and resistance
Edited by Elizabeth J Perry and Mark Selden

Ethnicity in Asia
Edited by Colin Mackerras

The Battle for Asia
From decolonization to globalization
Mark T. Berger

State and Society in 21st Century China
Edited by Peter Hays Gries and Stanley Rosen

Japan's Quiet Transformation
Social change and civil society in the 21st century
Jeff Kingston

Confronting the Bush Doctrine
Critical views from the Asia-Pacific
Edited by Mel Gurtov and Peter Van Ness

China in War and Revolution, 1895–1949
Peter Zarrow

Asia's Great Cities
Each volume aims to capture the heartbeat of the contemporary city from multiple perspectives emblematic of the authors own deep familiarity with the distinctive faces of the city, its history, society, culture, politics and economics, and its evolving position in national, regional and global frameworks. While most volumes emphasize urban developments since the Second World War, some pay close attention to the legacy of the longue durée in shaping the contemporary. Thematic and comparative volumes address such themes as urbanization, economic and financial linkages, architecture and space, wealth and power, gendered relationships, planning and anarchy, and ethnographies in national and regional perspective. Titles include:

Bangkok
Place, practice and representation
Marc Askew

Beijing in the Modern World
David Strand and Madeline Yue Dong

Shanghai
Global city
Jeff Wasserstrom

Hong Kong
Global city
Stephen Chiu and Tai-Lok Lui

Representing Calcutta
Modernity, nationalism and the colonial uncanny
Swati Chattopadhyay

Singapore
Wealth, power and the culture of control
Carl A. Trocki

Asia.com is a series which focuses on the ways in which new information and communication technologies are influencing politics, society, and culture in Asia. Titles include:

Japanese Cybercultures
Edited by Mark McLelland and Nanette Gottlieb

Asia.com
Asia encounters the internet
Edited by K. C. Ho, Randolph Kluver and Kenneth C. C. Yang

The Internet in Indonesia's New Democracy
David T. Hill & Krishna Sen

Literature and Society is a series that seeks to demonstrate the ways in which Asian Literature is influenced by the politics, society and culture in which it is produced. Titles include:

The Body in Postwar Japanese Fiction
Edited by Douglas N Slaymaker

Chinese Women Writers and the Feminist Imagination, 1905–1948
Haiping Yan

Routledge Studies in Asia's Transformations is a forum for innovative new research intended for a high-level specialist readership, and the titles will normally be available in hardback only. Titles include:

Critical Asian Scholarship is a series intended to showcase the most important individual contributions to scholarship in Asian Studies. Each of the volumes presents a leading Asian scholar addressing themes that are central to his or her most significant and lasting contribution to Asian studies. The series is committed to the rich variety of research and writing on Asia, and is not restricted to any particular discipline, theoretical approach or geographical expertise. Titles include:

Singapore

Wealth, power and the culture of control

Carl A. Trocki

Routledge
Taylor & Francis Group

LONDON AND NEW YORK

First published 2006
by Routledge
2 Park Square, Milton Park, Abingdon, Oxon, OX14 4RN

Simultaneously published in the USA and Canada
by Routledge
270 Madison Ave, New York, NY 10016

Routledge is an imprint of the Taylor & Francis Group

Typeset in Times New Roman by Taylor & Francis Books
Printed and bound in Great Britain by
The Cromwell Press, Trowbridge, Wiltshire

British Library Cataloguing in Publication Data
A catalogue record for this book is available from the British Library

Library of Congress Cataloging in Publication Data
Trocki, Carl A.
  Singapore : wealth, power, and the culture of control / by Carl A.
Trocki.
      p. cm. -- (Asia's transformations) (Asia's great cities)
  Includes bibliographical references and index.
  ISBN 0-415-26385-9 (hardback : alk. paper) -- ISBN 0-415-26386-7
(pbk. : alk. paper) 1. Singapore--Politics and government. 2.
Singapore--Economic conditions. 3. Social control--Singapore. I.
Title. II. Series. III. Series: Asia's great cities
  DS610.6.T76 2005
  959.5705--dc22
                                    2005003172

ISBN 0–415–26385–9 (hbk)
ISBN 0–415–26386–7 (pbk)

Taylor & Francis Group is the Academic Division of T&F Informa plc.

Contents

List of illustrations

Figures

All figures (except 4.2, 5.2 and 5.3) are by permission of the Syndics of the Cambridge University Library

Tables

Acknowledgements

This book is the result of a great deal of assistance and tolerance from many quarters, not the least of which is my family: my wife, children and grand-children have all suffered some degree of neglect while I attempted to research and write this book. I am also grateful for the generous support from the Queensland University of Technology, which provided me with a number of research awards toward the promise of this book, as well as the material support without which no work of this kind can be undertaken.

My many friends in Singapore, whose advice, comments, assistance and hospitality were invaluable aids to this effort, are owed a debt of particular thanks. I am grateful to the History Department of the National University of Singapore, which sponsored many research trips to Singapore and also provided me with material support and a forum for my ideas. Likewise the Institute of Southeast Asian Studies in Singapore was especially helpful in permitting me to use its library. I am grateful for the support and assistance of Ms Chng Kim See and Datin Patricia Lim Pui Huen, the latter not only for assistance at ISEAS but also for her friendship and many other kindnesses.

I must also acknowledge my debt to the National Library of Singapore and the library of the National University of Singapore. I have also made use of the US National Archives, the Library of Congress, the Library of the School of Oriental and African Studies, University of London, the Cambridge University Library, the National Library of Australia, and the Chiffley and Menzies Libraries at the Australian National University.

I am also grateful to Benedict Anderson and Mark Selden, who read portions of the text and offered helpful comments. They saved me from many errors, but I am responsible for what has finally appeared here. I am doubly grateful to Mark, who encouraged me to write this in the first place and who patiently waited while I did a number of other things before turning to this task.

Carl A. Trocki
Brisbane

Weights, measures and currencies

For the nineteenth century, the general currency in circulation was the Spanish dollar, which was the mother of all the other dollars and pesos that we have today. All references to dollars and currencies designated as $ for the nineteenth century are Spanish and later Mexican dollars. In the twentieth century, their place was taken by the Straits dollar, then by the Singapore dollar and the Malaysian ringgit. The dollar sign must be understood in its temporal context.

Pikuls and tahils refer to the Malay terms for Chinese measures of weight. These too were commonly used in the trading world of the nineteenth century. A pikul was 133⅓ pounds (about 60 kg) and was composed of 100 catties of 1⅓ pounds (about 600 g) , each of which was divided into 16 tahils, or in terms of precious metals and opium, "taels," which are 1⅓ ounces or 37.5 g.

Introduction

Singapore was my first experience of a tropical Asian city. I first arrived there in December 1964, and, like others, I was really on my way to somewhere else. I don't remember much about that first visit. I think I was struck most by the smells. In those days, Singapore smelled like a tropical city. It doesn't anymore. The city had a distinctly seedy appearance: old cream-colored shophouses crumbling slowly away, walls stained with tropical mildew and smoke from charcoal cooking fires. Some shops sold everything from toothpaste to used tires, while others were located in streets with scores of other shops selling exactly the same things. Aside from basic repairs and a minimal amount of rebuilding, not much seemed to have changed since the war – not that I was in a position to know this at the time.

There was an atmosphere of tension in the air. Singapore was still a part of Malaysia, but within less than a year it would be out. Already, the difficulties in that relationship were becoming clear, and future prospects seemed uncertain. Unemployment was high. The labor unions, student unions and intellectuals had, although I did not realize it at the time, recently suffered several rounds of intimidation and arrests by the government. However, the Left had not yet been defeated, and the sense of resentment and suspicion was palpable.

Perhaps I was sensing that first whiff of post-colonialism. The city lacked a sense of direction and a clear sense of identity. There was a vague sullenness in the air toward Europeans, and toward the government of Lee Kuan Yew. The colonial era was over, but the new world had not replaced it. Even the once genteel areas of the city were looking a bit run down. The Raffles Hotel was badly in need of remodeling and repair and had no air-conditioning. Freedom had brought only poverty and a deeper sense of disappointment. The Chinese masses, fed up with both Malaysia and the Lee Kuan Yew government, watched hopelessly as what remained of the left-wing leadership slowly self-destructed – with a helping hand now and then from the police and the ruling party. My last memory of the place, as I left it for that first time forty years ago, was of serried rows of red-tile-roofed Chinese shophouses interspersed with the deep tropical green of rain trees and mangroves as they flashed through holes in the clouds while our 707 banked over the city from Paya Lebar and headed out across the South China Sea.

I was happy to leave Singapore then after those few days and looked forward to my new life as a Peace Corps volunteer in Sabah. There, colonialism had just ended with an abrupt halt, and very little of the social upheaval, impatience and greed that would soon surface had yet shown itself. The towns were small, and the jungle was still beautiful and largely uncut. The beaches were clean and the water crystal clear, and the people were glad to see us. It hardly seemed to have changed since Agnes Keith wrote about it a quarter of a century earlier (Keith 1949). Unlike many other Peace Corps volunteers in those days, who often found themselves in hardship posts, we had been airlifted into paradise, and even though I was in my mid-twenties, I was still a child as far as Asia was concerned.

During the next decade, I grew up and learned about Southeast Asia and about China and came to understand something about imperialism and the struggles for independence and economic development among the people of the region. Between Sabah, Hong Kong, Bangkok, Johor and Ithaca, I repeatedly found myself in Singapore, either just passing through or getting stuck there for longer than I liked. Likewise, my research, which started out exploring Johor, kept dragging me back to Singapore. Even though my first book was about Johor and its Malay rulers, half was still about Singapore (Trocki 1979).

By the end of the 1970s, I began to understand Singapore a little better, or so I thought. I came to see it as a part of Southeast Asia that functioned as an important center for the political and economic life of the Malay world around it. I came to see Singapore as much the successor of the Malay *entrepôts* of the Straits as it was the brilliant innovation of Thomas Stamford Raffles. It was intimately linked to Johor, Riau, Sumatra, Borneo, Siam and the Indonesian archipelago. It was these continuing connections between Singapore and its surroundings that drew my attention. After all, one cannot cross the causeway from Woodlands to Johor Bahru on a regular basis without realizing that tens of thousands of Singaporeans and Malaysians cross there every day, and that thousands of tons of goods move likewise. The two countries are still intimately linked.

There are a number of problems one encounters in writing the history of Singapore. The first set relates to the essential diversity of the island's population. The British, the Chinese, the Malays, the Indians and all the others really seem to have separate historical paths. Although they intersected in Singapore during the nineteenth century, they separated in the early part of the twentieth, and while some of them re-converged later, some seem to have separated entirely.

For instance, the British administrative community, and the mercantile society that they came to serve as their main local constituency, had a well-developed sense of identity from the very beginning. As a result, the sources of its history and the shape of its narrative are already quite well developed, so much so that one might assume that it is the only narrative worth discussing. British Singapore loomed large until 1942, but then it virtually disappeared, and the history of Asian Singapore began. We need to understand the reasons for this disjuncture. Did a whole new set of people suddenly arrive with a new set of aims and priorities? It often appears that way. Part of the difficulty is in the sources and the way in which they have been used.

There is a wealth of documentation for the nineteenth century, including the considerable collections of British colonial records, both the Straits Settlements records from the India Office and the Colonial Office records, and there are English-language newspaper collections and a wealth of personal accounts of European life in Singapore.

Nothing of a comparable nature exists for the rest of Singapore's diverse peoples. In fact, the history of the rest, the majority of Singapore's societies, must often be largely written from these English-language sources. The British wrote about themselves, about their projects, their agendas and their plans. They described the world around them and offered their contemporaries and the historical audience their version of it. Much of what they reported seems fairly accurate, and much of it can be verified by a number of authorities, but there remain blind spots, and no matter how accurate, European voices are simply not Asian voices.

Much of the discourse changes in the postwar period, when the Asians take over the country. Asian voices become louder and take on a new authority. However, it is important to understand that the Asians were there all along and that the British involvement did not simply cease when the Japanese walked in. As a historian, I have always been interested in continuities. The past is not a blank canvas but complicated terrain that influences how we make the future.

I think I began to understand Singapore in a way that others had somehow missed when I looked at it from Johor. The accounts of Raffles, the British East India Company, free trade and the British governors of Singapore – topics that populate the books of Mary Turnbull (Turnbull 1989) and many other European and American writers – while important, did not satisfy me or resonate with the Singapore I knew. I was more interested in the Chinese *taukehs* who populated Song Ong Siang's *One Hundred Years' History of the Chinese in Singapore* (Song 1923). I became fascinated by Singapore's pivotal position in the Asian opium trade in the nineteenth century, and that became the topic of my second book (Trocki 1990).

Along with the wealthy opium farmers of Singapore, I came to see their connections to the vast populations of Chinese coolies that flowed through Singapore, a river of muscle and bone, most of which was ending up as part of the voracious Malayan rainforests. It struck me that the struggles between secret societies, between opium farmers and the conflicts between British rulers and the people they attempted to govern needed to be understood in a different way. Their conflicts were not simply the "old grudge brought from China" – the irrational fractiousness of "inscrutable Orientals" who had to be pacified by noble, disinterested Englishmen seeking only peaceful trade. Rather, I came to see that the conflicts were rooted in the economy and society created by colonialism.

I became convinced that these violent upheavals constituted a kind of class conflict between rich and poor, between the haves and have-nots. On the one side were the thousands of Chinese coolies whose labor would produce wealth, but who themselves in most cases would die in the mud, spending their last pennies on a puff of opium. On the other, there were the wealthy Chinese traders and merchants who managed the coolie trade, sold them opium and dealt in the goods they produced – tin, pepper, gambier, sugar, tapioca, etc. Their riches depended on a strategic alliance with the European rulers and the European merchants of Singapore, who likewise depended on the profits gained from opium sales to the coolies. They constituted what Lee Poh Ping has called the "free-trade society" (Lee 1978).

The coolies and lower classes of Singapore, who found solidarity in their *kongsis* and secret societies, made up what Lee called the "pepper and gambier society." They were laborers and smaller shopkeepers, mostly Teochew, bound together by oaths of sworn brotherhood and who inhabited the urban fringes and rural areas of Singapore. The societies flourished in the 1840s and 1850s, but gradually their leaders chose to join the wealthy Baba and Hokkien traders in the town and used their secret society muscle to gain a share of the opium farms for themselves. The *kongsis* were thus transformed from egalitarian brotherhoods into hierarchical secret societies run by the wealthy and powerful to oppress the workers. This was but a step on their way to becoming criminal gangs of extortionists and smugglers.

In time, the pepper and gambier frontier exhausted Singapore's land and forests and moved on to Johor and elsewhere. Plantation labor and the site of their conflict with colonial capitalism also moved. Singapore's Chinese society changed and came under the domination of *taukehs* who controlled the *huiguan* and the *pang* organizations. The coolie masses did not disappear but continued to arrive in increasing numbers until the 1930s. Some passed through on their way to Sumatra, the Malay states or elsewhere. Some returned on their way home to China. Some managed to stay in Singapore. Some became rich, but most did not. The Chinese masses became diversified according to dialect and occupation. They served as dock workers, coal heavers, rickshaw pullers, street vendors, craftsmen and water-carriers – skilled and unskilled laborers undertaking the myriad tasks of a thriving port city. While the elite sought to compete in the broader framework of the empire, the lower classes populated the slums of Chinatown and were thankful that they were not in Sumatra.

Class struggle did not end there but resurfaced, becoming a more and more insistent theme through the early twentieth century even as the actors, the ideologies and the balance of forces shifted. The rise of Chinese nationalism and later of communism both motivated the Chinese of Singapore and at the same time divided them from the other races in the Malay world. Class conflict spawned ethnic conflict. The Japanese occupation swept away the structures and legitimacy of imperial hegemony and brought the fundamental social conflicts into sharp contrast. Postwar Singapore was a time of intellectual, political and social ferment. Driven by the prospect of independence and social change, the struggle took the form of a multidimensional confrontation between the English-educated and the Chinese-educated for leadership in the post-colonial order. It pitted Malays against Chinese, rich against poor, and reactionaries against reformers against revolutionaries. The conflict was not limited to the territory of Singapore but also involved the European colonial powers, Malaya and Indonesia.

The conflict had barely been resolved when I arrived in Singapore. Lee Kuan Yew and the People's Action Party (PAP) regime had destroyed the left-wing leadership and succeeded in taking control from the British. It only remained for them to separate from Malaysia to achieve full independence and to settle differences with Indonesia. However, the task of economic reform lay ahead, with the creation of a new political economy that would ally the Chinese rulers of Singapore with international capital and provide them with the means to subdue the Chinese working classes once again. At the same time, however, it would give those Chinese a new country and a livelihood that would make Singapore, for a time at least, the most prosperous city in Southeast Asia, and it would provide opportunities for a better life.

In fact, within a decade after I first set foot in Singapore, the major social and economic transformation had occurred, and it was largely due to the strategies and efforts of Lee and his close group of associates that ran the PAP. They had done a paradoxical thing. They had allied with international capitalism to create a workers' paradise. The slums were gone, the streets were clean, crime had been greatly reduced, and the people had jobs and regular incomes. There was affordable and utilitarian housing for all, free public education, affordable medical care and a major improvement in basic security.

There were costs. Freedom of speech and expression had ceased to exist. The government controlled most forms of communication and had created an intensive system of surveillance. Opposition and dissent were forbidden, and even mild, constructive criticism was met with harsh reprisals. Government propaganda, hectoring and improvement campaigns became as intrusive and banal as in Maoist China or American TV advertising. The magazines, newspapers and journals that had flourished during the 1950s and 1960s, particularly the Chinese-language publications, were gone. Singapore's once-vibrant civil society had ceased to exist as even the mundane *huiguan*, the regional and dialect and occupational groups that flourished wherever Chinese settled, had been ruthlessly brought to heel. Their management and patronage of Chinese education and culture had been severely curtailed, and their sources of wealth and influence appropriated by government. What the city gained in material advancement it seemed to have paid for in intellectual and cultural sterility.

For the past forty years, I have been working in Singapore, writing about its history and thinking about its social and political development. While I have lived and worked in Lee Kuan Yew's Singapore, I have never really written about it. As a historian, I was interested in the past, and I was interested in reconstructing a past that had been neglected or misunderstood. Like James Warren, I believed that there was another version of the past than that which we had been given. His work on prostitutes and rickshaw coolies constituted an important breakthrough in the study of Singapore's past (Warren 1986, 1993). His version of history from the bottom up added additional pieces to the picture, but I still struggled with the task of how to fit them with the others.

Since finishing my book on Singapore's opium farmers (Trocki 1990), I had wanted to write this history of Singapore, but I did not know then how to connect the past of pirates, opium farmers, agency houses, coolies, and pepper and gambier with the present "clean, green" Singapore of Lee Kuan Yew, Housing Development Board flats, electronics industries and skyscrapers. I could intuit that Lee himself would have preferred that I did not. After all, he began his administration by pronouncing that history, in the form of class struggle and inter-party competition, was abolished. For him, the history of Asian Singapore had no relevance. However, I believed that the conflicts that had reverberated throughout the nineteenth and twentieth centuries have surfaced since independence. These have persisted despite the pacification of society that has come to characterize Singapore at the beginning of the twenty-first century. I have tried to draw my parallels along these fault lines. I hope they make sense to my readers and contribute to an understanding of the overall sweep of Singapore's history. As Karl Marx pointed out, we make our own history, but not as we like.

I would like to say a word about the format of this book. Aside from the introductory and concluding chapters, the body of this book is symmetrically divided into six paired chapters. The first three deal with the colonial era, essentially from 1819 (and a little before that) to 1945. The first chapter treats economics, the second society and the third politics. The second three chapters deal with the same topics but in reverse order for the years since World War II.

This is not merely a self-indulgent attempt at some sort of symbolic balance. Rather, it has to do with the manner in which I see Singapore's history unfolding. Singapore was founded for economic reasons. As Bill Clinton said of another epoch and another place: "It's the economy, stupid." And I accepted that. Society came next, in my mind, because social formations were determined by the economy, and ultimately society structured what passed for politics in the colonial era.

However, politics has always been in command in post-colonial Singapore. Thus it made sense to put that chapter before the others. It also makes possible the presentation of the general sweep of Singapore's political history in two consecutive chapters that occupy the center of the book. For the placement of Chapters 5 and 6, my thinking may seem a bit arbitrary. Why should social history precede economic history, especially when the economic system probably had more to do with shaping society than the other way around? Nevertheless, there was the question of the pattern and of symmetry, but beyond that, it struck me that the economy needed to have the last word. It often does. Singapore's future will depend on the economy. I hope that explains the structure.

My friend and mentor, Ben Anderson, has never tired of reminding me how incredibly boring he finds Singapore. Perhaps he and other readers will find this account more engaging and perhaps instructive. Singapore is a small place, and it may not be very important in the general sweep of global history. On the other hand, it may be seen as an interesting social experiment. Its successes and failures may provide examples for other developing, and even developed, countries. Beyond that, it ought to be important to the people who live there, many of whom are now beginning to write, or rewrite, their own history. I hope it will not be long before they can improve upon what I have written here.

1 The development of Singapore's colonial economy

There was more to the foundation of the British colony of Singapore in 1819 than a stroke of brilliance by Thomas Stamford Raffles, who is usually credited with the creation of the city. We are occasionally apt to forget that the city is located in Asia and is largely populated by Asians. At the time, it was also a vital part of the Asian maritime economy and should be seen as the heir of a long line of Asian maritime trading centers located in or near the Straits of Melaka. Singapore's history, properly understood, can be traced back to the Malay *entrepôts* of Srivijaya and Melaka. Moreover, it is clear from recent archaeological work that the island itself was the site of an *entrepôt* that flourished as early as the fourteenth century (Miksic 1985). Between then and the nineteenth century, there was always an important Malay *entrepôt* in the immediate vicinity. Whether at Riau, on the island of Bentan, on the Johor River or at Melaka itself, this part of the Straits was an area of vibrant economic activity.

Nineteenth-century Singapore played a number of roles: some traditional, some innovative. Much that has been written about the city has stressed its innovative aspects, often to the extent of exaggerating their importance. John Crawfurd, who was the Resident Councillor (then the chief administrative officer) of the colony from 1824 to 1827, emphasized the British role in the success of the colony: "Few as the British settlers of Singapore are [there were only eighty-seven resident Europeans in 1827], they constitute in reality the life and the spirit of the settlement; and it may be safely asserted, that without them, and without their existing state of independence and security, there would not exist either capital, enterprise, activity, confidence or order" (Crawfurd 1987: 553). While there is some justification for Crawfurd's boast, it does not fully explain the colony's early or continuing success. After all, there had been a number of attempts at founding British settlements in Southeast Asia during the late eighteenth century, and most of them were dismal, if not disastrous, failures.[1] Even Penang had never fulfilled its original promise.

Singapore's success owed much to its location, and because of this, it filled many of the roles played by the earlier Malay *entrepôts*. It drew together the east–west trade between China and India and points further west. It also acted as a gathering point for the products of Southeast Asia: the sea products of the islands and the coasts, and the rice, pepper, spices, forest produce, tin and gold of the inland areas. These commodities, many of them unique to tropical Asia, found markets throughout the world. From age to age, a port had arisen in this part of the Malay world. Whether located on what O.W. Wolters called the "favored coast" of eastern Sumatra or on the Malayan peninsula, or in the Riau–Lingga Archipelago, it serviced the trade and produced wealth, power and culture for its overlords. It was the city "below the wind" or *di-bawah angin*: the city at the end of the monsoons and the beginning of others, as Tome Pires called Melaka (Cortesão 1944). In the past, such cities had been dominated by Malay rulers and the maritime peoples of the region. In the nineteenth century, even though it was under British rule, Singapore shared fully in the trans-Asian, maritime trading culture that had a heritage of over fifteen centuries.

Singapore also partook of the heritage of another type of city. Since the sixteenth century, a new type of port had also arisen: these were the colonial castle towns of Melaka, Manila and Batavia. These were centers for the concentration of European power, bases for navies and imperial expansion. Their superior firepower and fortifications guaranteed a level of security for European activities that would have been impossible in other ports.[2] In particular, European companies and traders could amass wealth and dispose of capital on their own terms.

Even though Singapore had aspects of both types, there were key differences. For Raffles, Singapore was to be a refutation of the policies of monopoly, trade restriction and territorial expansion that he saw practised by the Dutch and Spanish. His focus was on free trade and the avoidance of territorial governance. Despite sporadic attempts at constructing fortifications, Singapore has never had a castle. In the stress on free trade, Singapore was more like its immediate predecessor, the nearby port of Riau. In fact, if we look more closely at eighteenth-century Riau, it may be argued that Riau was the real predecessor, bringing not only the traditions of the Malay port-polity but also a complex of Asian trading patterns and networks that had been newly established during the eighteenth century.

What was Riau? The eighteenth-century predecessor of Singapore was the Malay/Bugis center of Riau, located near the present town of Tanjong Pinang on Bentan Island, just 50 kilometers south of Singapore. Its formal ruler was the sultan of Johor, whose state was the inheritance of the Melaka sultans. Riau pulled together three of the major trading streams of eighteenth-century Asian commerce and allowed the emergence of a number of new features. First, although it was located in the Straits and populated by many Malays, Riau owed much of its commercial success to the Bugis. These were traders and pirates who had become princes[3] and had come to dominate the Malay *negri* of Johor/Riau in the eighteenth century. The Malay sultans, Mahmud III (*c.* 1760–1812) and his successors, were largely under the domination of the Bugis Yang di-Pertuan Mudas and their families. The other

Malay princely families, like those of the Temenggong of Johor and the Bendahara of Pahang, were pushed to the fringes. At Riau, the interlopers brought together the far-flung trading networks of the Bugis traders and warriors, whose activities made them a major force throughout much of island Southeast Asia (Andaya 1975; Trocki 1979).

The second principal element in the Riau economy was the Chinese junk traders and the large number of Chinese laborers who had settled on the island to produce pepper and gambier. During the eighteenth century, the Chinese junk trade of Southeast Asia, based largely in the ports of Fujian province and the Teochew areas of Guangdong province, had greatly expanded as a result of the Quangxi boom. So great was China's demand for Southeast Asian goods that it had become necessary to rely on colonies of Chinese laborers to produce them. By the end of the eighteenth century, the coasts of Southeast Asia were dotted with such outposts of laborers. Riau was thus part of this "water frontier" of Chinese expansion, which stretched around the coast of the South China Sea from southern Vietnam to Batavia (Cooke and Li 2004). There were tin miners in various parts of the Malayan peninsula and Bangka; gold miners in Pontianak, Sambas and Kelantan; and pepper planters in Chantaburi, Trat and other towns around the Gulf of Siam, Brunei, Terengganu and elsewhere. There were sugar planters in Kedah, and there had also been a thriving colony in Java until the massacre of 1740, when the Dutch killed most of them (Trocki 1990; see Figure 1.1 for details of the British trade route from Bengal to Guangdong and the Chinese settlements in Southeast Asia, *c*. 1780).

These settlements represented a new phase in the Chinese relationship with Southeast Asia. In addition to being a new and more productive presence in the region, their labor provided a new source of income and wealth for the indigenous and European colonial rulers. At the same time, the existence of large numbers of Chinese concentrated in specific locations, often far away from urban centers, would come to present new challenges in terms of assimilation and control for those rulers. For Singapore, the trade of these settlements and the flow of Chinese labor in and out of them would become the life blood of the port.

The colony of pepper and gambier planters at Riau would come to form an important element of Singapore's economy and population. Gambier was a shrub that was grown in conjunction with pepper, making both viable economic enterprises. The gambier leaves were boiled and the decoction reduced to a hard paste, which was packed and sent to China, where the highly astringent substance was used in tanning leather and as a dye. I have estimated that by the late eighteenth century there may have been as many as 10,000 Chinese settled on Bentan Island, most of whom would have been engaged in this industry (Trocki 1979).

The third new element in the economy of the region was the Europeans, in particular the British. Europeans had been an important presence in the region since the beginning of the sixteenth century, and they had demonstrated

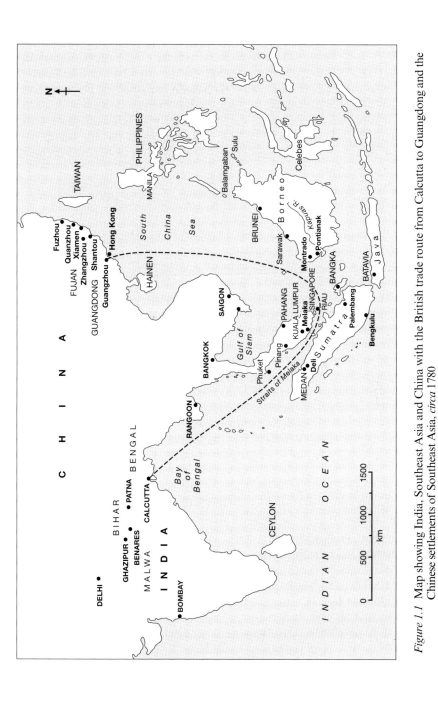

Figure 1.1 Map showing India, Southeast Asia and China with the British trade route from Calcutta to Guangdong and the Chinese settlements of Southeast Asia, *circa* 1780

an ability to carve out economic niches for themselves, sometimes to the disadvantage of Malay and other local rulers. Thus the Portuguese had seized Melaka, the Spanish had created Manila and the Dutch had set up Batavia. All functioned as fortified centers for the expansion of European power and the enforcement of monopolies. On the other hand, all had really opened themselves to the junk trade and despite monopolistic practices had provided a focus for the Malay, Bugis and other "native" trade. The Spanish and the Dutch, with their access to New World and Japanese silver, also brought important infusions of capital into the area. Sometime before the beginning of the eighteenth century, the Spanish silver dollar had become the universal currency of the South China Sea trading zone.

British activity in the second half of the eighteenth century added a new and significant element in the Asian trade. The forerunners of free trade, the British "country traders" came to form a key component of the triad of economic networks that had gathered around Riau. These traders, usually based in Bombay, Madras or Calcutta, carried cargoes of Indian produce intended for exchange for both Southeast Asian goods (pepper, spices, tin, forest produce, pearls, etc.) and Chinese goods, primarily silver. They made dangerous, epic voyages in large, well-armed vessels, "country wallahs" as their ships were called. These sometimes took two to three years to complete, with stops at both colonial and indigenous ports throughout the islands. Their ports of call included Aceh, Kedah, Phuket, Linggi, Melaka, Riau, Terengganu, Sambas, Pontianak, Banjarmasin, Brunei, Batavia and Sulu. By the 1780s, they had been joined by the Americans, who now came seeking their own supplies of pepper and tea (Furber 1951; Lewis 1995).

Until it was destroyed by the Dutch in 1784, Riau in particular was a crucial port of call. In addition to being strategically located at the entrance of the Straits of Melaka, it gave country traders the opportunity to meet Asian traders from all points to the east. They could turn over considerable portions of their Indian cargoes, particularly textiles, weapons, gunpowder and opium. At the same time, they could load up with Riau's pepper, Bangka and Selangor tin, and the usual range of forest and sea produce, all of which were in demand in China. Under its Bugis rulers, Riau was virtu-ally a free port, and charges were minimal; however, if it was low-cost, it was also somewhat insecure for European shipping.

In their Indian bases, the country traders formed partnerships with Parsees, Banjans and Muslim merchants on the one side and linked up with covenanted East India Company (EIC) servants on the other (Bulley 2000). They operated at first with the grudging sufferance of the EIC but later became indispensable to the company. They specialized in carrying certain products that the East Indiamen decided not to carry. In particular, they pioneered the opium trade. The security of this trade was probably one of the key motivations behind Raffles' decision to found a port at the eastern end of the Melaka Straits. He was, after all, a servant of the EIC and was operating under the direct orders of the Governor-General.

By the early nineteenth century, much of the British Indian economy had come to depend on the profits from the opium trade to China, control of the drug having fallen into British hands following the Battle of Plassey in 1757. Groups of EIC servants in the towns of Patna and Ghazipur had seized the monopolies over opium cultivation in the surrounding districts. In the 1780s, Warren Hastings had taken over the monopoly on the company's behalf, and Lord Cornwallis had then formalized the EIC's control of its production. Between 1780 and 1820, the EIC produced an annual average of about 4,000 chests of both Benares and Patna opium combined. Although the price had fluctuated considerably, by 1820 it was valued at over $1,000 per 140 lb (*c.* 63.6 kg) chest (Trocki 1999).

Although a good portion of the annual "provision" was traded in the various ports of Southeast Asia, the greatest bulk of it was sold, illegally and clandestinely, in China. The opium trade had been illegal in China since 1729, thus the EIC took no part in handling the contraband merchandise. The annual production of opium was gathered in Calcutta and was auctioned to the country traders and their agents in a number of lots over the course of each year. From that point on, the company ostensibly had no part in the trade. On the other hand, the country traders, after disposing of their illicit cargoes at Macau or Whampoa, found themselves with large amounts of silver on their hands, and rather than carry it back to India, they deposited it in the company's treasury in Canton. For their deposits they took bills of exchange, which were negotiable in Calcutta, Madras, Bombay, and ultimately in London, New York and elsewhere in the world. These "India bills" became one of the world's first truly global currencies. By the mid-nineteenth century, opium profits greased the commerce of the entire Western world. On the other hand, in Canton, the EIC could now use the silver to cover its annual tea purchases, thus wiping out what had been a chronic balance of payments problem for the company during most of the eighteenth century.

The opium trade, which in 1819 had come to represent an annual flow of silver amounting to about $8 million, was highly vulnerable. Despite their firepower, the country ships had no secure base between Calcutta and Canton. In 1782, the EIC ship *Betsy* was seized at Riau by combined French and Dutch forces (with the compliance of the Riau ruler), costing the company nearly 1,500 chests of opium among other things. Such experiences led the EIC to leave the country trade of Southeast Asia to the independent traders,[4] but they also strengthened the resolve of the EIC and interests allied with it to find a secure base in Southeast Asia for the China trade.

It was in the shadow of these events that the country trader Francis Light, working on behalf of the EIC, established the settlement of Penang in 1786. Outside this port, the British China trade, as it was euphemistically termed in the documents of the era, continued to be at the mercy of undependable native and unfriendly Dutch governments. It was thus the security of this trade, in actuality the opium trade, that Raffles and his Indian superior, the Marquis of Hastings, saw as one of their key responsibilities in the atmosphere of 1818–19. Not to put too fine a point on it, we can say that the founding of Singapore was above all about opium.

Following the Napoleonic wars and the re-establishment of the Anglo-Dutch alliance, the British government, ignoring the "narrow interests" of the EIC, had restored the Dutch to their position in Southeast Asia prior to the war, returning to them Java, Melaka and other Dutch territories seized during the war. After being required to hand Melaka back to the Dutch in 1818 and being out-maneuvered by Dutch agents in making a treaty with the Yamtuan Muda of Riau, Raffles and his associate, Colonel William Farhquar, sought to found a new British settlement. They surveyed a number of sites at the entrance to the Melaka Straits and finally decided to make the bold move of signing a treaty with Temenggong Abdul Rahman of Johor.

The Temenggong had been one of those Malay chiefs who had suffered a loss of status and influence as a result of Bugis power at the Riau court. He and his followers had left Riau and were then occupying a site near the mouth of the Singapore River; according to Dutch reports of the time, they made a living from small-scale piracy. The Temenggong had also welcomed the settlement of a small group of Chinese pepper and gambier planters on the island whose numbers would increase rapidly in the coming years. Given the recent treaty between the Dutch and the Riau ruler, Johor and its chiefs were technically off-limits to the British, but despite Dutch protests, the settlement went ahead.

Agency houses and junk traders

Although it was a British initiative, the new settlement, with its policy of free trade, became a natural focal point for the trading interests that had formerly gathered around Riau. In a matter of months, the Chinese junk traders, Bugis traders and British merchants began to flock to Singapore. The combination of these factors certainly made the initial success of Singapore quite spectacular. Within five years, Singapore's trade grew to a value of over $13 million annually (Crawfurd 1987: 537). John Crawfurd argued that Singapore had contributed greatly to an absolute increase in British trade in Asia. Answering critics that Singapore simply drew trade from Penang, he pointed out that in 1818, the whole of direct British trade with the Straits of Melaka, and generally with the eastern islands, excluding Java, centered at Penang, totaled $2,030,757. In 1824, however, the joint exports of Penang and Singapore were $9,414,464, $6,604,601 of which was exported through Singapore (*ibid.*: 549).

What was the basis of this sudden increase in British trade? Certainly an important share of it was opium. In 1823–24, $8,515,100 worth of opium was shipped to China. Even though not all of this was landed in the Straits, much of it was. Its location gave Singapore advantages that Penang could not match. In addition to serving as a base for British trade, it was better able to tap into the very active trade carried on by Chinese junks in the South China Sea and in the Gulf of Siam. Now, much of the trade that had formerly gone to Riau shifted to Singapore, and Dutch-controlled Riau became a backwater. It may have been true that British free-trade policies were an important attraction for Chinese traders, but so too was its open market in opium, which at that time was as negotiable as silver dollars all over Southeast Asia.

A second element related to the British presence was the arms trade. Throughout the first fifty years of its existence, Singapore and the other two Straits Settlements of Penang and Melaka were the major distribution points in Asia for arms and ammunition. In his description of Singapore's trade, an incidental chapter to his report of his embassy to Siam and Cochin China in 1827, John Crawfurd offered a spirited defense of the arms trade of Singapore. He argued that if the British did not sell arms to Southeast Asian countries, then other Europeans would: "For example the Americans now supply the whole pepper coast of Sumatra; and before the trade was tolerated at Singapore, they had supplied Siam, in less than two years, with above 30,000 stand of firearms." (*ibid.*: 547). He thought that the British government had no business forbidding the sale of arms to nations over whom they had no political control. He felt that wealthy traders and princes could better afford weapons for defense than could the "pirates." Moreover, he argued that:

> The effect of firearms in civilizing the barbarous tribes themselves, should not be overlooked. The possession of these gives the more intelligent and commercial tribes an advantage over their ruder neighbours, and thus a power is established, which cannot fail to tend more or less to the diminution of anarchy, and the melioration of law and government. If this reasoning is well-founded, and I think it would be difficult to controvert it, a law prohibiting the sale of munitions of war to nations and tribes over whom we exercise no control, and with whom we scarcely maintain any political relations, is to all purposes as inefficient as it is unwise and impolitic.
>
> (Crawfurd 1987: 547–8)

Somewhat similar rhetoric was deployed to defend the opium trade. Thus one might say that early Singapore's role in the economy of the British Empire was to serve as a marketplace for both guns and drugs.

It is interesting that almost as soon as Singapore was founded, the country traders settled down. Rather than continue to ply their trade throughout the islands, European merchants who had previously sailed as country traders quickly took up land in Singapore. They opened trading establishments that came to be known as "agency houses." Also, many newly arrived European merchants (mostly Scots) set up trading houses. These men had connections in India, Canton and Europe and acted as agents for the sale of goods shipped from the West. They also procured return cargoes of Asian goods for their "constituents" abroad. By the mid-1820s, such firms as A.L. Johnston, John Purvis and Alexander Guthrie had been founded, and a community of eighty-odd Europeans had taken up residence in the new settlement.

The agency houses became the fundamental outposts of the imperial economy in Southeast Asia. The East India Company's monopoly on the China trade did not apply to Singapore's trade. In 1833, the EIC gave up its monopoly on the China trade altogether and left the way open for private British firms to trade directly with Britain and other European ports west of the Cape of Good Hope. The agency houses thus handled the trade of India and Europe that would formerly have been in the hands of the EIC. In Singapore, the company was only the government and took no part in trade.

Far from enforcing a monopoly, Singapore was a free port. The English-language newspapers regularly carried a large headline just below the masthead or across the top of the pages devoted to "Prices Current" that stated: "Singapore is a Free Port and there are no charges or port duties of any kind." The port was also open to traders of all nations. This was a great incentive to the native trade and to the Chinese junk trade, which now flocked to Singapore's excellent harbour in large numbers. Raffles and his successor, Crawfurd, were deeply committed to Adam Smith's ideas of free trade, and they molded Singapore in its most formative years as a free port, and it stayed that way for the next century.

Singapore's status as a free port and as an outlet for British and Indian commodities in Southeast Asia gave it an important position in the region. The fact that it also occupied a geographically strategic site as well as a historic niche in the Malay world gave it numerous advantages held by no other trading center in the region at the time. Singapore had a place in the imperial calculus of British trade while filling a vital function in its immediate environment.

The key nexus of the port's economy was in the relationship that the agency merchants were able to develop with Asian traders, especially the Chinese, who would on the one hand distribute their goods and on the other provide the Europeans with supplies of local and Chinese produce. Initially, not all British merchants realized that this was their major opportunity. Many of them, formerly involved in the country trade to China or as former EIC servants, still had their eyes on the long-distance trade between India and China and the purchase of Chinese commodities for the European market. Those who managed to survive in the competitive atmosphere of free trade and open markets ultimately discovered that Singapore's role in the China trade, at least as they knew it, was one that would diminish over the near future. The trade to China continued to flourish, but it fell almost entirely into Chinese hands. The improvements in maritime technology that would come in the 1830s, particularly the advent of clipper ships, and after them of steamboats, and the inexorable increases in the opium trade, would limit the role that Singapore-based European merchants could have in the traffic.

The economy that developed in Singapore during the early nineteenth century was segmented and hierarchical. At the top – at least in terms of capital flows – was the handful of European firms. These had links to the global network of the British Empire. Their connections extended from Canton to Calcutta to Europe and the western hemisphere. As commission agents for these interests, they controlled the flow of capital goods into the colony.

Ironically, they had no direct links to the trade goods desired by their constituents or clients. Aside from a smattering of Malay, most spoke no local languages, and apparently none of them spoke (let alone read) any Chinese language. They were not equipped to deal in the small quantities of goods that were delivered and demanded by local traders. They needed intermediaries who spoke the local languages and who were ready to deal with a large number of suppliers, and who could consolidate large quantities of goods so as to organize reasonable loads for exporting. They needed intermediaries who could take large quantities of their own goods for extended periods of time and distribute them into the channels of the "native trade."

In the mid-1820s, the locally based native trade of Southeast Asia seemed far less attractive to European merchants. Nevertheless, a number of merchants, Alexander Guthrie and A.L. Johnston among them, saw the need to find local partners who could connect them with the native traders. It was also important for them to find people in whom they could trust and with whom they could communicate. As it turned out, these individuals tended to be Chinese merchants from the Straits Chinese community, often from Melaka. These traders, also known as Babas or *peranakan* (locally born), had the benefit of long experience in dealing with local traders and producers, and many of them had also learned a certain amount of English during the time that Melaka had been under British control from 1795 to 1818. With the founding of Singapore, considerable numbers of Melaka people, both Malay and Chinese, migrated to the new colony. This was especially the case between 1818 and 1824, when Melaka had been returned to the Dutch.

These merchants, most of whom were the children or grandchildren of Chinese traders from the coastal towns of Fujian province, also maintained links to the junk captains and other smaller locally based Fujian traders. In the local dialect, these people were known as Hokkien. Through these traders, the Baba merchants had networks that ramified throughout the trading and economic world of the Chinese, both inside Southeast Asia and in China itself. Key examples of this group were Chua Chong Long and Kiong Kong Tuan. The former was the son of the Kapitan China of Melaka, and the latter held the Singapore revenue farms for many years. Both were among the first Chinese to take out land titles in Singapore.

There were also traders and merchants from parts of Guangdong province, but many of these had much smaller businesses. These included Cantonese from the Pearl River delta region around Canton such as Tan Che Seng, who was one of the wealthiest Chinese of early Singapore, and Ho Ah Kay or "Whampoa." It also included the *kejiah* people, or "Hakka," from a number of specific regions in the province. Originally, however, the most numerous were people from the port of Shantou (formerly Swatow), in the Chauzhou region of Guangdong. These were the "Teochew," who dominated the pepper and gambier industry. Most important among this group were individuals such as Seah Eu Chin and later his brother-in-law, Tan Seng Poh. Finally, there were people from Hainan Island, the Hainanese, or "Hailam" people (Song 1923: 25).

As the Chinese population of Singapore grew, there came to be an ethnic division of labor together with a segmentation of the population according to wealth and power. Many of the largest and wealthiest merchants (or *taukehs*) tended to be Babas or Hokkien, although there were wealthy Cantonese, Teochew, Hakka and even Hainanese. Many of the smaller traders and shopkeepers were less affluent Hokkien and Teochew. Many of the craftsmen, the carpenters and builders, were Cantonese. In the early years, agricultural laborers, particularly the pepper and gambier planters, tended to be Teochew, although later there were both Hakka and Hokkien planters as well. Hailam people often dealt in food services, coffee shops and small food stalls. If some of these characterizations are stereotypical, there is a certain accuracy to the categories.

However, most important for the local economy was the pyramid of debt and exchange that came into existence. At its top were the European traders, who supplied capital in the form of European and Indian trade goods. These included opium, cheap cotton cloth, hardware, particularly agricultural and mining tools, weapons, and other foodstuffs. Such goods were often simply turned over to specific Baba or Hokkien merchants on credit. These wealthy *taukehs* in turn traded them to junk captains and other traders who sailed to Siam, Cambodia, Cochin China, Tongkin and China itself. They also lent the goods to smaller merchants, shopkeepers and commission agents, who traveled to small settlements in the islands, on Sumatra, Borneo and the coasts of the Malayan peninsula. In turn, these dealers lent goods to even smaller dealers in a chain culminating with individuals in charge of groups of Chinese laborers, Malay headmen and others who were in direct communication with the producers of the Southeast Asian trade goods in demand. These included forest and maritime produce, spices, pepper, tin, gold, tapioca, sugar and rice.

The labor forces, whether Chinese coolies, Malay peasants, forest people, or sea people, were often already in some form of dependency relation with the individuals who had access to these foreign goods. The provision of a regular supply of these goods, usually through restricted and more or less exclusive channels, guaranteed that the dependency relation would persist.

Most of these producers were offshore and resident in the Malayan peninsula, the Riau–Lingga Archipelago, Sumatra and Borneo.

There was thus a chain of indebtedness that stretched from the wealthy European merchants in their Singapore godowns (warehouses), through the Baba *taukehs*, to the middle-sized Hokkien merchants to the smaller Teochew and Hakka traders to the gang bosses of the labor crews and the headmen of Malay settlements in the upriver areas in the hinterland of Singapore and along the many sea routes leading from Singapore throughout maritime Southeast Asia. Many commodities, both Western and Asian, circulated down through this chain and brought back to Singapore the quantities of Straits produce that was in demand in China and elsewhere. This pattern of economic relations persisted until the 1880s and 1890s, when a number of other factors came into play.

The advantage for the Europeans was that they only had to place their inputs of capital with the leading Chinese traders and the task of collecting, processing and procuring goods was undertaken by others. That, too, was the disadvantage. Europeans had no control over the pyramid of debt. They had no direct or unmediated connection with the primary producers. They did not have much room to bargain over prices and often had to wait for three to six months before receiving their goods, and they occasionally found that they did not receive what they ordered. At times, even their choice of intermediaries proved unwise, these latter absconding altogether. This was, in the broadest sense, the way in which business in Southeast Asian ports had always been done.

There grew to be a community of forty to fifty very prosperous Chinese merchants who established shops in the town. Although the majority were Babas or Hokkien, there were also a number of Teochew, Cantonese, Hakka and Hainanese merchants who made it into this upper echelon of the local economy. They became economically, socially and politically important within the colonial structure. Song Ong Siang, an early twentieth-century descendant of this group, has recorded the life stories of scores of these men (Song 1923). Many came to Singapore with virtually nothing and managed to amass great fortunes in the British colony. Many of these settled permanently in Singapore and became naturalized British subjects, founding families that continue to play important roles in the city-state's economy. Many of the most successful of the China-born merchants managed to marry into more established families, thus bolstering their own prestige while reviving the fortunes of the local lineages.

In the nineteenth century, some of the most prosperous merchants occupied premises along Boat Quay Road, which followed the Singapore River and gave them access to the goods moving in and out of the port. By mid-century, Boat Quay was dominated by a group of Teochew merchants who controlled the pepper and gambier industry that had come to flourish in the interior of Singapore Island. Chief among them was Seah Eu Chin, a Teochew who had come to Singapore with a certain level of education, found employment as a clerk with a Baba merchant and got his start as a commission merchant. He traveled around the waters near Singapore collecting merchandise from the settlements and developing a network of contacts. Once he had acquired a little capital, he invested in pepper and gambier plantations in Singapore and thus made his fortune.

By the 1860s, Seah was one of the most powerful men in Singapore. He was also one of the richest and most respected. He was the unofficial headman of the Teochew community so far as the British government was concerned. He had also come to dominate the pepper and gambier industry of both Singapore and the neighboring state of Johor. He seems to have been one of the key organizers of a group known as the Kongkek, in English the Pepper and Gambier Society. This was made up of all or almost all of the pepper and gambier dealers of Singapore and Johor. At about the time the Kongkek was formed, the opium and spirit revenue farms of Singapore and Johor were taken over by his brother-in-law, Tan Seng Poh. Between them, the pair dominated the economic life of thousands of Singapore Chinese for a major portion of the nineteenth century.

Among the most important Chinese were the revenue farmers, particularly the opium farmers. They were able not only to win the confidence of individual European merchants but also to command the respect and cooperation of the government itself. Since Singapore was a free port and had very limited agricultural production, there were only a few ways to raise revenue. Ultimately, the most expeditious source was the taxation of "luxury" consumption: opium, spirits (as spiritous liquors were then known), gambling, pork, sireh or betel nut, coconut toddy, and cannabis. These were things that were consumed by a large majority of the population, mostly laborers. They were marketed through monopoly concessions known as "farms."[5] These were auctioned off to the highest bidder, who paid the government a monthly rental. In exchange, the "farmer" acquired the privilege of controlling the retail sale of one of these commodities or services. The most lucrative of these was the opium farm. For nearly a century, from about 1824 until 1910, it was the single largest source of revenue available to the government, yielding between 35 and 60 percent of its entire revenue, depending on the year.[6]

Even though there was an auction process, farmers also needed to be men with respectable backgrounds in whom the government could place its trust. As in the case of European merchants, the British government was most comfortable when dealing with Chinese who could speak some English, who could produce references, and who possessed roots in the Straits Settlements. This circumstance again favored the Melaka-born Babas. As a result, for nearly the first twenty years of the settlement's history, the opium and spirit farmers of Singapore tended to be Babas (Trocki 1990).

While Baba merchants had privileged links to Europeans and to the sources of capital, it was only a matter of time before members of other speech groups found ways around their monopoly. They only needed, as some said, to put on a clean shirt and turn up at a European godown to receive all they wanted in trade goods. This was an exaggeration, but there was some truth in the belief. Beyond this, the Babas lacked certain advantages that the China-born merchants possessed. The latter often had much more direct access to the labor force, and it was the laborers who produced the trade commodities. The Babas needed these small, China-born merchants for their access to labor and its products.

Access to the largest single labor force was the province of the Teochew merchants who were grouped around Seah Eu Chin. They dominated pepper and gambier cultivation on the island and, after the 1840s, in Johor as well. The large population of Teochew coolies who worked the plantations were also the major consumers of opium. On the plantations, where they were isolated from the town. the coolies were under the watchful eyes of the *kangchus* or managers of the pepper and gambier settlements in the interior of Singapore and on the rivers of Johor. These coolies made up the largest single population of Chinese in Singapore. According to Seah Eu Chin's brief article in the *Journal of the Indian Archipelago*, there were an estimated 10,000 Teochew pepper and gambier planters in 1848.

Coolies, gambier and opium

The coolies were at the bottom of the economic pyramid of Singapore. They came by their thousands from the very inception of the settlement. Many came willingly, seeking opportunity and hoping to return to China with wealth. Many came because they lacked even the opportunity for survival at home. Still others came because they were forced, tricked, kidnapped or otherwise brought against their will or better judgement. These were the "piglets," and they formed yet another key commodity of Singapore's trade. They were cheap labor. Many of them arrived in Singapore already in debt for their passage if nothing else.

They usually came on the "credit-ticket" scheme. By the 1830s, this seems to have been established as a fairly formalized system with its own infrastructure of recruiters, brokers, rooming houses, shippers, investors and employers. It was ultimately integrated into the system of secret societies and formed a part of the complex of economic interests that also governed the revenue farms and the mining and planting interests of Singapore and its hinterland. Often returned coolies or immigrants from Singapore would go back to their home villages and to other rural areas to find strong young men and recruit them for work in Southeast Asia. Someone in China, usually a coolie broker, paid their passage on a junk to Singapore. Often the recruits were kept together in rooming houses in the ports while awaiting a ship. The coolie was expected to reimburse the ticket price, with interest, once he had found employment in Singapore. The cost of a ticket was $7 or $8, and a coolie could expect to earn about $3 or $4 monthly. Ideally, the cost of living was about $2 per month. Theoretically, it should have been possible to pay off the debt and begin accumulating savings before the end of the first year.

However, this did not include funds that the coolie might need for his own tools, clothing and provisions that he would need before taking employment on a mine or a plantation. These too would be provided by a shopkeeper in Singapore, who had them through the line of credit from one of the European merchants. Usually, such goods were valued at four times their market price in terms of calculating the coolie's debt. Thus, before he began earning money, the average coolie could really be in debt for up to $20–30. However, even this was not too onerous, and with industry, it might realistically be paid off in the space of two years.

However, these calculations did not include the possibility that the coolie might fall victim to the temptations of life in the mines and plantations. There he would be living in a rude wooden shed together with twenty to forty others if on a mine, but only nine or ten if on a gambier plantation, who were young, single men like himself. Outside of their constant round of hard labor in the tropical sun and chilly nights in the tropical rain, they had only a few sources of comfort and entertainment. These included the local opium den, the gambling table, the spirit shop and, in some cases, a few prostitutes. These amenities were provided by the owner of the mine or plantation for whom the coolies worked, and who was not only their paymaster but also their creditor, having purchased their debts when he took them into his employ. He also owned, or controlled, the local provision shop.

Within Singapore, during the first four decades of its existence, many of the coolies landed there would be likely to find work on the island itself in the pepper and gambier industry. From the foundation of the port there had been pepper and gambier planters on the island. Once the British settlement was formed, significant numbers of gambier planters and shopkeepers seem to have moved there from Riau, and very quickly Singapore became the regional center of the industry. By the 1830s, it is clear that the cultivation had spread over large portions of the interior of the island and probably employed a significant proportion of the island's Chinese population (Trocki 1979).

Much of this development and settlement seems to have taken place without attracting very much attention from either the government or the European community. Aside from the social and linguistic distinctions that separated the various ethnic groups of Singapore, Europeans were not very interested in gambier as a trade commodity. Gambier was simply not on the European radar until the mid-1830s. Prior to that time, gambier was only in demand in China. As a commodity, it was produced by Chinese, handled by Chinese shopkeepers and carried to China in Chinese junks. The fact that it was cultivated jointly with pepper may have been the only aspect of interest for Europeans. About 1836, however, shipments of gambier began to be exported to Europe, and from that time it became a relatively common item of trade to the West for the remainder of the nineteenth century.

There thus came to be a symbiotic relation between opium farming and the pepper and gambier business. The laborers constituted the major population of opium smokers. By controlling both the industry and the opium farms, it was possible for the pepper and gambier *taukehs* to make a profit on both the production and the consumption of their workforce. What they paid the coolies in wages could be quickly recaptured through opium sales. The construction of a "company store" type of arrangement in each of the more or less isolated planting settlements of Singapore made it possible to monopolize the consumption of the coolies in each settlement, or *kangkar* (port or river foot) as they were called in the Teochew language. These terms were formalized in Johor, where the system was officially recognized by the Malay government of the Temenggong. Thus the headman was called the *kangchu*, or "lord of the port" (or river), and his settlement or headquarters was called the *chukang*. However, the same terms were already in use in eighteenth-century Riau and were applied in Singapore as well (Trocki 1979). Even today, the legacy of the pepper and gambier agriculture of nineteenth-century Singapore lives on in place names such as Chua Chukang, Peng Kang, Lim Chukang and Yeo Chukang.

Singapore and the Southeast Asian hinterland

Control of Chinese labor gave Singapore's wealthy Chinese merchant class the opportunity to engage in commodity production throughout Southeast Asia. Singapore's port acted as a clearing house not only for Chinese laborers for pepper and gambier in Singapore but also for labor demands in any part of Southeast Asia, particularly in the sparsely populated territories of the Malayan peninsula, Sumatra and Borneo. In all these areas, the Dutch, the British and Chinese merchants of the Straits Settlements and the "enlightened" rulers of the Malay states together embarked on aggressive programs of commodity production. In addition to gold and tin mining, and pepper and gambier planting, Chinese labor was engaged in sago, tapioca, sugar, tobacco and indigo cultivation.

John Cameron, in his description of Singapore written in the 1860s, remarked on the industry of the Chinese:

> In Singapore all the gambier and pepper produced is of their growth, and the sago is of their manufacture; in Penang and Province Wellesley also, the chief plantations are in their hands or worked by them; and in Malacca all the tin, all the sago, and all the tapioca is of their produc-tion. ...During the months of December, January, February, March and April, fleets of junks crammed with Chinese coolies arrive at the ports in the Straits from the different provinces of China. In Singapore, the arrivals for the first four months of the present year (1864) were 8,500 males and 109 females – and for the whole year about 14,000, which is not much above the average of other years.
>
> (Cameron 1865: 183–4)

Coolie ships unloaded their human cargoes in Singapore, and the "piglets" were herded into rooming houses and kept under guard while the coolie brokers sold their contracts to agents for plantations and mines on the Malayan peninsula, Sumatra, Borneo and the Riau–Lingga archipelago. Singapore was the major labor exchange center in Southeast Asia, and Singapore's merchants dominated the region's major strategic economic resource. As a result, they also came to control commodity production throughout the region. Raffles may have abolished slavery, but exploitative labor systems persisted in Singapore.

Behind the coolies came the other major resource, and this one was controlled by Europeans – opium. Opium flowed out into the region to serve the labor force. Initially, most of the commodities produced in Southeast Asia were destined for China. The reason Chinese had pioneered the production of tin, gold, pepper, gambier, sugar, tapioca and other commodities was to serve the home market, but when European country traders came through Southeast Asia in the eighteenth century, they too purchased these products, together with other jungle and sea products to sell in China.

Now, Europeans settled down in Singapore and began to invest in production in and around Singapore through the Chinese. Over time, they began to find markets for increasing numbers of these products in Europe itself. Around 1835, it is possible to see important shifts taking place in the movement of Southeast Asian commodities through Singapore. Whereas in 1819, virtually all of the goods labeled "Straits produce" were destined for China, by the mid-1830s much of the region's pepper production, tin production, and even gambier was being bought up by British merchants for the European market. For the remaining years of the nineteenth century, this continued to be the pattern. European merchants, even though many aspired to a variety of economic roles, could not break out of their niche in tertiary activity. Many would have preferred to run plantations and mines on their own, but this was not possible. They could not communicate with the labor force let alone control it, and they could not do business the way the Chinese did. The failure of nutmeg planting, sugar planting and other such efforts by Europeans in the early years of Singapore's history was in large part due to their inability to communicate and deal effectively with Chinese labor. It was not until the advent of Indian labor and different crops such as rubber that European merchants found it possible to move beyond the agency house as a form of successful business enterprise (Jackson 1968).

As Singapore's population grew, so too did its need for provisions and supplies simply to feed and clothe its workforce. Here, too, long-established Chinese networks and Asian trading patterns showed their continuing utility. Already by the early 1830s, two of Singapore's major trading partners were Bangkok and Saigon. The major products in these exchanges were rice and opium. Rice came from these larger, more densely populated, river basin states on the mainland and was exported to feed the growing numbers of

Chinese laborers in and around Singapore. Indian opium, flowing through Singapore, was among the major exchange commodities that paid for the rice, and ultimately even paid for labor and the commodities it produced.

Here, again, the established Chinese merchants in Singapore and the Straits dominated these exchanges. Men such as Tan Kim Ching, Cheang Hong Lim, Tan Hiok Nee, Seah Eu Chin, Tan Seng Poh, and later others like the Tan brothers of Saigon, Tan Keng Sing, Tan Keng Ho and Tan Keng Hoon, and their partner Banhap, controlled the rice trade of Siam and Cochin China with Singapore (Trocki 2004). It was this nexus of rice, opium and Chinese labor that gave a small group of Straits Chinese merchants and their Hokkien and Teochew allies, some based in Singapore, others in Penang and still others scattered around the ports of the South China Sea and the China coast, an international reach.

Singapore and the Industrial Revolution

From the 1830s, however, Singapore's triumphant position as an Asian trading hub came to be directly affected by the global links that had been created by the British Empire. The advances in European technology began to dramatically shift the balance not only of political power but also of social and economic power. These changes also began to affect the manner in which business was conducted in the region and thus struck very much at the heart of the dominant position of Chinese mercantile interests. In some cases, the Chinese were able to adapt and even take advantage of these shifts, but in the long run, their key advantages in control of labor and opium were eroded. The first great challenge came from advances occurring in European shipping.

Improvements in sailing technology as well as in armaments had by the 1830s made European-style square-rigged ships the champions of the sea. Square-rigged vessels were faster, more dependable and safer than other kinds of ship in Asian waters. With secure bases such as Singapore, European naval expeditions could map out the seas and coastlines and put detailed knowledge of the islands, winds, tides, currents, anchorages and sailing conditions of the whole South China Sea into published manuals and into the hands of European skippers.

The most spectacular of the new ships were the clippers. Patterned after fast American brigs like those used in the war of 1812 and American slave ships, they had slim hulls and carried only moderate levels of cargo under a veritable cloud of sails. They were the fastest craft of their age, and until the late twentieth century, nothing on the water could equal their speed. They revolutionized the opium trade, making up to three voyages per year between Bombay and Canton. The trip from Singapore to Macau and back was cut to less than three weeks; moreover, it could be done at any time of the year. With their ability to beat upwind, they freed Asian trade from the tyranny of the monsoons. They were heavily armed and sailed by large, well-trained

European crews. These were ships made for high-value, low-bulk cargoes like opium and tea.

In addition, there were many more ships, not necessarily in the express class, but still quite efficient, dependable and secure. Many such ships now engaged in the carrying trade between ports in China, within Southeast Asia, and to India and beyond. By the late 1830s, square-rigged shipping began to carry increasing amounts of trade, and, gradually, the tonnage of cargo carried by square-riggers rose above that carried in Chinese junks (Wong 1960: 123). Soon, even the wealthy Chinese merchants of Singapore began to purchase such ships to carry their own cargoes. The less affluent ones simply consigned their cargoes to European firms.

The impact of such ships in Singapore was immense. Aside from placing a much larger share of Asian commerce in European, primarily British, hands, the new ships increased the overall levels of trade, which in turn enriched many of the merchants of Singapore. On the other hand, they also reduced Singapore's role in the long-distance transshipment of goods, particularly valuable ones between other major ports. Clipper ships with cargoes of opium for China no longer needed to stop at Singapore. The same was true for tea ships coming back from China. They could load up in Calcutta or Bombay, sail straight through to Canton and later Hong Kong, and return without stopping at Singapore. Singapore's trade became restricted to its immediate hinterland. While this was no small portion, gaining a part of it took skill and some level of risk. It also meant greater involvement with local traders and engagement in the economic and later the political affairs of neighboring states. This last was something that had not really been part of Raffles' original vision for Singapore.

The next great advance was steam navigation. The first steam-powered ships in the Straits were relatively small ones, but they were immediately pressed into service in the war against piracy. The steam launch *Diana* was the first steam vessel to arrive in Southeast Asian waters, around 1836, and it was immediately useful for its surprise value, if nothing else. Later, in 1839, steam vessels were used in the First Opium War against China. During the next three decades, steam became a dependable but sometimes clumsy and slow alternative to sail, but with the completion of the Suez Canal in 1869, steamers brought Asia into much more intimate contact with Europe. The canal and the completion of a trans-Eurasian telegraph link made possible the closer integration of Western and Asian economies. With greater speed in the movement of goods and information, the economic shipment of bulk goods such as grains and metal ores over long distances became possible. Beyond this, steamships were eminently dependable, and by the late 1870s such lines as the Peninsular and Orient Shipping Company were making regular scheduled voyages to most of the major Asian ports.

These technological innovations also had a major impact on what was termed the "native trade" of Singapore: that carried in their *prau* by Malay/Bugis traders who sailed throughout the islands. Although the founding of Singapore had brought increased trading opportunities for all these traders, as the port grew, the major advantages accrued to European-style shipping. Wong Lin Ken has shown that the greater proportion of the trade of the archipelago was being carried in square-rigged ships by the 1840s (Wong 1960: 82).The native trade did not disappear – in fact, it continued to increase into the 1870s – but the great growth in trade was in Western shipping. As the century wore on, the economic role of Malayans was being progressively marginalized. Thus, John Cameron felt justified in pointing out that the Malays of Singapore had no significant economic aspirations (Cameron 1865: 135).

It seems likely that the growing prominence of square-rigged shipping was also related to the anti-piracy campaigns launched by the Singapore and Dutch authorities in the 1840s. In the attacks on "piracy," European naval forces seem to have destroyed and/or supplanted many Malaysian traders. Wong points out that the preponderance of square-rigged over Malaysian shipping coincided with the development of Sarawak by James Brooke and the establishment of British influence in Labuan (Wong 1960: 83; Trocki 1979).

Singapore's domestic economy

The economy of the Malay chiefs in and around Singapore suffered with the British attacks on piracy. In many respects, the political economy of the Malay states relied on raiding and control of shipping in and around their territorial waters. The activities of James Brooke, Admiral Keppel and Captain Congalton cut at the heart of the Malayan political system by depriving them of a major source of income. Economically speaking, only those Malayan princes who were able to understand and to take advantage of the opportunities presented by Singapore and the other Straits Settlements managed to survive as viable rulers. Thus individuals such as the Temenggongs of Johor, who were able to profit from their dealings with Chinese and European merchants, made significant gains. Temenggong Ibrahim, the son of the man who had signed the treaty with Raffles, began by introducing Chinese pepper and gambier planters into the otherwise sparsely populated territory of Johor. His son, Abu Bakar, later the sultan of "the State and Territory of Johor," was closely involved with individuals such as Tan Hiok Nee, a prominent pepper and gambier dealer in Singapore and also a major figure in the opium farming syndicate. Abu Bakar had also enlisted the services of the European firm of Ker, Rawson & Co. (later Paterson & Simons) as his agents. Similar but less successful projects were launched by Tengku Zia'udin in Selangor and Nga Ibrahim in Perak.

Johor was, in some respects, a parable for the fortunes of Malays. They could succeed if they left Singapore and its domination of international trade to the British and the Chinese, and, paradoxically, if they could somehow bring the wealth and administrative skills of both to aid them in their new states. There was no future for Malayan traders in Singapore; they could find employment only near the bottom of Singapore's economic pyramid. Malays could move their *kampongs* to the creeks and backwaters of Singapore. They could become boatmen or fishermen, or they could grow coconuts. They could be servants and scribes or grooms and gardeners. They could live on the fringe of European and Chinese affluence, they could pursue their traditional lifestyles and let progress pass them by, or they could leave Singapore and follow the Temenggong to Johor, or some other Malay chief.

Johor, in particular, was an important adjunct to Singapore. As Chinese pepper and gambier planters spread throughout Singapore, they gradually reached a point where the supply of readily available land and timber became exhausted. By 1845, the first settlers were leaving Singapore and moving across the straits to Johor. In the long run, the economy of Johor became a satellite of Singapore, with the major Singapore merchants and revenue farmers controlling large portions of the state and enjoying a close relationship with the Temenggong, and later the sultan, of Johor. Simultaneously, the same group of Chinese *taukehs* also controlled much of the Riau archipelago through the same mechanism.

Pepper and gambier planting had started in Riau and persisted in the neighboring islands even though the center of the industry had moved to Singapore. By the 1860s, pepper and gambier cultivation covered an area that included the Dutch islands of Riau, much of Singapore Island and most of south Johor. The capitalists who controlled the finances of all these plantations and who supplied the provisions and opium were all in Singapore. Singapore was also the site from which these commodities were exported and the gateway through which Chinese labor moved into the region. By 1870, the revenue farms of all three settlements and the British settlement of Melaka were all under the same syndicate controlled by three Singapore *taukehs*: Cheang Hong Lim, Tan Seng Poh and Tan Hiok Nee.

The relationship with Johor was, in fact, Singapore's future. Singapore came to excel as the *entrepôt* for the products of the Malayan peninsula. The second half of the nineteenth century saw the rise of the Asian commodity trade to Europe. The Asian port came to function as a gathering point for the raw materials and industrial commodities of the region and for shipping them to the industrializing West. Many of these products had only limited uses in the region and came to be produced only because there was a demand for them in Europe or the United States.

One of the first was gutta percha, the rubber-like sap of a local tree, which first became known to Europeans in the 1830s when a European merchant in Singapore noticed Malay coachmen using it for whips. In the mid-1840s, it was found to be the only substance capable of shielding marine telegraphic cables. It is still used today for golf balls, chewing gum and surgical tubing. Gambier, for instance, was used in tanning leather originally had no market in the West, but by mid-century it was no longer shipped to China but was a staple of the trade to Europe and America. With the development of the canning industry during the American Civil War, tin came to be in great demand. At the end of the century, the development of the automobile created a demand for rubber. It also became the port of entry for cheap manufactured goods coming from the West. In addition to cotton cloth, now mass produced in the mills of Britain and New England, Singapore introduced Asia to bicycles, sewing machines, bottled soft drinks and an increasing range of European manufactures.

The discovery of a process for successfully vulcanizing rubber led, in the 1890s, to the widespread planting of rubber trees in Malaya. Singapore became the major port for the movement of the substance to the world at large. It also became the distribution point for Indian labor, which was now used by Europeans on plantations. The longstanding problem of European involvement in successful plantation agriculture had been solved with the advent of rubber. The crop, which lent itself to long-term land ownership and substantial capital inputs (at least for large plantings) seemed much better suited to the demands of European capitalism than other forms of agriculture. It also became possible to import labor from India, a region under British rule. Unlike Chinese labor, the recruitment and dispatch of labor into the colonies could be controlled by Europeans.

While there had already been a small but significant Indian mercantile community in Singapore, the rubber boom brought a large number of working-class South Asians into the colony, mostly from the Tamil areas of southeast India and Ceylon. While most of these simply passed through Singapore on their way to plantations in the Malayan peninsula and Sumatra, some managed to find employment as unskilled laborers in Singapore.

With the rise of the rubber plantation economy, European merchants and other European economic interests were freed from their dependence on Chinese intermediaries for their access to the products of the Malay world. The Malay states of the west coast, Negri Sembilan, Selangor and Perak, had all come under the control of British residents after 1874, and in the 1880s a body of land and property legislation had been put in place that sharply favored European economic interests. It now became possible for European corporations to obtain rights on large blocks of property and clear them and place them under rubber cultivation using cheap gangs of docile Indian labor delivered by British-managed companies. This opened the door for large European and American corporations like Dunlop, Firestone, Goodyear and Goodrich to invest directly in primary production in Malaya. Again, while little rubber was planted in Singapore, the headquarters of the industry was located there, and the lion's share of exports passed through its port.

A technological breakthrough in tin mining had a similar result in that industry. The development of steam dredges and other mechanized mining equipment likewise eliminated the need to depend on Chinese labor and the Chinese merchants and revenue farmers who dominated the industry. These two industries, rubber and tin, became the life blood of British Malaya during the first half of the twentieth century. The value of Singapore's trade rose from $11.6 million to $147.4 million between 1824 and 1883, reached $975.7 million in 1923 and stood at a prewar high of $1,886.7 million in 1926 (Wong 1991: 51, 54). The construction of a railroad linking Penang and Singapore and running though the tin fields and rubber plantations of Malaya's west coast, accomplished in 1923, further strengthened Singapore's connection to its Malayan hinterland.

Developments such as these occurred in an atmosphere of intense competition between business models in the region: that is, between the Straits Chinese family/brotherhood networks and the European corporate establishment. The latter was successful in beating back the challenge of the Chinese. As always, the colonial state was final arbiter, and it tended to come down in favor of the Europeans. After the 1880s, structural changes in the Asian economy began to seriously affect the role of the Chinese. The old triad of opium, Chinese labor and Southeast Asian commodities was weakened with the advent of Indian labor and the increasing mechanization of the tin-mining industry. The opium trade, too, was changing. From the 1880s, European governments, especially the Dutch in Java and the French in Cochin China, began to abolish the opium farms and make the manufacture and distribution of smokeable opium a government-controlled monopoly (Rush 1990; Nankoe 1993). While Siam, the Malay states, Sumatra and the

Figure 1.2 Tanjong Pagar: Singapore's shipbuilding industry in the 1890s.

Straits Settlements retained the revenue-farming system until 1910, government authorities in Singapore began to place the farming syndicates under closer scrutiny (Trocki 1990). This meant that choice financial opportunities for Chinese capital had to be found elsewhere, and one of these new directions was in the establishment of Chinese banks and in finding some compromise with Western-style corporate organization while not entirely breaking away from the family business model of traditional Chinese enterprise.

Singapore and the making of a global economy

Singapore's European, mostly Scottish, agency houses came to dominate the local economy and from that base expanded into the global economy. They participated as intermediaries between the Southeast Asian hinterland and the developing economy of the world. Beginning as commission agents, they handled goods for European producers and took a percentage for their services. They used the goods as capital, advancing them to Chinese dealers in return for Straits produce and other Asian products. This was a trade that continued to be essentially a barter trade until the beginning of the twentieth century. Along the way, they also began to act, sometimes as agents and sometimes on their own account, for providers of economic services such as insurance, banking, shipping and commercial intelligence. Acting in concert with their constituent trading houses in Hong Kong, Shanghai, Manila, Batavia, Calcutta, Bombay and London, they created locally based financial institutions such as Barclay's, the Chartered Bank and the Hong Kong and Shanghai Bank. They also began to act as agents for local chiefs and governments. Companies such as Paterson & Simons, which had virtually grown up with Singapore, ultimately became the agents for the government of Johor, acting as its traders, lawyers, bankers, diplomats and advisors.

Groups like this were able to finance large projects such as the Tanjong Pagar Dock Company and major transportation companies like the Straits Steamship Company and the railroads. They also acted as agents for global rubber, tin, and soap and cosmetic companies as managers for their plantations and mines in the Malay world. Through their connections in Britain, they also advised and influenced the Colonial Office and Parliament on behalf of their interests in Asia. They protected the free-trade regime. They mobilized national armies and navies to combat pirates, break the back of Malay resistance, invade China, and intervene in Malaya, Burma and Siam. They were the key "agents of change" that created the empire and forged the global economy.

In their shadow, in a global sense, but still quite powerful locally were the large Chinese firms. By mid-century, a number of wealthy Chinese merchants had emerged as dominant figures in the Singapore economy. A part of their power derived from the fact that they led cliques of other merchants, mostly fellow members of their dialect groups or *bang*. In particular were individuals such as Tan Kim Ching, the Hokkien Baba from Melaka who led one of the Hokkien cliques, while Cheang Hong Lim led another. Seah Eu Chin and his brother-in-law, Tan Seng Poh, led an important Teochew clique. Ho Ah Kay, or Whampoa, dominated the local Cantonese. Later, there came to be others among the Hakka and Hainanese. Economically, the Hokkien and Teochew were the major figures in the Singapore economy. These men were also seen as the "headmen" of their respective language communities and were often appointed to positions on the Legislative Council or as municipal commissioners.

During the period between the 1840s and 1880s, two important cliques emerged to dominate the opium and spirit revenue farms. On the Hokkien side was Cheang Sam Teo and his sons after him, Cheang Hong Guan and Cheang Hong Lim. From 1845 to 1883, one member of this family was always a member of the revenue-farming syndicate. On the Teochew side was the Seah family and their affines: Seah Eu Chin; his sons Seah Song Seah and Seah Peck Seah; and grandson Seah Eng Keat; but most important was his brother-in-law, Tan Seng Poh. Seah Eu Chin himself was never listed as an opium farmer, but his control of the pepper and gambier industry was a crucial link. On the basis of this, and the Seah family's access to its labor force, they were able to create a place for themselves in the farming syndicates that otherwise would have been dominated by the Hokkien. Circumstances also suggest that until the 1880s, all these figures had close links with the secret society world of Singapore and the surrounding regions (Trocki 1990).

These Chinese merchants amassed great fortunes. By the 1860s, Cameron mentions individuals who were known to be worth $2 million and $3 million. However, what was more significant was their ability to dominate groups of other merchants. The revenue farms were, in fact, grand coalitions of the wealthiest Chinese in the colony. They were broken up into shares and held by members of large syndicates. Only such accumulations of capital could guarantee regular payment to the government of the large sums that constituted the rent of the farms. Conversely, the farms were probably one of the safest ways in which individuals could invest their capital. There were, as yet, no Chinese banks, and the Chinese did not fully trust Western financial instruments. There was also a better return on their investment (*ibid.*).

One example that gives some indication of the global reach of Singapore's wealthy Chinese is seen in the financial exploits of Cheang Hong Lim. In 1879, he went into partnership with a group of Singapore-born *taukehs* who had settled in Saigon. The key figures were Banhap and Tan Keng Sing, who together controlled the opium farms of Saigon, French Cochin China and Cambodia. With Cheang, they created a syndicate that successfully took the Hong Kong opium farms from the control of the established Cantonese syndicate. Their aim was not only the management of three major Asian opium-farming areas but also control of the lucrative Hong Kong-based trade in coolies and prepared opium to Hawaii, California, Australia and other parts of the Pacific. In other words, they aimed to create a cartel controlling the export of virtually all Chinese labor and all opium in most of Southeast Asia, the China coast and the entire Pacific rim. While the entire scheme failed within a couple of years, one cannot deny the vision and scope of Singapore's Chinese *taukehs* of the mid-nineteenth century (Trocki 2004).

These cliques created large accumulations of capital, which in time became the foundations for the major financial institutions of present-day Singapore. While it is difficult to trace the control of these accumulations through time, it is clear that ultimately the heirs, either natural or otherwise, of the revenue-farming cliques founded the first Chinese banks. A Hokkien group founded what became the Overseas Chinese Banking Corporation or OCBC. A Teochew group, operating with the capital of the Ngee Ann Kongsi, established the Four Seas Banking Corporation. The *kongsi* had been founded by the Seahs, but control of it, and the leadership of the Teochew community, was later wrested from them by Lim Nee Soon. However, the first Chinese bank, the Kwong Yik Bank, was founded by the Cantonese revenue farmer of Johor, Wong Ah Fook.

Beneath the world of global commerce, international corporations and wealthy merchants, however, there was a huge underclass. Singapore was still a "coolie town" more than anything else. James Warren shows that the wealth of Singapore still rested on the backs of multitudes of overworked and underpaid coolies, both Chinese and Indian (Warren 1986). In its early years, Singapore was a port town surrounded by settlements of agricultural coolies and planters. By the end of the nineteenth century, it had been transformed into a concentration of urban laborers. Singapore had become, overall, a city of rickshaw pullers, coal heavers, boatmen, stevedores, water carriers, fishermen and market gardeners. In many respects, these people had always been the backbone of the colony. In 1848, there had been 10,000 pepper and gambier planters resident on the island of Singapore out of a total population of about 50,000 (Siah 1847: 284; Saw 1991: 221), but fifty-four years later, Warren tells us, there were upwards of 22,000 rickshaw pullers in 1902, when the total population was 226,842 (Warren 1986:36–8).

These armies of mostly single young men turned the wheels of Singapore and made the great port function. If they were lucky, they earned about 40 cents a day in 1893 before deducting 8–10 cents for the rent of the rickshaw. By 1908, a puller could earn up to $2 a day, but by then there had been some inflation in the currency since the colony had gone onto the gold standard in 1906, so the cost of renting a rickshaw had also increased. This compared reasonably well with other working-class wages at the time. An ordinary coolie could earn only 50 cents a day, and a coal heaver could earn about $1. In the Malayan tin fields, a laborer earned 70 cents. The fares that rickshaw men could charge were fixed by municipal ordinance; thus in the late 1890s the fare was set at 6 cents per mile or 60 cents per hour, depending on whether they were hired by distance or time.

They lived packed into rooming houses in tiny cubicles scarcely more than two or three cubic meters in volume. Very often, these houses were rented to them by the same men who owned their rickshaws. Average rents were around $1 a month in the early part of the twentieth century. Warren notes that in 1914, fifteen rickshaw men living at 96 Queen Street were paying an average of $1.13 per month (Warren 1986: 45–7). They spent their lives, like most immigrant laborers, in a constant cycle of indebtedness, hard labor and grinding poverty.

The pullers were perhaps more fortunate than agricultural or mining coolies in the Malay states, or even worse, Sumatra, in that they received their pay immediately on completion of their labor and did not have to depend on the honesty of foremen or mine owners, who regularly cheated their workers (Wong 1965: 70–1; Stoler 1985). However, like the mining coolies, very few of the rickshaw pullers ever broke free of the cycle of sweated labor and poverty. In the 1840s, Seah Eu Chin estimated that only one or two coolies in ten ever returned to China, and from Warren's work, it is clear that things had not changed much by the twentieth century. Between the grueling labor of pulling a rickshaw in the tropical heat and the temptations of the gambling table, the opium den and the brothel, it was a major undertaking for an indentured *sinkeh* to pay off his debt and to actually accumulate some savings of his own.

> The rickshaw hire was 20 cents during the day and 25–30 cents during the night, which did not leave the puller very much. A rickshaw coolie made about $1 a day (or $24 a month) in 1924. He had to buy food out of that, for which a puller spent about 30 cents a day. That left him 40–50 cents to buy clothes, send money to China, pay the prostitute and buy opium, if he smoked. However, few pullers made more than $20 a month. Since the cost of living was $12 to $14 a month, the puller could count on $6–$8 clear to either remit or fritter away on opium, daughters of joy and gambling.
>
> (Warren 1986: 47)

Another army of laborers stood by to service these workers. Thousands of mobile noodle vendors and other food providers patrolled the streets and huddled in the verandahs to feed the multitude. Blacksmiths, metalworkers, carpenters, upholsterers and wheelwrights repaired and serviced their machines. Scribes wrote their letters home, and remittance "post offices" undertook to deliver their meager savings back to China. Beyond these were the opium shopkeepers, gambling house managers, spirit shopkeepers and brothel keepers to make sure that all their needs were met and that their pockets were always empty. Since these men were on their own in Singapore, they were ready customers for the 2,000 to 3,000 prostitutes who stood ready to serve them.

Warren has also written of these young women, mostly Chinese and Japanese girls who had either been sold by their parents or forced by their families' poverty to seek a living in the tropical port. Many of these were also under some form of indenture or debt burden that kept them in a state of virtual bondage. Between 1870 and 1905, prostitution was legal, and the government kept statistics on the number of brothels and prostitutes in Singapore. Warren points out that in addition to registered brothels, there were probably an equal number of unregistered establishments in the town. His figures show a total of 212 registered brothels in 1877 and 353 in 1905. In a number of selected samples in 1905, he calculated there were an average of 7.3 prostitutes per house in the brothels of Chinatown off New Bridge Road around Upper Hokkien Street and Upper Nankin Street, while further south in Sago Street and Sago Lane, there were 12.2 girls per house, while in the Japanese brothels of Kampong Glam, there were 5.8 prostitutes per house (Warren 1993: 44–9). It is also worth noting that Warren's maps in the inside cover pages of both books show that the brothel districts and rickshaw tenements were in close proximity to each other.

Global depression and global war

It was perhaps the exploitative and unbalanced nature of the economy that helped to bring on the global depression that struck the world in the late 1920s and 1930s. Singapore was typical of the colonized world in the incredibly low wages paid to the working classes. The disparities between the rich and poor in the colony simply mirrored the global imbalance between colonized states and imperial centers. As an *entrepôt*, Singapore had become a conduit for the flow of industrial raw materials from tropical Asia to the industrialized West. By the interwar period, the bulk of Singapore's trade with the developed world was flowing to North America. From 1915 onwards (except for the very depths of the depression in 1930–33), more than 50 percent of Singapore's trade with the West went to North America. The ultimate problem was that the reverse was not also occurring.

This shift in trade flows to the western hemisphere reflected a number of changing circumstances. The key aspect of this was the rapid industrialization taking place in both the USA and Japan. The USA was now reaching out across the Pacific, and the global trading community around that ocean was strengthening with the emergence of Japan as an industrial power. Particularly important was the expansion of automobile production and use in the USA that came with the development of Henry Ford's Model T assembly line and the creation of a mass market for the motor car. This absorbed increasing quantities of the rubber and petroleum of Malaya and the Dutch East Indies, most of which flowed through Singapore (Wong 1991: 54–6).

Singapore's connection to the global economy, always an Achilles heel for an *entrepôt* state, left it most vulnerable to the rapid shifts that came with the mid-twentieth century. In particular, its role in processing and shipping prime industrial raw materials such as tin and rubber were both its strength and its weakness. With World War I came a sharp rise in demand for both these commodities. Thus, in 1913, the Dutch East Indies and British Malaya

Figure 1.3 Boat Quay and the Singapore River in 1900, with Fort Canning in
   the background.

exported 7,000 tons and 33,000 tons of rubber, respectively. By 1919, the two
were shipping 88,000 and 200,000 tons, respectively. This response to
wartime demand led to an expansion of production that was hit by depression immediately following the war. The economy bounced back as US
automobile production boomed in the mid-1920s. By 1925, Malaya was
exporting $763 million worth of rubber and $175 million worth of tin; by
1929, the Dutch colony was exporting 255,000 tons of rubber and Malaya
was shipping 455,000 tons (Allen and Donnithorne 1957: 295). Although
production declined relatively little with the coming of the Depression, the
price of rubber on the London market fell sharply, going from 10¼d to 2⁵⁄₁₆d
a pound, thus losing 75 percent of its value (*ibid.*: 125).

   The large steamships that carried rubber, tin, copra, petroleum and other
industrial commodities from Southeast Asia to the West returned with
manufactures that had to be marketed in the colonized world. Even though
the availability of cheap raw materials helped to fuel this upsurge in industrialization, unfortunately, because of the wage structure in Singapore and
other colonies, there simply was not enough purchasing power to draw down
the inexorably growing quantities of mass-produced consumer goods. With
their markets oversupplied, Western manufacturers began to cut production,
lay off workers and reduce their orders of raw materials.

Singapore's trade hit a high point in 1926, peaking at $1,886.7 million, with more than half its exports going to the West and 60 percent of that going to the USA. The following year, trade values began to slide, and by 1933 the total value of Singapore's trade stood at $512.8 million. It would not be until after more than a decade and a half of depression and war that Singapore's economy would begin to revive, and not until the 1950s that the levels reached in the 1920s would be matched.

The problem of overproduction led to a number of schemes whereby the Dutch and British producers attempted to limit production, but this led the American companies to seek other sources of supply. Thus Ford initiated rubber planting in Brazil and Firestone in Liberia. The 1930s also brought a number of protectionist schemes such as Imperial Preferences, the Hawley–Smoot Tariff in the USA and restrictions on foreign shipping in the Dutch East Indies, all of which cut into the vitality of Singapore's *entrepôt* trade. The Depression also had the effect of forcing smallholders in Malaya and Indonesia to simply stop production, while the estates, with large over-heads and permanent staff, had to continue producing (Allen and Donnithorne 1957: 125). While this led the large producers to cut costs and increase efficiency, the cuts in staff led to rising unemployment. Many of these individuals left the Malay states and came to Singapore looking for work. With no more opportunities available in Singapore, the government was faced with growing populations of unemployed coolies. For the first time in its history, it was forced to formulate schemes to repatriate immigrant labor.

Around the end of the nineteenth century, the British and Dutch governments began to take steps to protect their national shipping lines from competition. The Batavia Freight Conference and the Straits various agreements aimed at reducing competition and stabilizing rates between Europe and the Straits or to New York. For Chinese firms and Singapore merchants not acting as agents for European shippers, these agreements were largely detrimental to Singapore's trade, but little was done to combat them. After World War I, there was general stagnation of international shipping, which led to further restrictions.

In addition to Chinese shipping firms based in Singapore and the other Straits Settlements, these restrictive agreements also hit the Japanese, who were rapidly expanding their merchant fleet in the 1920s and 1930s (*ibid.*: 212). These restrictions on Japanese shipping, together with the imperial preference schemes, which hurt Japanese manufacturing exports to Southeast Asia, were among the circumstances that fueled Japanese ambitions to establish themselves as a great power in Southeast Asia. At the same time, Japan was among the few countries that were beginning to invest heavily in the development of new mining ventures in the region. By the late 1930s, Japanese firms were mining iron in Johor and other states in Malaya, and in 1938 they exported 1.6 million tons of ore, much of it through Singapore. By this time, Japan was also mining bauxite and manganese in

Malaya (*ibid.*: 166). Japan's growing needs for Southeast Asia's raw materials and the barriers to the products of Japan's industry created a sense of frustration among their business leaders that brought them to support the adventurous policy of the Japanese military and provided a set of causes for going to war.

The Pacific War was an economic disaster for Singapore. While it continued in its role as an exporter of raw materials from colonial, or in this case, occupied Southeast Asia to industrialized Japan, it reaped even less than before in the way of profits. All Europeans were interned, and the Chinese were faced with a range of extortionist schemes to provide "donations" for the Japanese war effort. Thus the business community was seriously weakened and impoverished. Manufactured consumer goods did not flow back through Singapore's markets to the countries of Southeast Asia, and the demands of the war meant that Singapore's infrastructure of dockyards, repair facilities, shipbuilding, refining and processing industries were not kept up, and they gradually deteriorated. Its roads, railroads and bridges likewise fell into disrepair. Singapore would emerge from the war in very poor condition. Its infrastructure was outdated and badly damaged, short of capital and flooded with unemployed workers who were now mobilized by a dynamic Communist Party.

2   Colonial society

In examining Singapore's social order, it is important to remember two things. The first is that in the world before nation-states, when populations were not motivated by the sentiment of nationalism, linguistic and cultural diversity was not always seen as a "problem". The development of print capitalism and mass society demand a certain level of homogeneity, and often the value of diversity is called into question. This process of movement from what might be called a "traditional Indian Ocean port society" to a colonial "plural society" is one of the major social developments that have shaped Singapore's social order. There is a certain irony here, because at the very time the sentiments of nationalism were developing, the various populations were becoming more similar than ever before.

The second point is that Britain ruled Singapore, and the Europeans, primarily the British, wielded a high level of social and economic power. On the other hand, Europeans were a very small part of the population, and thus their influence and exercise of power were always somewhat diluted. There was a large gap between intent and result. Although they were only dimly aware of it, they had placed themselves in the midst of an ongoing situation, and many of the social forces around them were out of their hands.

Singapore was largely an immigrant society, and the island's social order emerged as a highly diverse mosaic. Aside from the obvious differences of race and national origin of both the original inhabitants and the immigrant settlers, there were further distinctions of both locale and class that need to be considered. Within the basic divisions of Europeans, Chinese, Malays and Indians; of Muslims, Buddhists, Hindus, Confucianists, Jews, Christians, Daoists and animists; there were numerous subgroups that make these broad classifications quite inadequate. Emigrants from China, for instance, were more likely to identify themselves as Hokkien, Teochew or Cantonese, while people from different parts of the Malayan peninsula would see themselves first as *Orang Kelantan* or *Orang Kedah* rather than as Malay. The same was true for natives of South Asia. Moreover, once groups settled in Singapore, differences in lifestyle, caste, education, wealth, power and place of residence in the population made the picture more complex. Add to this the continuing process of change over time, which did not take place evenly among the different communities of Singapore, as well as the interactions between and among the various groups that came to inhabit Singapore and the situation becomes truly intricate.

Finally, there is the question of consciousness of identity, which was a crucial factor in the development of sources that would permit the creation of a narrative. Here, one of the key difficulties is that many of the narratives have been structured around the European discourse. Most of the sources for the history of Singapore's society are in colonial records, newspapers and general descriptions, most of which are in English and present a European point of view. It is thus necessary to look at these sources, but also to try to look through them and past them when necessary and, when possible, to supplement them with information derived from other sources.

The Indian Ocean maritime port society

As soon as Singapore was founded, thousands of traders, mariners and adventurers immediately flocked to the place; within five years, the population had already exceeded 10,000. It included Chinese, Malays, Indians and other Malaysians (e.g. Filipinos, Javanese, Madurese, Bawaenese, Bugis, Minangkabau, Acehnese, other Sumatrans and Borneans, as well as those from the eastern islands). There were also Siamese, Cochin Chinese, Cambodians, Burmese or Mons, Arabs, Armenians, Parsees, Jews and others. Aside from the local Malays and some of the Europeans, the population was at first largely male. This was a typical mixture that had probably characterized most of the Indian Ocean and South China Sea ports and port polities for a considerable prior period, although it is possible that in earlier times there would have been a higher proportion of local women acting as traders and as temporary wives (Reid 1988: 154–6, 164–5). The exact proportion of various races and nationalities depended on how close to China, India or the Arab Gulfs the port was located. Within the port, each group lived in its own quarter of the town and was often ruled by its own headmen and under its own laws and customs, in so far as they did not conflict with the local rulers.

That is to say, Singapore itself, and the population that arrived there after 1819, were not really new phenomena but rather represented a perennial pattern that had a longstanding tradition behind it. We must assume that a similar social mix would have characterized Riau fifty or sixty years prior to the 1820s. It would also have been true of Palembang, Jambi, Aceh, Ayuthaya, Patani, Brunei, Saigon and others. This was an aspect of what Kwa Chong Guan called the *alam Melayu*, or the "Malay world":

> Much has been made of the 'plural society' which was established in Singapore from 1819 onwards. But plurality was also a defining feature of the *alam Melayu*. Located within a maritime environment, this *alam Melayu* was an open world into which not only non-Malays but also

Malays outside the *alam Melayu* crossed into. For the Malays of the Riaus, this was *jemberang*, crossing to the other side of the Straits of Singapore, Melaka or the various passages of the Riaus. This movement of people created complex issues of who then are the indigenous and exogenous population of a locality? What are the factors determining the degree of indigeny and exogeny in a community and shaping its identity? These issues of indigeny and exogeny link Singapore to its roots in the *alam Melayu*.

(Kwa 1998: 23)

Going back even further, it is clear that some sort of Malay emporium existed at Singapore during the fourteenth century where both Chinese and Indian traders met merchants from all over Southeast Asia. John Miksic's re-examination of the literary sources on Singapore's history in that era, together with his archaeological work at Fort Canning Hill, provide significant evidence to demonstrate the existence of an important Malay port-polity on the island.

It was an active Malay emporium and ceremonial centre from the fourteenth century, when it was at its height, to the end of the seventeenth century. His work reaffirms the perennial importance of not only Singapore Island but also of the Riau–Lingga Islands and the south Johor region in the historical consciousness of the Malay people (Miksic 1985: 19–35). It thus seems probable that the polyglot population of traders and mariners that characterized Singapore in the nineteenth century were also typical of Malay emporia of the past.

We get some idea of the diversity of the population in the early part of the century from Edmund Roberts, the American envoy to Siam and Cochin China, who visited Singapore in 1833 and offered a breakdown of the population (see Table 2.1). Roberts' statistics can be compared with the estimates given by John Crawfurd two decades later. The number of females in the population had increased considerably by 1833 to nearly one in four, but we have no breakdown of their ethnicity. One would assume that most were Malays, possibly as many as 3,000 or so. As the indigenous population, their sex ratio would have been the closest to 50:50 of any of the ethnic groups listed. Perhaps as many as 4,000 Chinese would have been among the "country and plantation" dwellers. This large population of Chinese laborers made a difference. Because of them and the unassimilable lump that they represented, they constituted a different element to that which had characterized earlier settlements. In addition, the fact that their presence made Singapore a labor exchange as well as a trading center brought a new element into the mix.

What is interesting here is that over 50 percent of the population did not live in the town prior to 1850, and this remained the case for some years afterwards. In fact, the proportion of rural dwellers, particularly those on the plantations, was relatively high. This is of great importance when

Table 2.1 Singapore's population: sex, ethnicity and location, 1830–60.

	1830	1833	1840	1850(a)	1850(b)	1860
Sex						
Male		15,181			52,000	
Female		5,997			7,500	
Ethnicity						
European	92	119	167	360	360	2,445[a]
Eurasian	–	90	–	922	–	–
Native Christian	300	–	–	–	–	–
Armenian	–	35	–	–	–	–
Jew	–	2	–	–	–	–
Arab	–	96	–	–	–	–
Malay	5,173	7,131	9,032	12,206	13,800	10,888[b]
Chinese	6,555	8,517	17,179	27,988	31,800	50,043
Indian	1,913	2,724	3,159	6,261	8,400	12,971
Malaysian[c]	3,571	–	–	–	4,200	
Other	–	39	–	–	–	–
Location						
Rural and plantations	–	7,362		–	34,000[d]	–
Islands	–	1,072	–	–	–	–
Town	–	12,544		–	26,000	–
Total	16,634	20,978	39,681	59,034	60,000	80,792

Sources: Mills (1925: 217) for 1830, 1840, 1850(a), 1860; Roberts (1837: 323) for 1833; Crawfurd (1971: 400) for 1850(b).

Notes
a This figure probably includes Eurasians, Armenians, Jews, etc.
b This seems far too low and probably indicates that much of the kampong and outer island population was not counted.
c Here "Malaysian" means natives of the Indonesian/Malayan archipelago (i.e. Javanese, Bugis, Balinese, etc.), whereas "Malay" refers to Muslim natives of the Riau–Lingga Archipelago, the Malayan peninsula and Sumatra.
d Includes islands.

looking at the Chinese and Malay populations of Singapore. At about this time, the rural parts of the island were essentially *terra incognita* to the European population. Given this, it is possible that the statistics themselves may be questionable. Although G.W. Earl was exaggerating when he said that there was an independent Chinese community living in the interior of the island that no European had visited, he was perhaps not far wrong (Lee 1978).

In comparing Crawfurd's statistics with Roberts', it is noteworthy that the population had nearly tripled, and the pattern of increasing Chinese dominance in the numbers was beginning to show by 1850. Their numbers, as well as those of the Indians, had increased nearly fourfold, and the Chinese had already become the majority group in the population. While Crawfurd does not give details, we may assume that the greater part of the Chinese were working on pepper and gambier plantations. Crawfurd also points out that the male:female ratio had shifted again. In the 1850s, he claimed that there were seven men to one woman overall, and among the Chinese the ratio was 18:1, which he described as "a source of much immorality and disorder" (Crawfurd 1971: 400).

It was the appearance of this rural population of migrants, most of whom worked in some form of commercial agriculture, that made Singapore

Figure 2.1 Commercial Square in about 1906.

different from earlier port-polities that partook of the Indian Ocean maritime cultural complex. While it is clear that Riau actually pioneered this innovation, Riau does not seem to have become a center for labor exchange in the same way that Singapore did. In fact, it was this population and the coolie trade that was built upon it that made the long-term function of Singapore and British Malaya unique. In addition to being an *entrepôt*, Singapore would also be a bridgehead from which the Malayan interior would be opened up to commercial agriculture and mining ventures. In the future, these would be a major source of the port's prosperity. While these were largely economic functions, they had major social implications for Singapore and for Malayan society in general, because the main actors in these developments were Chinese and, later, Indians.

British mercantile society (Scotsmen, sailors and agencies)

The European population of Singapore was like that of most Asian colonies: minuscule when compared with the Asian population. In 1824, when the overall population was over 10,000, there were only eighty-seven Europeans in the colony. Over a century later, in 1931, when the total population numbered almost 570,000, there were just over 8,000 (Braddell 1934: 42–3). Despite their small numbers, they possessed decisive military strength and unity of purpose; they also controlled the flow of capital.

The Europeans constituted the social elite of the town. Virtually all of them were wealthy, and even if they were not, they lived well. In fact, the British in Singapore believed, as did their colleagues in India, that their power depended on prestige, and that prestige could be maintained only if all Europeans kept up the most affluent of appearances. Thus, as John Cameron pointed out in the 1860s, Singapore was no place for poor or working-class Europeans (Cameron 1865). Aside from the fact that a European craftsman could not compete with a Chinese, it would never do for the natives to see a European doing physical labor, or worse yet, living in poverty. In fact, the European residents took pains to make sure that such "unfortunates" did not get stranded in Singapore.

> It would be a mistake however to imagine that the Straits Settlements present any field for the industry or enterprise of the working classes at home. ... Two Chinese carpenters will generally do the labour of one European, and their wages together will amount to less than a half of what it would cost the European to live in even the meanest condition. ... There is no more pitiable sight than to see, as are sometimes to be seen, strong able-bodied men willing to work whom accident has cast on these shores, seeking in vain for employment. ... It is not only painful, but in a place where it is essential to keep up the prestige of the European, it is humiliating to witness the straits to which these men are sometimes brought (Cameron 1865).

This was at a time when the average Chinese unskilled laborer earned between $3 and $6 per month, while the skilled carpenter or mechanic could expect a monthly wage of $10 to $15. The average European inhabitant of Singapore, according to Cameron, supported a "turn out" of a horse and carriage, which itself could be valued at about $100. He lived in a house set on one to two acres of land, which, if he did not own it, would cost him about $60 per month to rent. Chinese coolies in "Chinatown" often lived ten to fifteen men per room (Leung 1988). Economically and socially, Europeans and Asians lived in very different worlds.

Although there was a constant concern for European sailors, who were regularly stranded in Singapore, there were special arrangements for them. They could stay in the sailors' home while they waited for a berth on an outgoing ship. In their own part of the town, with their own drinking houses and brothels, they were but birds of passage and, except for the ships' officers, did not form part of European society. Some of this manufactured prestige was eroded when Asians students visited Europe and studied in British universities, but it was some time before the masses actually saw large numbers of whites in demeaning circumstances. For many, this did not occur until 1942.

The core of European society was the group of Scottish merchants who controlled the most prominent agency houses in the town. Men such as A.L. Johnston, W.H. Read, John Purvis and James Guthrie were counted among the leading lights of the colony during the middle years of the nineteenth century. The generation that came after them, such as William Patterson, Henry Minchin Simons, W.G. Gulland and William H. Shelford, dominated the municipal government and served as members of the Legislative Council in the years after 1867, when Singapore and the other Straits Settlements were taken under the Colonial Office. They controlled the Chamber of Commerce, the Masonic Lodge of Zetland of the East and whatever else passed for "society" in Singapore. They had race days, amateur theatricals and yacht races, and they promenaded on the esplanade. Charles Burton Buckley's *Anecdotal History of Old Times in Singapore* is a catalog of their doings (Buckley 1903). Their firms recruited young men, mostly from among their own extended families in Britain, and sent them out as junior members expecting them to spend the greater part of their lives in Singapore.

It is also of significance that they controlled the flow of information, not only about themselves but also about their fellow inhabitants of the colony. We know a great deal about their entertainments, sports and, of course, trade, which is what they were there for. Beyond that, they were quite limited and insular. Few of them (after the first generation of country traders) seem to have traveled much in other parts of Asia. Aside from smatterings of bazaar Malay and perhaps bits of Hindi or Persian, none of them spoke any Asian language, least of all any of the Chinese dialects. Nonetheless, they had fixed opinions about lazy, bloodthirsty, devious, polite Malays; greedy, opium-soaked, industrious, voluptuous Chinese; and untrustworthy, over-educated, litigious Indians. We learn a lot about the morality or lack thereof among the Asians around them.

On the other hand, we know virtually nothing about the family life of the Europeans or their sexual preferences. This was an important issue, since in the late 1820s the sex ratio of the population was 17:1, men to women. We hear little about Eurasians, other than comments about the rather limited community of long standing that was mostly of Portuguese or Dutch origin. There appear to have been relatively few European women in Singapore, but the question of what most European men did for sex is rarely raised in the studies. Still less do we hear of the social consequences of the interracial liaisons that one assumes must have existed. It was not until the early part of the twentieth century that significant numbers of European women began to reside in Singapore and that European family life began to assume an important place in local society.

Until that time, it seems that European society was really quite homogeneous. Aside from the merchants, there were some administrators and military personnel. These were supplemented by a small corps of professionals: lawyers, surveyors, architects, doctors, missionaries, a few teachers and some journalists. It was not until the turn of the twentieth century that the European population became more diverse. In particular, with the arrival of significant numbers of European women – the spouses of merchants, colonial administrators, plantation managers, missionaries and others, as well as young women from England out to find a wealthy husband – European society began to diversify considerably. The development of steam travel in the last quarter of the nineteenth century made communications with the metropole much more expeditious and convenient. By 1900, the voyage from Britain to Singapore was only a matter of weeks rather than of months. It also became common for colonial civil servants to be moved at regular intervals within the empire. This not only increased the size and diversity of the community but also increased the rate of turnover and transience.

As diversity began to develop within European society, so too did social and cultural stratification begin to exhibit itself among the whites. No longer was it enough to simply be white to be "one of us"; one also needed a level of wealth, education and connections to move in the higher levels of European society. Also, with the more rapid turnover of the population moving, entering and leaving the colony, it became more difficult to readily identify the "right sort" of people. This development of patterns of discrimination in European society was also reflected outwards into their relations with the non-European masses. As John Butcher has pointed out in his perceptive study of the British in Malaya, at the very time when one of the great goals of British imperialism was being achieved – that of educating and "civilizing" the natives by which they adopted more and more of the language, culture and practices of Europeans – we find Europeans erecting a color bar and systematically beginning to exclude Asians from their company (Butcher 1979).

In order to be like Europeans, Asians learned English. They learned to play cricket, tennis and football. They dressed, ate and drank like Europeans. The Chinese abandoned their traditional dress and cut their queues: the Indians did likewise and cut their beards, threw aside their turbans and dhotis and ignored the dietary and avoidance rules of their castes. They scorned those Asians who clung to the old ways, only to find that Europeans were increasingly hostile to their advances. Asians were excluded from sports clubs and similar social organizations throughout Singapore and Malaya. They had become "wogs".

It is important to understand that many of these restrictions did not originally exist but were implemented gradually and more and more rigorously around the beginning of the twentieth century. During the early part of the nineteenth century, for instance, wealthy Chinese merchants were accepted as members of the Singapore Chamber of Commerce. By the third quarter of the century, however, they were excluded. This is why later it was necessary for the Chinese to establish their own Chamber of Commerce.

While dinners, dances and other such social gatherings, which included guests from the various communities, were infrequent during the first half of the nineteenth century, they did occur. Buckley and other writers describe such occasions, but by the end of the century, such events were no longer being held.

Taukeh town

Most Chinese did not come to Singapore to build a new society or to found a "community." They came to make money and then return to their homes as quickly as possible. Everything else was subsidiary. However, they did create social structures. Of great importance were the secret societies, or triad organizations, which it may be argued, Chinese settlers originally intended for their own welfare and security and to serve as a sort of "temporary society" in a foreign land (Trocki 1990). The earliest triads were probably indistinguishable from the *kongsis* organized by coolies and *taukehs* to facilitate joint economic ventures such as mines, or in Singapore, pepper and gambier plantations. These allowed for the pooling of labor and capital and allotted shares in the venture to each participant. These were usually formalized by traditional Chinese oaths and rituals of sworn brotherhood as a substitute for kinship relations. Within a few years of its founding, there came to be a number of fairly isolated settlements in Singapore's interior. This was Lee Poh Ping's "pepper and gambier society." He distinguished them from the "free-trade society" of the town, grouped around the European agency traders (Lee 1978).

Initially, the Asian portion of the free-trade society was dominated both economically and socially by the Straits-born Chinese, most of whom had come from Melaka, although there were also some from Penang. Overall, these families displayed considerable staying power, managing to increase their wealth and prestige over the course of the nineteenth century. In contrast to the newcomers, these did belong to a recognizable "community", and as they settled in Singapore, they created a replica of the Melaka/Penang social formation there as well. At the same time, with the constant influx of immigrants there was always a continuing level of competition from successful *sinkehs* whose wealth demanded an accommodation within Straits Chinese society.

It is important to remember that in the nineteenth century, most of the Chinese in Southeast Asia were of lowly origin, and social status was determined largely by the wealth that one was able to acquire in the marketplace. Scholars and gentry-class Chinese did not emigrate, thus it was merchants who constituted the elite of Singapore's society, both Chinese and European. By contrast, most of the Europeans who came to Singapore in the nineteenth century were from established mercantile families in Britain, whereas except for the Babas, most Chinese were self-made men.

Possessed of some capital, knowledge of English and connections to the European rulers on the one hand, and knowledge of Malay and connections to various segments of Malay and other nearby Southeast Asian societies on the other, the Straits-born merchants flourished in the early years of the settlement. Even those without much capital could depend on the Europeans, for whom they could work as compradors or alternatively on the wealthy but less well-connected Chinese merchants who spoke no English.

The wealthy traders of the town established their reputations as leaders through charitable works and public donations. Thus Tan Tock Seng, one of the early Melaka Chinese who came to Singapore, founded a pauper's hospital. Tan Kim Seng built the Chinese Free School (Chui Eng Si E). Cheang Hong Lim, the opium and spirit farmer, also founded a school, as well as a park and a temple, and maintained a fire brigade. Kim Seng built a road and donated $13,000 toward a waterworks. Such undertakings were necessary in a society where the government provided virtually no services. These men became the founders of the Straits Chinese society that came to dominate Singapore throughout the nineteenth century.

They also selectively cultivated close relations with successful but newly arrived Chinese, hoping to feather their own nests. In addition to their access to European capital, they also possessed another important asset: women. Given the male:female ratio among Chinese of 18:1 in 1850, Straits Chinese families with marriageable daughters could attract the most successful China-born merchants to ally with their families. Straits-born merchants could organize powerful *kongsi* organizations to protect the wealth and welfare of their families and clans over the long term, providing for education, burials, support for the destitute and other social benefits.

Such alliances could also be of great benefit to the newcomers. The career of someone like Seah Eu Chin is instructive. He was a Teochew and came to Singapore in 1823 from Swatow. Since he had had some education in China, he was able to find employment as a bookkeeper and a commission merchant for Yeo Kim Swee, a Straits-born "Baba" Chinese. Not only was Seah able to get a start in business but on Kim Swee's death, Eu Chin became his heir and was able to take over his land and assets (Song 1923: 19–20, 43). In the 1840s, Seah married the daughter of Tan Ah Hun, the Teochew Capitan China of Perak. When she died prematurely, he married her younger sister. The girls also brought along their younger brother, Tan Seng Poh, who, on Seah's retirement in 1864, took over the family's pepper and gambier businesses and became famous as one of the most powerful opium farmers in Singapore. He was also a municipal councillor and controlled extensive landholdings and the Alexandra Gunpowder Magazine, and he held shares in the Tanjong Pagar Dock Company (Trocki 1993).

Seah's sons succeeded to control of the family business in the 1880s after Tan Seng Poh's death in 1879. Seah Liang Seah, Seah Peck Seah and Seah Chiu Seah were recognized as leading lights in Straits Chinese society in the 1880s and 1890s (Song 1923). In addition to dominating the pepper and gambier business and opium farming, the Seah/Tan family exercised a controlling influence over a large section of the Singapore Teochew community. In the 1850s, Seah Eu Chin had emerged as a leader of the Teochew community and was seen by the British as one of the "headmen," who was responsible for the general conduct of the remainder of the community. The major community institution for the Teochews was the Ngee Ann Kun, later called the Ngee Ann Kongsi. Through their position as directors of this temple and burial association, the Seah family dominated the Singapore Teochew *bang* until the 1890s.

The *bangs* were the other major Chinese social grouping in Singapore. *Bang* membership was determined by language grouping and place of origin. Thus in addition to the Teochew *bang* there were Hokkien, Cantonese, Hakka and Hainanese *bangs*. Each was dominated by the wealthiest and most influential merchants of that group, and these men were recognized by the British as the "headmen" of their respective communities. However, the list of the five *bangs* is a simplification. The solidarity of the *bangs* was often a tenuous thing, and there were occasional splits and conflicts among leadership cliques and subethnic groups.

The waning of the opium/pepper and gambier complex undermined the social and political position of groups like the Seahs. On the one hand, the Seahs and the Teochew Tans had always been in competition with the Hokkien for dominance in Singapore. Sometime in the mid-1850s, the Hokkien achieved numerical domination in Singapore and have maintained it to the present. This shift in population numbers occurred about the time of the Hokkien–Teochew riots of 1854, when there was an influx of Hokkien and Teochew fighters from uprisings in China. This led to the move by a large number of Teochew to Johor. In the next two or three decades, the pepper and gambier society and the Teochew expanded across the straits into Johor. There the Ngee Heng Kongsi found a congenial home with the Temenggong and his descendants.

However, there were divisions within the Singapore Teochew community that the Seahs never fully defeated. During the 1860s, a number of clans (surname groups) broke away from the Ngee Ann Kongsi federation. These were the Lim and Chua clans. The Chua group was of particular importance, since it was also known as the Ghee Hock Society and was led by Chua Moh Choon, an important Ghee Hock–Ghee Hin headman, merchant and coolie broker. These groups kept up a continual opposition to the Seahs and the Tan clan throughout the period 1860 to 1890. During the 1890s, a new generation of outsiders led by Lim Nee Soon challenged Seah control of the Ngee Ann Kongsi and forced a change in the leadership. In succeeding years, the Teochew coalesced around the Sze Hai Tong, or Four Seas group, which later established a bank and became the financial core of the wealthy Teochew merchant clique.

There were also conflicts within the Hokkien *bang*. The major fracture line was the division between migrants from different regions, in particular the Quanzhou and Zhangzhou people. Ultimately, lines were drawn between the Haizhang group led by Tan Tock Seng and later by his son, Tan Kim Ching, who represented most of the Melaka-born Hokkien. On the other side was the Zhang Hai group, led by the opium and spirit farmer Cheang Sam Teo and later by his son, Cheang Hong Lim. The conflict between these various groups, reflected in their support for rival burial societies, temples, schools and other charitable institutions, has been discussed by Yen Ching Hwang (Yen 1986: 181–91).

From the mid-nineteenth century, another sort of social grouping began to develop alongside the triads and their component clan and *bang* groups. These were the *huiguan*. These were smaller and more specifically oriented organizations that brought together individuals of the same lineage, place of origin (whether village, district, or group of districts), occupational group, etc. These too began to offer a range of social services to the new immigrants, such as temporary housing, employment and burial. Ultimately, they also founded temples, schools and cemeteries. These were supported by charitable donations from wealthy members and naturally fell under the leadership of the *taukehs*. By the last quarter of the nineteenth century, these had begun to aggregate themselves along *bang* lines, and they came to make up the components of more broadly based groups such as the Hokkien Association (Hokien Hui Guan) and the Teochew Association (or Poi Ip (Eight Districts) Hui Guan). Control of these groups gave the merchant elite a vehicle for social and economic control of specific constituencies, and the hierarchical aggregation of the groups provided an avenue through which the colonial government could access the Chinese population.

An important shift occurred in the leadership groups of Singapore society around the turn of the twentieth century. On the one hand, groups such as the opium farmers, pepper and gambier dealers, labor brokers, rice merchants, ship owners and other pillars of what might be called the "old economy" began to decline in wealth and, concurrently, status. In addition to well-heeled merchants from prominent Straits Chinese families, a group of aggressive newcomers sought wealth from the emergence of the rubber economy. The older families and many of the newcomers tended to be Hokkien. A small group of them rapidly made vast fortunes in rubber and in the establishment of Chinese banks. Men such as Tan Kah Kee, Lee Kong Chian, Tan Lark Sye and Lim Nee Soon became the leading lights of the Chinese community in the late nineteenth and early twentieth century (Visscher 2002).

Ultimately, men such as these became the leaders of the five *bangs* and managed to come together to form the Singapore Chinese Chamber of Commerce. At the beginning of the twentieth century, the wealth and power of the upper echelons of Chinese business leadership was represented by this group. By this time, however, wealth and entrepreneurship were no longer the only markers of status.

The educated members of this group were also important in the process of re-sinification that began to occur toward the end of the nineteenth century. Individuals such as Lim Boon Keng rediscovered their roots, studied Chinese and began to promote the revival of Confucian culture among their fellows. These efforts came at a time when China was undergoing an anti-dynastic and reformist movement that would ultimately be overtaken by Sun Yat-sen's revolutionary nationalist movement. The schools, newspapers and voluntary organizations of the Chinese community would soon find a political focus.

While the wealthy merchants in their mansions would take leading roles in these movements, they came to depend increasingly on the growing numbers of middle-class Chinese: smaller shopkeepers, clerks and professional men. Many of these were English-educated and came to develop a middle-class lifestyle in suburbs such as Katong. Many continued to form an important second echelon of community leadership between the wealthy elite and the masses of the laboring population.

Coolie city

While Chinese coolies were among the first to arrive in Singapore, they did not come to comprise the largest single group in the overall population until about 1850, when Chinese became the most numerous group in the population. At first, it would seem that most of them moved through the town quite rapidly and out into the gambier and pepper plantations of the island's interior. Certainly, the first form of social order they would have encountered was the Ghee Hin or Ngee Heng *kongsi*, the local version of the Heaven and Earth Society, the Tiandihui. For most of the first sixty years of the settlement's existence, this was the major social group on the island in that it was the largest and most powerful.

The society appears to have evolved over time from a relatively egalitarian brotherhood of laborers and small capitalists to an exploitative institution run by the wealthy *taukehs* and aimed at intimidating the labor force and controlling the revenue farms. The first notice we have of the society's presence in Singapore is the description by Munshi Abdullah bin Abdul Kadir of an initiation that he witnessed in about 1824 or 1825 (Abdullah 1970). The society seems to have dominated the life of ordinary Chinese until at least the 1880s, when it was finally banned by the British government. Until that time, it would be incorrect to call it a "secret" society, although that is the term that was generally used, since its rituals were secret as were its membership lists, but everyone knew it existed, and it was tolerated by the colonial government. It was a key element of what Lee Poh Ping has termed the "pepper and gambier society" that comprised the mass of Singapore's rural population in those years.

The *kongsi*, a form of organization that Wang Tai Peng has described as a native form of Chinese democracy, was initially structured as a corporate brotherhood (Wang 1995). It is probable that the Ngee Heng or Ghee Hin reflected a similar ideology and practice in its early years in Singapore and was intimately connected with the economic and social organization of pepper and gambier agriculture. It appears that the *kongsi* exercised a fairly high degree of autonomy throughout the first half of the nineteenth century. If it bore any resemblance to the *kongsis* of Hakka miners in Borneo, it

Figure 2.2 Singapore's workforce. A group of Chinese and Malay coolies gathered at Tong Cheong Tailor in about 1900.

offered laborers shares in their enterprises, a sense of social solidarity and a measure of self-defense in their isolated communities. My own studies of the *kangchu* system in Johor show that each pepper and gambier settlement was organized around a *kongsi* made up of the capitalist and the planters. This was the organizational pattern exported from Singapore and that had probably been pioneered in Riau during the previous century. As time passed, shopkeepers and capitalists took control of the *kongsis* and the settlements, and coolies and planters were reduced to wage laborers.[7] This shift in power and wealth was probably at the root of some of the conflict in the Chinese community around the middle of the nineteenth century.

The triad also reflected Singapore's wider Chinese society in that it was, or at least came to be, divided into ethnic components, or *bang*. There were also ethnic and linguistic subdivisions among these general categories. They were also divided by "clan," or more correctly by surname group, but all these subdivisions were seen as but components of the overarching Ghee Hin.

Recent research by David Chng has revealed some little-known facets of the organization and leadership of the Ghee Hin (Chng 1999). His study of the funerary tablets stored in the Five Tiger Shrine, or Shekong Temple, on Lavender Street in the Rochore district of Singapore town shows a well-organized and ideologically coherent institution that flourished between the 1830s and the 1880s. It also exposes an entirely new stratum of middle-level Chinese leaders. The funerary tablets commemorating these men show that they carried a variety of ranks and titles. Most were styled "patriotic guardsmen" (*yishi*) of the Ming, but while thus reasserting the triad society's fundamental aim of opposing the Qing dynasty and restoring the Ming, there is little evidence of their anti-Qing campaign in Singapore. Rather, Chng shows that the use of terminology reflecting the pro-Ming ideology did not come into use until after the Small Sword Society uprising in China in the early 1850s (*ibid.*: 42–7).[8]

These men were highly influential in local social and economic matters. In 1860, the Ghee Hin society, combining its various *bang* branches, had a membership of about 27,500 (*ibid.*: 50). At that time, the total population of Singapore was 80,792, with 50,043 Chinese, thus the society comprised about one-third of Singapore's population and over half of all Chinese in the colony. These "patriotic guardsmen" no doubt constituted the "political" or charismatic leadership of the society. Some of them were undoubtedly wealthy *taukehs*, but the evidence suggests that many of them were martial arts specialists and individuals who were capable of providing military leadership for the defense of the rural communities.

J.D. Vaughan, who wrote a fairly detailed and knowledgeable account of the Chinese in the Straits Settlements, claimed that the society represented a "government" for the Chinese, providing for welfare and burials, settling disputes, and judging and enforcing its own laws in its own courts. As the power of the government grew and the tendencies toward rationalization increased, the power of the society was seen as a threat to the government's power. By the late 1860s, the government had begun to take steps to register and regulate, and ultimately to ban the secret societies, particularly as they came to be seen as sources of public disorder and as criminal organizations.

Secret societies continued to be a prominent element in Singapore, but after the 1880s they were cut off from the main sources of wealth in the colony (the revenue farms, the coolie trade, and pepper and gambier agriculture). Subsequently, they fragmented into small-scale criminal gangs involved in illegal drug trafficking, prostitution, gambling rackets, extortion and kidnapping. At the same time, the laboring segment of Singapore's urban areas tended to grow. Dock workers, construction laborers, rickshaw pullers, water carriers and a wide range of similar occupations demanded a large, cheap workforce located close to the major economic activities of the city and port. As these men settled into urban neighborhoods, they began to seek the comfort of conjugal relationships. The Chinese government began to relax the bans on the emigration of women, and by the early twentieth century even the humble working-class Chinese were establishing families and households in Singapore.

By the 1920s, a new social formation had come to characterize Singapore's Chinatown slums. There were large numbers of working-class Chinese families living in the crowded three-story row houses of the inner urban area. James Warren has styled these "elemental families" (Warren 1984). They inhabited tiny cubicles containing a bed and space for a few belongings. They were often walled off from each other by nothing more than a piece of cloth, and residents of one building shared kitchen facilities and bathing and toilet facilities with twenty or thirty others. Barrington Kaye's study of Upper Nankin Street in the late 1940s gives an idea of these parts of the city by the time of World War II (Kaye 1960).

The *kampong* coast

Singapore had been a site of Malay settlement prior to the arrival of Raffles and Farquhar in 1819. There was said to be a Malay settlement on the Singapore River gathered around the residence of Temenggong Abdul Rahman. There also seem to have been other Malay or "aboriginal" villages at places like Kallang and other river mouths around the island. J.R. Logan has left descriptions of the *orang biduanda kallang*. Settlements such as this were not mentioned by Crawfurd or other early settlers, and it is probable that most of these "native" Malay peoples escaped the notice of Europeans in these years. As European settlement expanded, the Kallang people and others moved to other parts of the island or to the southern islands flanking the Singapore Strait. Throughout the nineteenth century, there was a gradual expansion of Malay settlement into the rural parts of the island.

Within the urban area of Singapore and its immediate environs, there came to be two important Malay settlements. One was that of the Temenggong

Abdul Rahman, which, following the establishment of the European town and the treaty of 1823, was removed to Teluk Belanga to the west of the town. The other was on the east side of the town in Kampong Glam. The center here was the palace of Sultan Hussain, the prince whom Raffles had recognized as the "sultan of Singapore." The two princes received pensions from the British government and appear to have supported themselves, their families and their followers with these funds. Although the two had cooperated to effect the British settlement, and a marriage link existed between the two families, there seem to have been few contacts between them, and an atmosphere of hostility and competition arose between them.

Munshi Abdullah bin Abdul Kadir, the Malay scribe who followed Raffles to Singapore from Melaka, has drawn a stark picture of Malay life in Singapore during its early years. He contrasted the Malays of Melaka with those in the Temenggong's following. The latter were men of violence who went about armed and were accused of committing acts of violence and intimidation in the town as well as piracy at sea. The Melaka people, unlike the Temenggong's maritime followers, were town-bred men of commerce or agricultural villagers, and although skilled at using their fists, they knew nothing of dagger tactics (Abdullah 1970: 159). Both Raffles and Crawfurd had paid large amounts of money to the Temenggong to finance the movement of his people from their original site on the Singapore River to the more isolated area at Teluk Belanga, but they did not move until about 1824, and only after much coaxing from the British authorities. When they did move, Abdullah notes that the community split up and that while sixty or seventy households moved to Teluk Belanga, others went to Kampong Malacca, or to Tanjong Katong and Teluk Kurau (*ibid.*: 177).

In the 1820s and 1830s, many Europeans considered the Teluk Belanga *kampong* to be a pirates' lair. It is certain that the sea people or maritime Malays of the Riau–Lingga archipelago who came to Singapore gravitated there. Although there are no descriptions of the *kampong* in that period, it was made up of the Temenggong's residence, those of his wives, his followers and extended family, and the homes of *orang laut*, who were seen as "slaves" of the Temenggong. We must also assume that there were a number of fairly committed women and truly dedicated followers in the grouping. Abdul Rahman, the Temenggong who made the agreement with Raffles, died in 1825 and was succeeded by his son Ibrahim, who was only about 15 at the time. During the next decade or so, the Malays of Teluk Belanga reinforced their reputation for piracy. Various groups of *orang laut*, particularly those of the Gallang *suku*, were notorious pirates.

By the 1840s, however, things had begun to change. The Temenggong and his men began to grow wealthy, first from the trade in gutta percha and later from the increasing settlement of Chinese pepper and gambier planters in Johor.

A few years ago, Teluk Blangah only presented the appearance of a very dirty Malay village, the royal residence being merely distinguished from its neighbours by being of brick, and if possible dingier and dirtier than the rest. Now everything has put on a new face. The money, which has flowed so copiously into the Teluk Blangah coffers, through the successful dealings of His Highness and his followers in the gutta trade, has been more judicially applied than is generally the case when Malays become possessed of a little cash, and instead of being expended on evanescent shows and spectacles, or squandered at the gambling-table and cock-pit, it has been laid out in improving the outward appearance of Teluk Blangah. His Highness has built for himself several extremely neat houses and *baleis* in the European style, which are gay with green and white paint, and many of his followers have done the same, their smart, green venetianed, tile-roofed houses, being an extreme contrast to the rude huts in which they formerly were content to live. The old palace, now the residence of the mother of the Tumonggong, has also been cleaned up and white-washed, and altogether has a very nice appearance.

(Buckley 1903: 495–6)

In addition to the new houses for the Malays, a number of European and Chinese merchants began to settle in nearby areas, and a number of these developed close links with the Temenggong. Key among them were James Guthrie, William Wemys Ker and the Teochew cloth peddler Tan Hiok Nee. These links provided the young Temenggong Ibrahim with an entrée to both European and Chinese mercantile circles, connections that were to assure the fortunes of the Malay ruler. By the 1850s, the Christian missionary Benjamin Peach Keasberry had set up a Malay school in Teluk Belanga, and Munshi Abdullah and his son Ibrahim were employed as teachers there. Among their pupils were the son and successor of the Temenggong, the young Abu Bakar and the next generation of Teluk Belanga Malays, who would leave Singapore and take over the administration of Johor. Keasberry had also set up a printing press, which in addition to publishing a range of local English-language publications, also functioned as one of the first Malay-language presses in Southeast Asia.

Sultan Hussain and his family in Kampong Glam were less fortunate. They lost the political battle for continued recognition from the colonial powers and languished in genteel poverty for much of the nineteenth century. Likewise, the other Malays of Singapore, both those who came from Melaka and those who came from Sumatra, the Malayan peninsula and the surrounding islands enjoyed less of Singapore's burgeoning afflu-ence than did many of the other newcomers. Although the Malay population of Singapore continued to grow and remained a considerable portion of the overall population, they did not grow rich. Cameron, in his discussion of the Malays of Singapore, pointed out:

Though there are numerous Malay traders arriving throughout the year from all parts of the Archipelago, it is somewhat remarkable that as yet in none of the three settlements are any Malay merchants to be found. Parsees, Chinese, Klings and Bengalese have mercantile establishments that closely vie with those of Europeans, but the Malay never rises to be more than a hawker; and this is the result, no doubt, of that want of ambition to be rich which I have noticed before. It cannot be from want of education, for the larger proportion of them here can both read and write their own language.

(Cameron 1865: 135)

Despite the appearance of numerous *kampongs*, most Malays continued to live in the urban areas. In 1901, 26,000 of 36,000 "Malaysians" (including peninsular Malays, "other natives of the archipelago" and Javanese) lived within the municipality, a large proportion of them in Kampong Glam (Roff 1967: 33). By 1931, Singapore Island was dotted with forty or fifty *kampongs*, and a population of nearly 120,000 people, about a fifth of the entire population, lived in the rural areas.

Here there were both Malay and Chinese villages. In fact, one noticeable feature was their distinctive characters. The Malays built their houses from timber with attap roofs and raised them off the ground. Often near the shore or along river banks, the village precincts were seen as neat, with well-swept sandy grounds, and were populated by peaceable people in the their sarongs, gathered around a small *surau* or mosque and living with their cats and goats among the coconut trees. The Chinese *kampongs*, many of which had originally been pepper and gambier settlements, now grew pineapples or rubber. There were also villages of market gardeners and pig farmers, who lived by supplying the town with produce. Here, in the Chinese villages, the houses, also of timber and attap, were built on the ground, and the village was remarkable for the smell of pigs and the barking of dogs. Two very different and very separate lifestyles had developed in rural Singapore, and these marked some of the line that were deepening within Singapore's society as the twentieth century opened.

Indians in Singapore

The Indian population of Singapore has always been a minority; nevertheless, the natives of the Indian subcontinent have always constituted an important segment of Singapore's social tapestry. They always made up an important element of the mercantile community and likewise occupied key positions in the workforce. For them, Singapore was not only the sort of Indian Ocean port with which South Asian merchants and mariners had long been familiar; it was also part of the network of ports that made up the British Empire, of which India was a part. Indians thus moved into

Singapore along with the British, and they constituted a component of Singapore's economic connection with India.

Just as it is incorrect to view the Chinese or Malay populations as a uniform ethnic group, so too is it wrong to see the South Asian population as without diversity. The major distinctions have been those between Hindus and Muslims and those between north and south Indians. Over time, the majority of the Indian population has come to be made up of Tamils, the dark-skinned Hindus from the southern tip of the subcontinent and the island of Ceylon, now known as Sri Lanka.[9] In local parlance, these were often known as "Klings," while north Indians were styled "Bengalis." South Indian Muslims from the Coromandel coast were variously known as "nanaks," "mamaks" or "tulikans," while south Indian Muslim merchants were called "chuliahs." Malabar Muslims were "mopahs" or "kakaks", and Gujeratis were "Orang Bombay" (Siddique 1990: 8).

Beyond those who were largely voluntary migrants were thousands of transported convicts, another legacy of the British Empire. From 1825, when the first lot of convicts were brought to Singapore from Benkulu, until 1878, when the last convicts were released, they were an important presence in the colony. They came from virtually all parts of British India and included members of all castes, religions and language groups. In Singapore,

Figure 2.3 Malay children at Kampong Kallang in about 1900.

they performed a great deal of the heavy labor of clearing roads and leveling the hills and reclaiming the shallows. When released, it seems that the vast majority of them remained in Singapore rather than return to India. Many, particularly the Muslims, may have married Malay women and thus become a part of Jawi Peranakan society. This was a hybrid group, unique to the Straits Settlements and Malaya. made up of Malayo-Indian Muslims. Individuals such as the famous Munshi Abdullah bin Abdul Kadir were members of this group.

Yet another legacy of the empire were the garrisons of Indian troops that were a regular part of the social make-up of British Malaya. Throughout the nineteenth century, sepoy regiments were regularly posted to the Straits Settlements and formed an important element in the British military position in the region. On those occasions when it was deemed necessary, colonial governors had the option of employing the sepoys at their command. Whether to subdue rebellious Malays, Chinese secret society battles or to intervene in the political life of neighboring Malay states, the Indian regiments were an important asset to British colonial domination. Although the regiments themselves were constantly being rotated between various British possessions in Asia, they formed an enduring presence in Singapore and the other settlements and thus constituted an important element in the economy and social atmosphere of these towns.

Like the other races of Singapore, the Indians tended to group in specific sections of the town. Initially, Chulia Street and Market Street were areas where Indian merchants, particularly Chettiar moneylenders and cloth merchants, established themselves. In the mid-nineteenth century, areas of Indian settlement developed near the various harbor areas of Singapore, including Boat Quay, Tanjong Pagar and the Rochor Canal, as many Indians worked as laborers in the shipping industry. In particular, Indians dominated the lighter business carrying cargo from ships in the roads to the docks. Likewise, the areas in which convicts were housed as well as the garrison areas took on a distinctly South Asian character.

With the establishment of the rubber industry around the turn of the twentieth century, thousands of Tamils were brought to Malaya as estate laborers under the contract system. While there were few rubber estates in Singapore itself, these migrants moved through Singapore, and the business of managing this labor supply was centered in Singapore. This flow of labor did much to reinforce the Tamil presence in Singapore and to increase their numbers.

Also, because many Indians could speak and were even literate in English, they found minor positions in the civil service, particularly in the post office and the railroad. Together with the merchants, these formed the basis of an Indian middle class. Many of their children sought educational opportunities in the English schools opened by the government and Christian missionary groups. Along with Eurasians and Straits-born Chinese, a significant number of Indians came to make up the English-educated professional classes of Singapore in the early twentieth century. Partly as a result of their skills in English and their over-representation in administration, Indians were among the first Singaporeans to become politically active, both as individuals and organizationally.

In the late nineteenth century, the area known today as Singapore's "Little India" along Serangoon Road was still something of a suburban fringe area on the northeast side of the city. The region was located near the minor port area of Geylang Serai and was at the beginning of the road to the headwaters of the Serangoon River and the northeastern parts of Singapore Island. It became a center of Indian life in Singapore because it came to be dominated by Indians involved in the trade in cattle and horses. It also became a center for abattoirs, stables and the leather trade. In the early twentieth century, the area became a residential center for middle-class Indians and retirees from the civil service, and it drew increasing numbers of merchants and shopkeepers specializing in providing goods and services to these communities. These included restaurants, goldsmiths and sari shops, as well as Indian temples and various voluntary associations. The region thus became a true ethnic enclave, but it was also an area to which members of other communities gravitated when they wished to obtain anything from a fish-head curry or Indian vegetarian meal to Indian medicines, cloth or other specifically Indian goods (Siddique 1990).

The plural society

Singapore's diversity, certainly a constant element in the social history of the place, has led it to be described as a "plural society."

> In Burma and Java, probably the first thing that strikes the visitor is the medley of peoples – European, Chinese, Indian and native. It is in the strictest sense a medley, for they mix but do not combine. Each group holds by its own religion, its own culture and language, its own ideas and ways. As individuals they meet, but only in the market-place, in buying and selling. There is a plural society, with different sections of the community living side by side, but separately, within the same political unit. Even in the economic sphere there is a division of labour along racial lines. Natives, Chinese, Indians and Europeans all have different functions, and within each major group subsections have particular occupations. There is, as it were, a caste system, but without the religious basis that incorporates caste in social life in India. One finds similar conditions all over the Tropical Far East – under Spanish, Portuguese, Dutch, British, French or American rule; among Filipinos, Javanese, Malays, Burmans and Annamese; whether the objective of the colonial power has been tribute, trade or material resources; under direct rule and under indirect. The obvious and outstanding result of contact between East and West has been the evolution of a plural society.
>
> (Furnivall 1948: 304–5)

It is true that the term, as well as our understanding of the phenomenon, dates only from the mid-1940s, when J.S. Furnivall coined and defined it. However, we should question whether the condition really had been present since the founding of Singapore. There has been ethnic diversity, but its content changed over time. Furnivall's point about the role of colonialism is an important one. His experience was primarily of British Burma and secondarily with the Dutch East Indies, yet he argued that the concept applied to all colonial territories (*ibid.*: x–xi).While the meaning of the term has since been broadened to take in other societies, the colonial circumstance remains an important element. This is partly because of the policies of "scientific" racial classification that came into use in the nineteenth-century European colonies, partly due to the economic, political and social segregation that developed in the colonial environment and partly due to the sense of nationalism that arose in these societies in the immediate post-World War II era.

His perception of this phenomenon was also formed at a time when all of these societies were on the verge of becoming independent nation-states during and immediately after the Pacific War. The nationalist awakening in these countries involved the sharpening of ethnic distinctions and brought the power of the state behind consciousness of kind. Certainly, the existence of plural societies and the problematic obstacle that they present to aspirant nationalism is something that became depressingly familiar to the world during the twentieth century with our experience of the Holocaust, the partition of India and its associated violence and violent legacy, and widespread ethnic cleansing. As a result, we may have a tendency to read them back into the past when they may not have had the same resonance. On the other hand, a place such as Singapore does offer an object lesson in how such a social order comes into being.

Although Furnivall did not analyse the psychological roots of this phenomenon, we need to see it within the context of the sense of isolation, difference and perhaps of collective paranoia that the British and all Europeans experienced as ruling classes in Asia. If we look at some of the more recent studies of racism and colonialism such as those by Jean Gelman Taylor, John Butcher and Ann Stoler, we get an idea of the manner in which colonialists consciously erected barriers between the races, writing into law their perceptions and prejudices (Butcher 1979; Taylor 1983; Stoler 1989).

It is perhaps too much to say that European policies and practices alone placed barriers between the various ethnic groups of Singapore, but the peculiarly European consciousness of kind that developed in the colonial setting had a pernicious knock-on effect. Common sense tells us that there were already clear lines demarcating the communities. The distinctions between Muslims, Hindus, Buddhists, animists and Christians were as real as those between Chinese, Malays, Indians and Europeans. There were, through the nineteenth century, conflicts between certain ethnic groups or, more correctly, subethnic groups such as Hokkien and Teochew over economic preserves, but there was also a certain informal fluidity to one's identity.

In contemporary Asian port-polities, there was a tendency for the ruling group to set certain cultural norms. Moreover, there was a tendency for successful resident migrants to assimilate and to marry into the ruling class, when possible. It was simply a matter of traditional sexual politics. The Malays even had a term for the process: *masuk Melayu*. This was the process by which non-Malays converted to Islam, adopted Malay dress and custom and were thus accepted as Malays. This same phenomenon happened in Siam, Vietnam, the Philippines and other parts of Southeast Asia. For instance, we hear of Chinese merchants at the court in Palembang in the eighteenth century who converted to Islam and married into the sultan's family. It goes without saying that this sort of thing did not happen in Singapore. That is, wealthy Chinese did not intermarry with the English, or even with the Malays for that matter. However, they did form relations with Straits Chinese families. Foreign Muslims such as Arabs and Indians inter-married with Malays, as did other Malaysian peoples. However, they too did not intermarry with the British.

However, the process of European education did offer what appeared to be an entrée into the ruling class. There was also the prospect of conversion to some form of Christianity. The English schools presented European civi-lization as the global standard of progressive modernity. It was perhaps only natural that students would develop a respect for European cultural norms and thus aspire to become full participants in the culture and, by extension, in the life of the empire. What they did not understand was the racist subtext of European imperialism and the scientific aura that it had acquired in the nineteenth century. Asians would need to learn their place in the evolutionary hierarchy of the races.

Beyond that, the fundamental racist impulses of many Europeans, partic-ularly those of the lower strata of the ruling class, threw up more rigid barriers. These individuals found themselves in direct competition with Asians, or were working with Asians who sometimes knew more than they did, and they may even have been better educated. The attitudes expressed by the members of the "club" in George Orwell's *Burmese Days* were not unique to Burma but were quite consistent throughout the Raj by the twen-tieth century. Of particular concern to many English-educated Singapore Asians was the system of discriminatory pay scales in the civil service, which privileged Europeans. The dual standard of salaries and privileges was a constant source of comment in journals such as the *Malayan Chronicle*.

Moreover, there was a heavily reinforced "ceiling" that Asians could not penetrate. Butcher's study shows that colonial officials and members of the "unofficial" class (i.e. businessmen, merchants and planters) tended to come from the same social backgrounds in England and had gone to the same public schools. Many continued these relationships in Malaya, often joining old boys gatherings, taking membership in the same clubs and playing the same sports, particularly cricket. By the early twentieth century, the clubs and other informal meeting places were the sites where government decisions were influenced and the network of contacts within the power elite of European society were maintained. Obviously, there was no place here for Asians. Such social contacts became increasingly important to Europeans as certain Chinese and Indians became wealthy, wealthier in many cases that most Europeans.

A key element in the development of these characteristics in European society in Singapore was the arrival and longer-term residence of increasing numbers of European women. This reinforced the impulse to draw sharper lines separating the races to eliminate social contact as much as possible, particularly between European women and Asian men. Obviously, such liaisons did occur, and when they did it was cause for concern, but these have received little notice in the official record. One must look to literature for the facts of colonial social life. The novels and short stories of authors such as George Orwell, Somerset Maugham, J.G. Farrell and Anthony Burgess, plus a host of lesser lights deal, with the scandals that periodically broke the surface of the regimented life of the colonial master race.

Women and the new social order

For most of the nineteenth century, Singapore was a man's country. It was populated by immigrants, most of them sojourners in search of wealth and

Figure 2.4 A European family arriving in Singapore in about 1910.

dreaming of a return to their homelands, and Singapore's female population was always a minority. As late as 1860, women still constituted less than 10 percent of the total population, and most of these were probably Malay women who lived in the *kampongs*. For most of the population, family life was non-existent in Singapore; only the Malays and the wealthier Babas, Eurasians and a few of the Europeans lived with their wives and children. In the case of the working-class Chinese, the sex ratio was the most imbalanced, standing as high as eighteen men to one woman at times during the nineteenth century.

This imbalance to some extent may help to explain certain features of Singapore's social order during the nineteenth century, in particular the power and prevalence of triad societies among working-class Chinese. Men worked together and lived together and had little else in the way of society. The groups, with their bonds of sworn brotherhood, to some extent functioned as fictive families and support groups.

The absence of women also accounts for the high incidence of opium use among the same groups of Chinese. Although there are no reliable statistics for the period, anecdotal evidence suggests that as many as 60 to 70 percent of Chinese laborers and even skilled workers were regular users of opium, if not actual addicts. One must recall that the state itself was in large part supported by revenue derived from the sale of opium to the local population.

Table 2.2 Singapore's population: sex, ethnicity and location, 1871–1931.

	1871	1881	1891	1901	1911	1921	1931
Sex							
Male	72,183	104,031	138,452	169,243	215,489	280,918	352,167
Female	22,633	33,691	43,150	57,599	87,832	137,440	205,578
Ethnicity							
European	1,946	2,769	5,254	3,824	5,711	6,145	8,082
Eurasian	2,164	3,094	3,589	4,120	4,671	5,436	6,903
Malay	26,148	33,102	35,992	36,080	41,806	53,595	65,014
Chinese	54,572	86,766	121,908	164,041	219,577	315,151	418,640
Indian	11,610	12,138	16,035	17,823	27,755	32,314	50,811
Other	617	1,339	1,776	2,667	3,660	5,717	8,295
Location							
Rural and islands	–	–	28,871[a]	35,466	43,711	–	119,004[c]
Municipality	–	–	155,683	193,089	259,610	304,815[b]	447,741
Total	97,111		184,554	228,555	303,321	418,358	557,745

Source: Yeoh (1996: 38, 140 and 317).

Notes
a These figures for the rural and islands population are calculated.
b This is the figure for 1917, not 1921.
c These figures for the municipality and rural populations are from Braddell (1934: 42–3); however, his total population figure differs from that given by Yeoh by 10,002. He gives the same figure for Chinese but gives 71,177 for the Malay population and 8,147 for the European.

For the remainder of the male population without wives, the options were abstinence, same-sex relationships and the use of prostitutes. European writings occasionally suggest that there were fairly high levels of homosexuality among the Chinese laborers. Again, the record is not very explicit, but one finds references to "immorality" and "depravity" among the Chinese as a result of the scarcity of women.

> How different would be the condition of the people of this island if instead of spending on Opium $417,884 yearly, they knew not the vice; that money hardly and honestly toiled for would be spent in clothes, in food and better houses, the men could afford to marry, a taste would be formed for finery, and something more would be required than bare rice the necessary of life … instead of 40 or 50 living under one roof, too often a mass of iniquity, a man and his family, or one or two individuals could afford to live in a house of their own.
>
> (Little 1848: 73–4)

Little's words are both ironic and prophetic. Singapore was not to attain that level of society until the 1920s. In the meantime, boys and young women, both often sold into some form of debt slavery, serviced the larger male population of Singapore.

James Warren's study of prostitution in Singapore during the 1870s and 1880s shows that the sex trade was well developed during those years. It should also be stressed that his focus on those years is indicative of the fact that the practice was legal only in that period. Thus we have some official records of the numbers, locations and social character of Singapore's brothels. It should be assumed that they existed prior to and after this period despite the lack of statistics. The illegality of the practice simply meant that no records were kept (Warren 1993).

Technically, it was illegal under Chinese law for women to emigrate until the twentieth century. This did not mean that no women left China, but it does mean that legal avenues for emigration did not exist. There were illegal avenues, and the women that did leave were usually younger Cantonese women who had been kidnapped, deceived or sold by their families and then smuggled out of the country and to Singapore to be held in virtual slavery in the illegal brothels that existed during the earlier part of the nineteenth century. These women were almost exclusively for the use of Chinese men, and apparently they would not take non-Chinese customers. There were, it seems, European prostitutes who serviced other parts of the population.

During the 1870s, another group of women appeared in Singapore. These were the Japanese, the *Karayuki-san* as Warren describes them. Missing from our earlier discussion of prostitution. they were available to the remainder of the population throughout the latter part of the nineteenth and into the twentieth century. Like the Chinese women, they too were seduced, kidnapped or sold by their families into a life of prostitution. Like the

others, once in Singapore, they found themselves entrapped in debtor relationships with brothel owners and more or less caught in a never-ending
cycle of compounded obligations.

Their presence also reflected a growing Japanese element in Singapore's
overall population. Many of those listed as "Other" in the late nineteenth-
and early twentieth-century censuses were probably Japanese settlers. In
addition to the merchants, pharmacists and optometrists, there were several
groups, such as hairdressers, dressmakers, cloth dealers and photographers,
who made a significant part of their living by providing services to the
Japanese prostitutes, not to mention the brothel owners themselves.

In addition to the Japanese and Chinese prostitutes, there were also a
group of European women who found their way to Singapore in the nineteenth and early twentieth century. These were Eastern European women,
many of them Jewish, but also Russians, Poles and others. Thus, in the
marketplace of Singapore, where most men were valued for their labor,
women too became commodities, valued for the price of the services that
they provided for the laboring population. It may seem somewhat sordid
and grim when we think of Furnivall's comment that the people of this
society met only in the marketplace, but for Singapore that seems natural. It
was, after all, an economic establishment; it was a marketplace.

The printing press and the plural society

Perhaps the strongest forces in creating the plural society were the appearance of newspapers and other printed matter in the local languages. The
printing press and newspapers had been a part of Singapore almost from the
beginning, but their scope was limited due to the low levels of literacy in the
population of laborers, small traders, fishermen and peasants. It was not
until a significant level of education existed among the mass of the population that the printed word began to work its effect upon the multicultural
landscape of Singapore.

The first newspapers were English-language journals such as the
Singapore Chronicle, which first appeared in 1824 as a weekly, followed later
by the *Singapore Free Press* and *Straits Times*. All three tended to focus on
matters related to trade and foreign news, with a few items of local interest
and local advertising, and were aimed mainly at the European, English-
speaking community.

It was the Protestant missionaries who established themselves in
Singapore, first to preach to the Chinese and later to the Malays, who began
publishing in local languages. In 1834, Ira Tracy, who was later joined by his
brother Joseph, arrived in Singapore to take charge of the printing press
(Abdullah 1970: 287, fn 5–7). Much of what was published was religious
tracts, translations of the Bible and translations of other scientific or educational material from English. Publishing in Malay was carried on by the
Mission Press, founded by the Rev. Benjamin Peach Keasberry, who also

established the Teluk Belanga Malay School. Keasberry also wrote and printed his own textbooks for the school. He thus educated the family and followers of the Temenggong and trained the first generation of Johor administrators (Turnbull 1977: 63).

Publishing by Malays for Malays does not seem to have begun until 1876 with the appearance of the *Jawi Peranakan*, which was founded by Mohammed Said bin Dada Mahyiddin. It was printed in *jawi*, Malay in Arabic script, and lasted for twelve years. It focused on translations from Arab and Egyptian newspapers as well as the English and was an important voice in awakening the Malays of Singapore. It also testifies to the leadership role in the Malay community, which was, at least for a time, assumed by the *jawi peranakan* people (Mulliner 1991: 290). Singapore, along with nearby Riau, became important centers of Malay publishing during the late nineteenth and early twentieth century, printing editions of classical Malay manuscripts and Islamic tracts.

Another early Malay newspaper was *Sekolah Melayu*, published by Munshi Mohammed Ali bin Ghulam Al-Hindi, which focused on students in Singapore's Malay schools. In addition to general news, it stressed language issues, including standardization of spelling and usage and the modernization of the Malay language. By the 1920s, newspapers such as *Utusan Melayu*, *Warta Melayu* and *Lembaga Melayu* were circulating not only in Singapore but also in the rest of British Malaya. Malays in the British colonies were not only being politically and culturally awakened; they were also rediscovering their cultural links to Sumatra and the Dutch colonies, and to the Muslim world of western Asia. An important voice for Islamic reform was *Al Imam*, published by Shaikh Al-Hadi, who received financial backing from a group of Indonesian and Arab merchants. Although it lasted only a few years, it was but the first of other such journals with an Islamic reform agenda (*ibid.*: 291).

For a variety of reasons, during the late nineteenth and early twentieth century, Singapore continued to be an important center of Malay literature and culture. Because of the large concentration of Malays resident there, because of the influence of Arab and Indian Muslims who concentrated there for the trade, and because of the importance of Singapore as a staging post for pilgrims to Mecca, Malayo-Muslim culture flourished there. In the early twentieth century, Eunos Abdullah (the Singapore-born son of a Minangkabau trader), the editor of the *Utusan Melayu* and later of *Lembaga Melayu*, was the acknowledged leader of the Singapore Malay community. He represented the Malays first on the Municipal Council and later on the Singapore Legislative Council. He was also a founding member of the Singapore Malay Union.

The publication of *Bintang Timor* was another significant development in Singapore, since it paralleled developments in the Dutch East Indies, where Malay-speaking *peranakan* Chinese began to publish in romanized bazaar Malay.[10] In the Dutch possessions, this version of Malay was the forerunner of Bahasa Indonesia, or "revolutionary Malay" as Ben Anderson has styled it (Anderson 1990). In Singapore, the future was less grand. Song Ong Siang, the chronicler of Singapore's Straits-born society and the publisher of *Bintang Timor*, never aspired to create a national language, and it lasted only nine months.

The first Chinese newspaper in Singapore was founded in 1881. This was *Lat Pau*, which was founded by Melaka-born *peranakan* See Ewe Lay. Even though he started the paper, it seems that much of the impetus came from China. The paper was patterned after other Chinese newspapers in Hong Kong and China and adopted a conservative posture. It also received a level of backing from the Chinese government. The paper continued publication for forty years and circulated among the population of literate Chinese shopkeepers, assistants, merchants and clerks. By the end of the nineteenth century, a number of other Chinese newspapers had appeared, some with revolutionary or reformist agendas.

The newspapers became vehicles through which the local elites, whether merchants, intellectuals or religious leaders, exercised some control over the cultural development of their respective communities. Newspapers brought news and events from the wider world to the Singapore communities. Most specifically, they brought news from the parts of the world that mattered to their readers.

Malays were put in touch with the Islamic world and with the various currents of the Islamic reform movements in the Middle East. They were a part of the world of Arab, Persian and Turkish nationalism. The issues of concern to the Muhammadiyah and Malay tradition were fought out in their journals, and the place of Malays and Malay culture in the colonial world became the issues of concern. While the mass audiences for these struggles often lay beyond Singapore, the colonial port was often the free center where publications and leaders could speak without fear of censure by the Dutch colonial government or Malay rajas in the native states. It was in Singapore that the seeds of Malay nationalism were sown.

With the rise of Chinese nationalism and the anti-Manchu movement, Singapore Chinese became a part of the struggles then going on in China. The impact of the May Fourth Movement in particular swept into Singapore and sowed divisions among those supporting the Guomindang and those favoring the Chinese Communist Party. Likewise, the Tamil press, although quite limited in the nineteenth century, put non-English-speaking Indians in touch with the nationalist movement in South Asia. Most of all, the newspapers were modernizing forces, but each sector – English, Mandarin, Malay or Tamil – pursued its own version or variety of modernization. It was this type of modernization that laid the foundation for Singapore's plural society.

For the English-speaking community, whether Indian, Straits Chinese or Eurasian, the most important newspaper was the *Malayan Tribune*. In a recent master's thesis, Chua Ai Lin has studied the impact of this paper, which was published between 1914 and 1942 (Chua 2001). Unlike the other English-language newspapers of Singapore, which saw the government and the European community as their prime constituencies, the *Malayan Tribune* spoke to the "English-speaking domiciled community" of both Singapore and the other territories of British Malaya. It was, in fact, this newspaper that coined the term "Malayan" to distinguish between those Asians who made Malaya their home and the Malays.

Linguistic divisions were often quite ambiguous in Singapore. Perhaps the English-educated read the *Malayan Tribune* and saw themselves as partaking of the greater English-speaking world. On the other hand, they were also Indians, Chinese and Eurasians. People of Indian background often spoke Tamil or some other Indian language at home, even though they may not have been literate. Chinese spoke Hokkien, Teochew, Cantonese or another Chinese dialect, or Malay at home or perhaps yet another language in their place of business. People like Lim Boon Keng and Song Ong Siang probably spoke a version of Hokkien with their families. They also spoke bazaar Malay and were educated in English. Lim was also a Chinese scholar. Most Eurasians spoke Malay as well as English. Among the China-born and India-born, linguistic identity was not always a clear-cut thing. Even for Malays, there were many dialects and usages, and many different places of origin.

Education in Singapore

As in the case of newspapers, there had been schools in Singapore since shortly after its founding; like the press, they were also aimed largely at the small European community. Raffles had created an endowment of over $17,000, made up of his own donation and subscriptions from the EIC and the merchant community for what he hoped would be an exemplary educational institution in Singapore. He envisioned a school where the children of native princes could be educated along with company servants and where the local languages could be studied and their literatures preserved. This idealistic plan was a complete failure. It was not until the 1830s that a group of Singapore merchants revived the Singapore Institution (renamed the Raffles Institution in 1868), but even then the school struggled along through difficult times until late in the nineteenth century. During those years, a handful of missionary schools were set up, including St Joseph's, St Margaret's, Raffles Girls' School and the Convent of the Holy Infant Jesus. They, too, struggled through this period when there was little support for education in Singapore.

The growth of Singapore's economy and its growing connections with Europe after 1870 led to an increased demand for education. However, there was little support from the colonial government. Aside from a few government-sponsored English-language and Malay schools, most were the result of private initiatives. Of greatest importance were the Chinese schools, which received no support at all from the colonial government but which, by 1942, constituted the largest and most vibrant sector of education in Singapore.

Chinese merchants in Singapore had had an interest in education, at least so far as their own immediate circle of clansmen were concerned, since the early days of Singapore's history. However, these efforts rarely amounted to any sustained institutional development and lasted only as long as particular individuals cared to support them. There were about fifty such "schools" by 1890, and most of them followed a traditional Confucian method and content and were taught in Hokkien or some other local dialect. Song Ong Siang claims that the standard in these schools was quite poor (Song 1923). One of the Baba reformers, Lim Boon Keng, began classes in Mandarin in 1899, and other groups such as the Chinese Consulate and the Straits Chinese Recreation Club later set up classes. By the beginning of the twentieth century, reformists among the Straits-born Chinese had set up a number of modern-style Chinese-medium schools in Singapore.

The rising tide of revolutionary nationalism in China and political instability led a number of Chinese intellectuals to flee to Singapore in the first two decades of the twentieth century. Many of these found employment as school teachers in the new schools being founded as expressions of patriotism by wealthy Chinese merchants. With the rise in the Chinese population and the increase in the number of locally born Chinese, we find an increasing number of Chinese families in Singapore whose children were in need of schooling. This population of young Chinese born to immigrant parents emerged at about the same time as the May Fourth Movement in China. In 1919, Tan Kah Kee, one of Singapore's first rubber barons, founded the first Chinese middle school, Nanyang Hua Chiao Chung Xue (Turnbull 1977: 119, 134).

These schools used Mandarin as the medium of instruction and stressed a China-oriented curriculum. Since Chinese students and teachers had been at the forefront of the anti-Japanese movement in Singapore in 1919 and 1920, the colonial government, for the first time, examined the curriculum and teaching materials of these schools and found that they contained politically subversive information. As a result, in 1920 the Education Ordinance was passed, which required the registration of all schools, teachers and managers. Although the government forbade teaching in Mandarin or *guoyu*, there was little support for this policy among the Chinese, and there is little evidence that it was respected; they continued to teach in Mandarin. During the 1920s, the Chinese-medium schools became important centers for the spread of Chinese nationalism and progressive political ideas. They also became centers of conflict as the fracture lines of Chinese politics, particularly those between the Communists, the Guomindang Left and the Guomindang Right, also appeared in the schools and other institutions of the Singapore Chinese community. It was also at this time that the divisions between the Straits-born elite and the Chinese-educated began to grow.

By the beginning of the Pacific War, Singapore possessed a significant and vibrant educational sector. There were schools teaching in each of the four languages: Malay, English, Tamil and Chinese (Mandarin). On the one hand, they tended to homogenize differences within the communities, but they also drew sharper lines between the linguistic communities. A significant number of scholars in the prestige English-language school had obtained university degrees in England. There was a growing community of well-educated Asian doctors, lawyers and other professionals, who would play important roles in independent Singapore.

Colonial society on the eve of war

By the beginning of the Pacific War, Singapore's social order had taken a form that was to be of great significance for the remainder of the century. In particular, there was the enormous Chinese majority, which though divided by speech groups, place of origin and wealth, was now gaining coherence through the Chinese educational system. Mandarin, an interest in China and Chinese politics, and a clear sense of Chinese identity were drawing them together in ways that were a new source of concern for the colonial government. They were the majority, not only of the Chinese population but of the entire island, and their sense of identity as Malayan Chinese was shared by millions more in the other Straits Settlements and the Malay states of the peninsula.

They included dock workers, laborers, mining and agricultural coolies, craftsmen, small shopkeepers, rickshaw pullers, wealthy *taukehs*, and a small group of important professionals such as school teachers, journalists, clerks, lawyers and government servants. Their social organization was structured around the *bangs*, the temples, the burial societies and ultimately by the Singapore Chinese Chamber of Commerce (SCCC), which was founded in the 1890s and by the immediate prewar period had become the elite voice of the Chinese community. It was this group through which the government maintained its contact and exercised control over the Chinese population of Singapore (Visscher 2002).

Although organized by and for businessmen, the SCCC ran the schools, unified the dialect groups, managed the endowments of temples and cemeteries, and its leaders employed most of the Chinese in the colony and in Malaya. They subsumed the many divisions of the community, including the various political parties and factions that had come into being. Outside of the SCCC were the communists, now a part of the Malayan Communist Party, and the labor unions, which although not yet legalized were beginning to exercise an important influence among the workers.

Chinese schools, Chinese newspapers and Chinese politics, as well as an important but not fully recognized interest in and influence over local affairs, were all part of the place of the Chinese-educated, or the "Chinese stream," in Singapore's society. They comprised the mass of the workers and lower and middle classes as well as many of the wealthiest. They were building a world quite separate from that of the Malays, or the Indians, and also from the other most influential social group, the English-educated.

The English-educated group was in some respects much less clearly defined, since almost none of them were native English speakers. What they did have in common was the experience of English schools in Singapore and also in the other Straits Settlements. Most of these were Christian missionary schools like St Joseph's or St Margaret's, or elite government schools like the Raffles Institution. The mission schools, which had struggled through the dark ages of the nineteenth century, were then, and remain, the elite schools of Singapore. A few of the Chinese and Indians were from Christian families, as were most of the Eurasians, but outside of these, most of the students were "pagans" when they began and remained so when they left. For a variety of reasons, only one of which was Christianity, Malays avoided these schools.

By the early part of the twentieth century, many of the Straits-born Chinese had become a part of this English-educated group. In 1899, Governor Cecil Clementi Smith established the Queen's Scholarship, which allowed one of the best graduates of an English school to pursue university study in Britain. Lim Boon Keng (a medical doctor) and Song Ong Siang (a lawyer) were among the first to take this opportunity, and they became the first of the "new generation" of English-educated professionals and intellectuals. They came to see themselves as the "Queen's Chinese" and were among the founders of the Straits Chinese British Association. They organized the Singapore Volunteers, the Boy Scouts and the Social Purity Union. They pursued an agenda of modernization for their class and preached against opium use and "decadent" festivals such as the "*chinggay*" and other celebrations. They criticized the cultural syncretism of the Baba lifestyle and the limited opportunities for women. They saw inspiration both in Western "scientific" ways and in the resurrection of "true" Confucian education. Finally, they came to see themselves in a new light: "In a place such as Singapore, the Straits-born have a peculiar right which even Europeans there, English, Scotch, Irish, have not, for they can claim the place as their country. The British were all, more or less, birds of passage, but to the Straits-born the Colony is their native land" (Song 1923: 417).

In the 1920s, with the appearance of the *Malayan Tribune* and the spread of English-language education, the idea that Malaya was the homeland of people who could call themselves "Malayans" began to take a firm hold among the Indians, Jews and Eurasians who were products of these schools. They began to constitute a class of professionals and clerks that were a godsend to the colonial government and large business firms, which needed a source of cheap but educated employees. On the other hand, for British colonial "society", they were "wogs", against whom it was necessary to erect a wide range of barriers to keep them out of clubs, football teams, swimming pools and other venues.

This was a class of no clear origin, other than the schools. They partook of some aspects of Western culture, they shared a diversity of Asian backgrounds, and they aspired to a brand of modernization that was not fully a part of the other two. They were ambiguous about their identity and in later years, Lee Kuan Yew, who was himself a member of this class, would say: "they are devitalised, almost emasculated, as a result of deculturalization. The syllabus in the English schools in pre-war Malaya had pumped in a completely English set of values" (Barr 2000: 144).

The new "Malayans" had also come to seem problematic to another group, both in Singapore and on the peninsula: these were the Malays. The latter now came to see themselves as the true "sons of the soil," and they were also being made aware that their claim to possession of that land was now under threat. The ground had shifted from under the Singapore Malays as nationalist movements in the Dutch East Indies called for unity around the nation of Indonesia. At the same time, in the Malay states, a more parochial call was being made to subjects of the sultans. In Singapore, there were few Malays of great wealth or stature to unify the *kampongs* of fishermen, farmers, laborers and small traders. The Temenggong's descendants had become the sultans of Johor and had taken with them the cream of Teluk Belanga, while the children of the other sultan, deprived of any share in the wealth of Johor, found themselves in the crumbling palace at Kampong Glam.

It remained for leadership to arise from new quarters. Muslim scholars, literate Indian Muslims, *jawi peranakan*, Arabs and others now came to the fore. The earliest Malay newspapers were often sponsored by wealthy Arab or part Arab families. Writers, scholars and journalists were Indians, *jawi peranakan* or others not really in the mainstream of Malay life, which was itself a backwater. Nevertheless, with several Malay newspapers publishing regularly in Singapore during the 1920s and 1930s, and with a growing number of Singapore Malays gaining at least a rudimentary education, the community was beginning to awaken to the challenges of modernity and of emergent nationalism.

A significant number of Singapore's Indian community had come to occupy a well-defined territory along Serangoon Road. The area where a number of Indian cattle- and horse-rearing groups had established themselves toward the end of the nineteenth century had evolved into "Little India." It was a place of temples, restaurants, Indian specialty shops and, above all, residences dominated by South Asians. This was the place to which new emigrants from India gravitated. This was where they came for lodgings, for work opportunities and for their cultural needs.

The appearance of such cultural/ethnic enclaves was nothing new for Singapore. There had always been Chinese areas, Malay areas, European areas and Indian areas. This was partly because in Indian Ocean port cities, and in most Asian cities of this era, occupations tended to group together, and since control of many occupations had been taken over by certain ethnic groups, ethnic enclaves were a natural outcome. By the 1920s and 1930s, however, occupational specialization was no longer the deciding factor. With the rise of identity politics, the possession of specific territories now became an important issue. Singapore became divided into ethnic neighbourhoods: Malay *kampongs*, Chinese *kampongs*, Teochew neighbourhoods, Cantonese streets, Hokkien areas, Straits Chinese suburbs, Indian, Hainanese and Hokchui neighbourhoods. It was a linguistic and racial kaleidoscope displaying the cultures of all maritime Asia, from the Hadramut to Hokkaido, from the Himalayas to Halmahera. However, its peoples had not yet gained the power or the right to speak for themselves, but that was beginning to change.

Community consolidation

During the 1920s and 1930s, Singapore's Asian communities were in a process of both modernization and consolidation that would have major political consequences in the postwar period. The influence of schools, newspapers, and political and social movements in the world around Singapore tended to dissolve subethnicities and to create cultures and communities spanning these differences. These influences also brought the communities into a version of modernity as consumers, workers and nationals. Thus the use of Mandarin in the Chinese schools, the Chinese newspapers, and the offshore activities of Chinese nationalists and Chinese communists pulled together Hokkien, Teochew, Cantonese, Hakka and Hainanese. They also created a taste for new hairstyles, dress styles, cosmetics, cars, houses and entirely new, modern, lifestyles. From within, the creation of bodies such as the Singapore Chinese Chamber of Commerce provided a forum for the leaders of a Chinese community that could speak for all Singapore Chinese.

There were also Malay newspapers and schools that had similar impacts on the Malays of Singapore, whether they were from Sumatra, one of the peninsular states, Java, Celebes, Borneo or some other part of the archipelago. The nationalist movement in Indonesia, Islamic movements from various parts of the Muslim world and pan-Malay movements all defined a new super category of Malay that drew together a host of regional identities and subethnicities. In fact, the strength of movements external to Singapore, both in the Malay states and in Java, led to a major shift in the centers of influence during the 1930s. The Singapore Malays were thus marginalized by broader movements around, both inside Singapore and elsewhere.

Indians, too, felt similar calls, but because of their smaller numbers in Singapore and the movement of so many of their leaders into the English-educated camp, consolidation tended to lag. However, Indians were significant because of their prominence in a number of key industries and professions. Their presence in the labor movement, in the law and in government service gave them an influence far beyond their actual numbers. There would also be many who would respond to the call of radical Indian nationalism promoted by the Japanese.

It was the English-speaking domiciled community that Chua Ai Lin has identified that would prove to be influential far beyond their numbers (Chua 2001). Bringing together Indians, Straits Chinese, Eurasians and others, they advanced rapidly as a community during the 1920s and 1930s. Through such organs as the *Malayan Tribune* and the experience of English-medium schools they developed a common culture and consciousness. With the presence of so many of their number in the professions of law, medicine and government service, they seemed to be the "natural" leaders of not only their own groups but of all Singapore. They were among the first, along with the Malays, to develop a sense of ownership in Singapore and the Malay states. The heirs of this hybrid group would emerge as a key power group in postwar Singapore.

They would be the group from which modernist leadership in Singapore would arise; however, they would also suffer in a number of unexpected ways when the Japanese took over Singapore. On the one hand, the markers of status that they had come to value – their command of English, their skill at cricket and other British pastimes, their Anglo-modern lifestyles – all these would clash with the radical anti-Western culture of the Japanese occupation. They would, at least vicariously if not literally, suffer the same humiliations as the British, who were interned and degraded by the Japanese. Some, in fact, were interned and were treated as enemy aliens. They would also find themselves torn, as a group, between the nationalist call of their group of origin and the hybrid Anglo-Asian culture that had come to form their modern identities.

Like Lee Kuan Yew, they would at once hate the British for their failure to defend Singapore and its peoples against the Japanese but still speak their language, study in their schools and become expert in their laws. At the same time, Lee and his fellows would both admire and fear the Chinese-educated, especially the charismatic firebrands like Lim Chin Siong and the dedicated, selfless leaders of the student and labor movements in postwar Singapore. They would stand up to and resist the Japanese, taking up armed struggle against them during the war. They would also claim leadership of the Chinese-educated masses. They had something that Lee and his class seemed to lack, and something they would need to tap if they were to succeed the British.

3   Politics in colonial Singapore

One can look at the question of politics in a colony like Singapore in a number of ways. On the one hand, there were the politics of the imperial power. On the other hand, there were the political lives of the dominated and the politics of their relationship with the colonial state. Another, perhaps more sensible, way of looking at it is to see Singapore as a sort of joint venture, a partnership or condominium between a shifting group of players, or power brokers. In general, these included the British administration, the European and various groups of Chinese merchants, and the Malay chiefs. They were bound together, both in conflict and cooperation, in a joint enterprise. They organized the exploitation of the material and human resources of the Malayan peninsula, including the peoples who migrated there over the course of the nineteenth and early twentieth century. They also created a system of domination, deciding how government would operate. Although it is important to understand that some decisions and policies came from Calcutta or London, these were tempered in many respects by the situation on the ground, at least in the early part of the nineteenth century.

The growth and transformation of the colonial "partnership" went through several stages and several generations of players. Relations between the parties were not always smooth, and the rules of engagement changed occasionally, but that did not mean that there was no joint enterprise. If they fought, it was more over a division of the spoils than over the principles of their activities. Towards the end of the century, and during the early decades of the twentieth century, outside influences came to have a greater impact on local affairs. At first, perhaps, the forces from Britain were the most powerful, but these were soon answered both by local actors and by influences emanating from China, India and other parts of Asia, not the least of which was Japan.

A less accessible feature is the political lives and movements of the peoples of Singapore, what James F. Warren calls history from the bottom up. Few of the ordinary people, the shopkeepers, boatmen, coolies, secret society fighters, hawkers, carpenters, planters, dock workers, rickshaw men, prostitutes, soldiers or the thousands of other people of different types who lived and worked in Singapore have left any written account of themselves. Nevertheless, we know that there were riots, mutinies, strikes and other outbursts from the masses, or from specific groups, that signaled their displeasure with the status quo, or some unwarranted change to it. We have to accept that they too played parts in the political life of the colony, and we should try to understand what circumstances gave rise to these activities.

The "joint venture" approach makes it possible to blend the accounts of the internal and external politics of Singapore both as a civic entity and as a fulcrum of empire. At the same time, it is possible to look at the factors that created a common ground for political action on the part of its leaders and its peoples. Finally, the approach stresses a continuity of structures and actors that has heretofore been ignored. There has been a tendency for the rulers of independent Singapore to suggest that there was no relationship between themselves and the political order that preceded them. While there are certain obvious differences, there have been significant elements of continuity.

These inquiries alone will not tell us much about the mechanisms, structures, traditions and attitudes or mindsets, of both rulers and ruled, that developed over the one 123 years of Singapore's prewar colonial existence. Thus, before looking at the processes of Singapore's political life, we should understand the political structures that were already in place when Raffles arrived. Beyond that, we should look at the administrative machinery created by the East India Company and Britain to rule Singapore, and at the structures and practices that grew up around them. Finally, we need to understand how these functioned.

The structure of the colonial state

It may seem contradictory, but it is important to understand that even though there was no real port or native urban settlement on Singapore Island in 1819, the island was part of a larger port complex. The chief who lived there had connections with the broader Malay world, particularly with the courts in Riau and Lingga. As we have seen, Riau was the major *entrepôt* in the region prior to the Dutch attack in 1784. The port of Tanjong Pinang on the island of Bentan, 50 kilometers to the south, continued to serve as a small port. At the time, Singapore could be seen as a sort of suburb of Riau. Given the mobility of trade and sea peoples at the time, it was a small matter to move one's base operations a short distance. As I have argued elsewhere, the economic patterns that had been established at Riau in the eighteenth century were resuscitated at Singapore with the arrival of the British.

Temenggong Abdul Rahman also maintained a *perentah*, a position, a territorial base and a following that gave him a political voice in the affairs of the old Johor–Riau empire. Even though the British were inclined to dismiss them as pirates, he and his followers constituted a power in the region around Singapore, and they possessed a claim to a kind of owner-ship, both to the island of Singapore and to other neighboring islands as well as to the tip of the Malayan peninsula known as Johor. Even though the British signed treaties, it would take four or five decades to rid them-selves of the influences and actual power of the Temenggong and the Sultan. Although they had signed away the island, the Malay peoples who lived there continued to be "their" subjects, *de facto* if not *de jure*.

Second, the Chinese also possessed networks and systems of governance and status that pre-dated the British arrival. The so-called secret societies, or triads, or *kongsis*, were already in existence in Riau, and the Chinese who came from Riau to plant pepper and gambier in Singapore brought these structures and their trading networks with them. They brought large "part-nerships" made up of both labor and capital that made and enforced laws and kept order and fought wars and provided security for the planters and their backers. They brought a variety of ethnic affiliations, especially the ambivalent links between the Hokkien and Teochew. In short, they brought their own political system (Trocki 1979).

The Melaka and Penang Chinese also brought their traditions of "kapi-tancy" developed under the Dutch and earlier British regimes. They brought the debt structures and family links that constituted networks of power and economic exchange. They also brought the understanding of systems of revenue farming and other political and economic practices that made enti-ties such as Singapore functional. Singapore was not a *tabula rasa* when Raffles arrived, and despite his claim, he did not have everything to make anew. Large, prefabricated components of the Indian Ocean *entrepôt* culture already existed and were ready to slide into place when Raffles cut the ribbon.

From the British point of view, the structures noted above often seemed insignificant objects of "clutter" in their grand design. To them, the colony of Singapore was established by Thomas Stamford Raffles on 26 February 1819 on behalf of the East India Company. And, from that time until 1867, Singapore was under the EIC or its successor in the India Office. The India Office ruled Singapore as a part of the Straits Settlements, the other two settlements being Prince of Wales Island (Penang) and Melaka.[11] In 1867, the government of the Straits Settlements was transferred to the Colonial Office, and they were ruled on that basis until 16 February 1942, when the Japanese took control of British Malaya. Between 1867 and 1942, the British colonial enterprise in the Malay world expanded to include the Federated Malay States (FMS) of Pahang, Negri Sembilan, Perak and Selangor; and the unfederated states of Johor, Kedah, Perlis, Kelantan and Trengganu. Protectorates had been established over the Borneo territories of Sarawak and Brunei; and north Borneo (now Sabah) was under the control of the Chartered Company. This is the story that one can find in all of the "colonial" histories of Singapore, particularly those by Mary Turnbull and others (Turnbull 1972, 1989). This is an important part of the Singapore story, but it is not a complete one.

Singapore was the center of this patchwork empire. The pieces had been acquired at different times and under different circumstances and were subject to separate treaties and conventions. The entire conglomeration was known informally as British Malaya and in 1942 was ruled by a governor who was resident in Singapore. One may say, then, that Singapore was the capital of British Malaya, but from 1895, Kuala Lumpur was made the headquarters of a resident-general, who governed the FMS under the authority of the governor (Sidhu 1980: 42–6). This marked the first step in the process of creating a separate political enterprise on the Malayan Peninsula. However, true administrative and political separation of Singapore from the peninsula did not come until 1942.

Turnbull has described the growth and development of the colonial administration and the role of Singapore as an imperial center. She has noted that there was never an intention on the part of any of the Indian powers to spend much money in Singapore, or the Straits for that matter. Singapore and its sister colonies lived on a strictly limited budget. This was another factor that left the administration even more dependent upon indigenous systems of political control. Singapore's strategic value was largely dependent on Britain's dominion of the seas in the first place. There was thus not much incentive to fortify the place or to enlarge its military installations. Without prior command of the seas, Singapore was indefensible in any case, as the Japanese proved in 1942. Despite its supposed strategic significance to Britain, no naval squadron or base was established at Singapore until much later in the nineteenth century, although British warships did routinely stop there on periodic cruises in Asian waters. The port did not even have Admiralty jurisdiction until 1836 and was thus forced to send captured pirates to Calcutta for trial.

Singapore's real value was economic. It was a free port, and at least so far as Raffles and those of his generation were concerned, not meant to be more than an *entrepôt* and a place where British shipping that traveled between India and China could safely resort. It was also a place where the traders of the islands and other parts of Asia could gather under the British flag. Although Raffles was not able to spend much time laying the foundation of his brainchild, his like-minded colleagues set the new colony on its path.

In 1824, John Crawfurd, Raffles' one-time subordinate in Java and the East India Company's envoy to the courts of Siam and Cochin China, became the Resident Councillor of Singapore. He was largely responsible for putting the administrative and fiscal structures of the colony firmly in place. In 1830, the Presidency of the Straits Settlements was abolished. Before then, Penang (which had been founded in 1786) had been considered the more important settlement, and the governance of Singapore was left to a Resident Councillor. When Singapore's size and prosperity began to outstrip Penang, the governor moved his base there. The first governor to reside permanently in Singapore was Sir Samuel George Bonham, who took over in 1836. He later went on to become governor of Hong Kong.

On paper, the Straits Settlements were under a system of direct rule.[12] That is, all formal structures were newly created by the colonial power and more or less patterned after those in British India, of which the Straits Settlements were a part. No authority remained in the hands of the prior Malay rulers, and none was given to Asian and other migrants who came there to settle. Authority was vested in the governor, and laws were made in India. Judges, police officials, magistrates and harbormasters were appointed by Calcutta and later by London. There was a garrison of sepoys, which was periodically rotated to other parts of Britain's Indian empire and replaced by other regiments. A local police force was made up of Indian and Malay "peons" and other lower ranks under the command of European officers.

However, direct and authoritarian rule in Singapore was more a technicality than a reality. Although there was no formal organizational allowance for representative government or any recognition of native authority or other local groupings of the colony's inhabitants, rule within Singapore was largely indirect and decentralized as a simple matter of necessity. The colonial government lacked the capacity to enforce its will without the voluntary collaboration of the informal power structure of the community. Malay chiefs retained considerable authority over their followers, especially those who lived within their own *kampongs*, but also many others in different parts of the island and offshore were seen to be under their authority. Locally settled communities of traders, including the Bugis and the Chinese, tended to be governed by their headmen, although there were no formal procedures for identifying or appointing such individuals, and no system of "kapitans" was ever established in Singapore.[13] Although British law was supreme, few Asian inhabitants understood it or had access to it, and most were governed by local custom so long as there were no blatant conflicts with British law. A great deal of authority was exercised by the Chinese revenue farmers, who collected most of the colony's taxes, and they seem to have worked largely through the agencies of the Chinese triad associations or secret societies, which themselves exercised considerable power within the Chinese population (Vaughan 1971).

The European merchant community, though able to communicate directly with the ruling authorities on an informal level, did occasionally develop a "public" presence. When matters of concern arose, such as the possibility of levying taxes or the threat of increased piracy, European merchants, like their Asian counterparts, held public meetings to convey their sentiments to the government and drafted petitions to the authorities. Buckley gives accounts of a number of instances on which such events took place (Buckley 1903: 301). European merchants organized a Chamber of Commerce in 1837 aimed at advancing their interests.[14] They also exercised considerable leverage through their constituents in Calcutta, Bombay and Hong Kong, and their connections in London, where they made up part of the very formidable "India interests" that played a major role in guiding the

EIC and later the British government in the development and exercise of imperial policy in Asia (Philips 1961).

Singapore and the Straits Settlements maintained this minimalist regime until 1867, when the colony was finally removed from the authority of the long-defunct East India Company and placed under the Colonial Office. At this time, the Straits were placed under a governor, who ruled with an Executive Council of his key administrators and the advice of a Legislative Council made up of both official and unofficial members. The "unofficials" were members of the European mercantile community together with Chinese and later Malay members who were appointed. Outside of this were the prominent merchants, Malay chiefs and other "headmen," who functioned on an informal level to manage the various communities.

In 1869, the Chinese Protectorate, which was intended to deal with matters touching on the secret societies, the coolie trade and the welfare of Chinese women, was established. It functioned largely as an arm of the police and enforced the Societies Ordinance, which attempted to restrict the formation of Chinese organizations, especially the secret societies. These were banned entirely in 1889. In the same year, the government also established the Chinese Advisory Board (CAB), which formally represented the five major Chinese *bangs* to the government. The CAB mirrored the structure of the Singapore Chinese Chamber of Commerce (SCCC), which was formed at about the same time (Visscher 2002).

These structures, with the periodic addition of specific officers for public works, health, sanitation, education and telecommunications, were the bare bones of government in Singapore. With little elaboration, they functioned until the coming of the Japanese. Until then, not only was there no plan to prepare Singapore for independence, there was no awareness on the part of the authorities that such a situation might ever occur. Even though varying levels of political consciousness were developing among different groups of Singapore's inhabitants, they too hardly considered the prospect of an independent Singapore.

The imperial politics of Singapore

As a part of the British Empire, Singapore exercised political influence in a number of directions. One was as a strategic outpost of British military and economic power in Asia. Here its governors and metropolitan authorities were agents of Britain within the arena of the global politics of Europe. It thus represented British interests against the imperial projects of the Netherlands, France, Spain and the United States, and later of Germany and Japan. Even though it welcomed trade and traders from all nations, Straits authorities had a role both in influencing the formation of international treaties and conventions affecting Asia and in implementing them. Even though it was not intended to be a territorial empire, Singapore came to serve as a platform from which British power, both political and economic, expanded into neighboring regions.

Singapore thus played a role in Malay politics, both as a base for the extension of British economic and political power into the surrounding states and waters and as a center of Malay political life in the region. This began with the very foundation of the settlement. To Raffles' advantage, there had been a succession dispute in the Riau–Johor court since the death of Sultan Mahmud in 1812. Although the leader of the "Bugis" faction, Yamtuan Muda Raja Ja'afar, had engineered the coronation of Tengku Abdul Rahman as the sultan, he was the younger of Mahmud's two sons, both of whom were by non-royal consorts. The "Malay" faction, led by the Temenggong and the Bendahara of Pahang, had supported the other son, Tengku Hussain (also known as Tengku Long), for the office, but they had been outmaneuvered by the Bugis. In fact, it was while Tengku Hussain was in Pahang marrying a daughter of the Bendahara that Mahmud had died suddenly (some said by poison) and Raja Ja'afar pre-emptively crowned Tengku Abdul Rahman. To complicate matters, the royal regalia (the crown, drum, sacred kris and other implements) were still in the hands of Engku Putri, the late sultan's royal, but childless, consort, who supported Hussain (Wake 1975). Raffles would have preferred an alliance with Raja Ja'afar, and Farquahar had already signed an agreement with him in 1818, but a few months later the Dutch returned and convinced Ja'afar to disregard the British overtures.

Raffles, who with Farquahar had arrived on Singapore Island in late January 1819, took the bold step of quickly signing a provisional agreement with the Temenggong and then, with the Temenggong's assistance, had Tengku Hussain brought to Singapore, where a more formal treaty was drawn up (Buckley 1903). The Malay prince was now recognized as the "Sultan of Johor and Singapore," but Temenggong Abdul Rahman was also dignified with the title of "Ruler of Singapore" (Trocki 1979: 36–53). The political implications of these rather dubious agreements became a long-running issue that continued to plague Singapore's political life into the twentieth century (Pang 1983). In any case, the acquisition of Singapore and the recognition of these two chiefs constituted a major intervention in the politics of the Malay world, irrevocably dividing the ancient kingdom of Johor and giving legitimacy to a different group of chiefs.

In each of the treaties, aside from the cession of Singapore and other matters relating to the status of the two chiefs, there was a clause by which each Malay ruler undertook to suppress piracy within his domains. The drive to combat piracy on the part of the Straits government was, in the final analysis, a major project of British imperialism. It served as Britain's primary excuse for intervening in the affairs of the Malay states of Southeast Asia. The anti-piracy campaign was actually launched by Raffles himself but was faithfully carried out by all of the succeeding rulers of Singapore and was particularly significant during the first half of the nineteenth century, ultimately having a devastating impact on the local political dynamics of maritime Southeast Asia.

The campaign represented a direct assault upon the overall political economy of the Malay world. Raiding by, or on behalf of, Malay chiefs was not only an "honorable" practice, it was crucial to the state-building process in the region. Malay rulers obtained resources, both material and human, by seizure.[15] They claimed the seas as well as the lands as their domain, and the people on it (except for foreign traders) were their subjects. They thus claimed the right to apprehend and relocate these resources in order to build up their own power. To Europeans, these policies smacked of theft and slavery rather than as taxation and government service.

The Anglo-Dutch Treaty of 1824 set the precedent for the two powers to agree that each would deal with the "problem of piracy" within their own areas. That is to say, the Dutch would police Sumatra, the Riau–Lingga Archipelago and the west coast of Borneo, while the British would deal with the Malayan Peninsula. On the whole, once the two powers had developed working arrangements – these began to fall into place by the mid-1830s – they began to cooperate against virtually any Malay leader or group seen to be in opposition to the broad colonial agendas (Tarling 1963 :48–9).

There was a certain irony here, since the rise of piracy was connected to the very presence of Singapore. As trade expanded, the local and imperial aristocracies sought to enforce their claims to the wealth of their subjects. James Brooke, in his "Letter from Borneo," decried the system whereby the sultan of Brunei or his *pangerans* would collect revenue from the people by

> sending boats to take the produce at a price merely nominal, the residue being left to the inhabitants, who were, and still are in theory, mere slaves. As the government, however, has become weak, and the mercantile class been stimulated by profits to be gained at Singapore, the people, or rather the local governments, have shown great reluctance to part with their riches, and, generally speaking, the Sultan and his pangerans have been content with a very diminished revenue, rather than coerce countries which they had no means of keeping permanently in subjection. The class of nakodahs [ship captains], taking advantage of this, are yearly busy in making engagements for the following season for the Singapore market.
>
> (Tarling 1963: 117)

These moves on the part of the local chiefs to either control or clamp down upon this opening of trade with Singapore brought about the naval violence that the British and Dutch called "piracy."

For the first twenty years of the settlement's existence, the followers of the Temenggong and the sultan both treated Singapore as their private domain and regularly attempted to interdict Malay and sometimes Chinese traffic moving in and out of the port to collect "taxes," presents, and sometimes the entire cargo and crew. The followers of the Temenggong of Johor were seen as a particular problem. Especially between 1825 and 1836, that is, following the death of Temenggong Abdul Rahman and before Temenggong Ibrahim had attained his majority, there was apparently no effective leader of the following. Various groups of *orang laut* and residents of Teluk Belanga were suspected of preying on native trade coming to Singapore. The same was true of groups associated with Sultan Hussain at Kampong Glam.

In 1835, a "commission" on piracy was established in Singapore, and a number of expeditions were undertaken by the gunboat *Andromache* and the steam gunboat *Diana*, operating out of Singapore. The *Diana* ventured into the Dutch-controlled areas of the Riau–Lingga archipelago over the objections of the Dutch authorities. In one instance, it raided an *orang laut* village on the island of Galang, where they discovered a 300-ton Cochin Chinese junk. Not long afterwards, the people of Galang came to Singapore seeking refuge with the Temenggong. The *Tuhfat al-Nafis* reports the raids in somewhat different fashion, claiming that the *Diana* was roaming the islands indiscriminately shooting at native craft. After these raids, the Temenggong is said to have come to Governor Bonham offering to lend his assistance to suppress piracy.

The Temenggong did not abandon his practice of intimidating native traders. In fact, his boats began to patrol the waters around Singapore and themselves seized cargos, particularly of gutta percha,[16] claiming that they were the produce of Johor and therefore his property. It was in this fashion that the Temenggong both smoothed his relations with the British government and at the same time became wealthy by trading in gutta percha with a number of favored British merchants (Trocki 1979). Other chiefs were not so fortunate.

The governors of Singapore found themselves committed to a necessary but sometimes unwilling cooperation with the Temenggong. As a price for relaxing his grip on the seas around Singapore, the Singapore government backed him in his expansion into Johor. The Temenggong formed alliances with a faction of European merchants and gained support from an important clique of Teochew merchants. An added feature of the period from the 1830s to the 1860s was that Singapore's European mercantile community was split into two factions, one supporting the Temenggong and the other, Sultan Hussain and later his son, Tengku Ali.[17] In the long run, the Temenggong was able to gain British recognition for his possession of the state of Johor, while Tengku Ali was left with only the strip of territory between the Muar and Kesang rivers. Even that was later lost to the Johor ruler. Prominent merchants such as W.H. Read were vocal supporters of the rights of the sultan's two sons, and they kept up a continual propaganda campaign, claiming that the Temenggong was an upstart and accusing him of involvement in piracy, but their arguments were ineffective.

In 1862, Temenggong Ibrahim's son, Abu Bakar, a product of the Teluk Belanga Malay School, succeeded his father and changed his title to "Maharaja."[18] A few years later, with the blessing of the local government and his merchant friends, he traveled to London and began his lifelong friendship with Queen Victoria. In 1885, again with the recognition of the Singapore governor, Abu Bakar took the title of Sultan of Johor. Even though he grew rich from the pepper and gambier agriculture in Johor and founded a capital for his state at Johor Bahru, Abu Bakar continued to maintain a palace at Tyersall in Singapore, and a residence, mosque and burial ground at Teluk Belanga. Tengku Ali and his brother and their descendants wasted away in genteel poverty at their crumbling palace in Kampong Glam, while the descendants of the Temenggong are the present royal family of Johor.[19]

During the nineteenth century, Singapore functioned as the center of the Malay world. As the center of British power, it was the place to which dissident chiefs came for the settlement of their claims. Both European and Chinese merchants treated Singapore and the other Straits Settlements as the platform from which to launch their economic adventures into the Malay states. In many of these affairs, the Temenggongs played significant roles, often behind the scenes. In the end, while they ultimately withdrew entirely from Singapore, they did gain the state of Johor, over which their descendants preside to this day.

Even before Britain's "forward movement," which saw the intervention in the "tin wars" in Perak and Selangor, Singapore governors had established a pattern of continuous involvement in the affairs of the Malay states such as Pahang and Trengganu. They used Penang as a base to expand into Kedah and the southern Siamese states. The piracy wars went on against the maritime Malays until the 1850s, when most "renegade" chiefs and most of the available or willing *orang laut* had either been either killed or intimidated to the point where it was clear there was no future in such a lifestyle.

The major turning point in this campaign came with the activities of James Brooke and the British naval expeditions under Captain Henry Keppel in *HMS Dido* in the 1840s. Their actions were a response to the more or less continuous drumbeat of demands by British traders for military intervention against the "pirates," whether in Riau–Lingga, Borneo, Sumatra or Malaya. Brooke, with Keppel's aid, launched a well-organized campaign against the "pirates" of Sarawak. These were mostly Ibans who had established relationships with Illanun, Bugis or Arab traders to procure slaves and trade goods for the Singapore market in "violation" of the claims of the Brunei ruler and his own *pangerans*. Annually, their fleets of war canoes swept the shores of northern and western Borneo from Brunei to Banjarmasin. Brooke's solution was ultimately to carve out his own little kingdom in Sarawak in the face of objections from both Brunei and the Dutch. This was done with official British support, both from Singapore and the Foreign Office. Brooke's moves brought the Dutch into cooperative military expeditions to suppress piracy and to exercise hegemony over the native states within their sphere of influence. They also came to accept British influence in northern Borneo.

The British, for their part, did not interfere with Dutch attempts to destroy the Malay governments that blocked their expansion. Thus in the 1850s we find that the British in Singapore were reluctant to support the "rebel" ruler of Lingga, Sultan Mahmud IV, in his campaigns to throw off Dutch hegemony. They also worked to thwart his attempts to establish alliances with the Temenggong of Johor, the sultan of Trengganu or even the king of Siam. In the 1870s, the British looked the other way as the Dutch used "piracy" as justification for their assault on Aceh. It is important in this context to understand that while the ostensible aim of the policy was to suppress piracy, it was clear that any "recalcitrant" Malay prince was liable to find himself tagged with that label. In the end, the maritime Malays virtually disappeared, and those who survived were those who, like the Temenggongs, actively cooperated with the colonial power and who were able to find alternative sources of income.

The British and the Chinese

Aside from the Malays, who inhabited the fringes of the colonial "bubble" that was Singapore, the Chinese were the other political challenge to British authority. The population figures show how rapidly and dramatically the other races of Singapore were outnumbered by the Chinese. Their economic and social dynamism, although admired and welcomed by the rulers of the port, was also at times a threat. Given the system of *laissez-faire* imperialism that was practised in nineteenth-century Singapore, the government was in something of a quandary. If it wanted direct control over the Chinese population, it would be necessary to invest in police forces and to develop an infrastructure that reached into the community. Apart from their unwillingness to spend money on such activities, the British lacked the expertise.

This was the reason for the headman system; however, it was only a short-term solution to the problem of governance. There were long-term disadvantages to the system. On the one hand, it created a class of privileged individuals and families who would come to enjoy power as a birthright. If British recognition acknowledged the power they already had, it also confirmed and, to a large degree, legitimized and institutionalized that power and added to it. As the only means of communication with the masses of the population, the headman system placed considerable leverage in their hands over which the British had no check. The British were thus often dependent upon this small group of individuals.

The other flaw in the system was that the individuals upon whom they relied lacked power in certain areas. Most of these men were, in the first instance, Straits-born Chinese from Melaka whose main qualification was that they spoke English. They were at a disadvantage when dealing with newly arrived *sinkehs*, particularly the ones who spoke no Hokkien. As a result, the thousands of Teochew, Hakka and Cantonese coolies who flooded into Singapore during the first three decades after 1819 were, for the most part, beyond their ken. The Baba headmen needed to form alliances with others who could communicate with these newcomers. It was thus necessary for them to share power with these individuals to some degree. As it turned out, this resulted in a power structure that ultimately incorporated the triads or secret societies into the system of government.

A key element in the power structure was the government's need for revenue, most of which was collected through the taxes on opium and spirits. These were the responsibilities of the revenue farmers, many of whom also functioned as the headmen of their respective communities. Here again was another contradiction in the system. The revenue farms, to be an effective source of income for the government, had to be let out by a system of competitive bidding, thus the farmers' positions were somewhat insecure and dependent upon their ability to gain control of the farms.

Since there was no set procedure for appointing headmen in Singapore, there was no need for these persons actually to be revenue farmers or to hold any specific position *vis-à-vis* the state. Individuals such as Choa Chong Long, Tan Tock Seng and Ho Ah Kay did not always hold official positions; although some were revenue farmers at times, and others were magistrates at times, none was permanently in such a post. Likewise, many of the revenue farmers never held any other official position; in fact, the names of many of them have been completely forgotten.[20]

An interesting case is the one of Lau Joon Teck, who held the opium farms from 1847 to about 1860, one of the longest periods on record. He is not mentioned in Song Ong Siang's history of the Chinese in Singapore; nor is his name to be found in any other published source. However, it did appear on some official correspondence in the Straits Settlements records (SSR) (Trocki 1990: 99–103). He does not appear to have been a Straits-born Chinese or even have been able to speak English. My original assumption was that he was a Teochew, but David Chng now suggests that he may have been a Hakka (Chng 1999). Chng has also found that Lau's name seems to have been included among the tablets of the tiger-generals of the Ghee Hin Hui or Tiandihui (the main Singapore secret society) in the Lavender Street temple.

Lau, together with Cheang Sam Teo, had taken the opium and spirit farms over from Kiong Kong Tuan and Tay Han Long (a.k.a. Tay Eng Long). This shift, I believe, represented a major change in the power structure of Singapore's Chinese society. Cheang and Lau displaced a syndicate led by a well-entrenched group of Straits-born Chinese.[21] Cheang Sam Teo, although he was a Hokkien and had also been a partner of Tay Han Long, seems to have been part of a different Hokkien faction.

In addition to this change in revenue farm ownership, the appearance of Lau Joon Teck in the syndicate suggests an alliance with a secret society leader. While earlier farms probably had some affiliation with the triads, this seems to have been the first occasion on which one had risen to be the acknowledged major partner in the syndicate. When he died in 1859, the resident councillor described him as "the principal monied man of the farms" (Trocki 1990: 122) It is also significant that he had returned to China just prior to his death. It thus seems clear that he was not a Straits-born Chinese.

The change in revenue farm ownership that occurred in 1846–47 also paralleled a period of instability and apparent leadership change in the secret societies. In 1846, the so-called Chinese funeral riots broke out during the funeral procession of the former leader of the Ghee Hin Hui. The riots were also clearly connected to the growing shortage of land and decreasing opportunities in pepper and gambier agriculture on Singapore Island. At the same time, the movement of Teochew pepper and gambier planters to Johor began to take place. There is credible evidence that the opening of Johor was actually led by the Teochew elements of the Ghee Hin, or the Ngee Heng as it was called in Johor.

Here we see all the elements or major political actors or forces of Singapore facing a multifaceted set of crises. As already suggested, the Temenggong of Johor was facing a problem. If he abandoned piracy, he would need an alternative source of income. In Singapore, pepper and gambier agriculture was facing a surge of immigration following the Opium War in China. Planters were fighting over land, while the government was in the process of attempting to extend its influence into the interior of the island (where it had had none) by surveying the land and attempting to issue title deeds. At the same time, there was a clear breakdown in the authority and power once exercised by the clique of Straits-born merchants. They had lost control of the opium distribution network, and new and aggressive leadership in the secret society world was now clamouring for recognition; it seems that a split in the society or societies was developing.

Thus, in 1846, a large group of Teochew planters moved from Singapore to settle on the Tebrau River under the leadership of Kapitan Tan Kye Soon of the Ngee Heng Society. This move confirmed that an alliance had been formed between the Temenggong and a group of Teochew *taukehs* who financed these planters, and with their affiliated secret society. In Singapore, the revenue-farming syndicate was reorganized under the leadership of the Hokkien *taukeh* Cheang Sam Teo and his partner Lau Joon Teck, another Ghee Hin leader. A third element in the revenue farms, which also linked with Johor, was the union of the Johor revenue farm with that of Singapore. The manager of the Johor opium farms was taken into the partnership with Cheang and Lau.

It is less clear how someone like Seah Eu Chin fitted into these shifts. It may have been that Lau Joon Teck was allied with Seah, who had already risen to wealth and power largely through his involvement in the pepper and gambier agriculture in Singapore. He had gotten into the business in the late 1830s and was now on the verge of becoming the most powerful Teochew leader in Singapore. He had also come to control the Ngee Ann Kongsi, which was the largest Teochew *bang* association in Singapore and the repository of considerable wealth. Later evidence shows that he was a major investor in Johor's pepper and gambier agriculture.

It is difficult to see clearly into the somewhat murky affairs of that age, but subsequent developments show that Singapore's powerful merchant cliques were coalescing at this time. One was the Hokkien Ch'ang T'ai clique around Cheang Sam Teo, which was not the only Hokkien clique but was the one that controlled at least part of the Singapore opium and spirit farms until 1880. The other was the Hai Ch'ang clique of Tan Tock Seng, controlled by a Melaka-born group of Babas. The other great coalition was the Ngee Ann group of Teochews under Seah Eu Chin.

The expansion of pepper and gambier agriculture was also an important development for the British in Singapore. On the one hand, it insured the gainful employment of the large numbers of coolies who were then arriving in Singapore. On the other, the links between the English-speaking Chinese mercantile elite and the masses of the population that were established in the revenue-farming syndicate of Cheang and Lau guaranteed that the taxes from that large population of opium-smoking coolies would flow steadily into government coffers. Finally, the expanded production of the island was now a crop that could be profitably shipped to Europe and America and thus become a source of profit for the European merchant community, which not only purchased the commodity but also supplied Singapore's opium farmers with their needs.

The final plank in this political and economic structure, which would serve Singapore for the next four decades, was the opening of Johor. The income (again collected by Chinese opium farmers) now flowing into the Temenggong's treasury made it possible for him to abandon piracy and turn to the management of an agricultural territory outside Singapore. He was the first of the new model of Malay rulers, fashioned largely by and for Singapore and its economic interests. In the coming years, he would be held up as an example to other Malay chiefs of how to become wealthy and powerful and not come to be seen as an obstacle to European advances. Although in later years he would become a different kind of obstacle, in the mid-nineteenth century he was clearly the sort of Malay chief with whom European colonists felt comfortable (Trocki 1979).

The continuous expansion of Chinese enterprise, in the form of pepper and gambier planters moving from Singapore into Johor, would continue into the 1880s. Not until the 1890s, when the bottom began to fall out of the gambier market in Europe and America, would the movement slow down. At the same time, the same group of Singapore *taukehs* were also spreading the cultivation and their influence into the Riau archipelago, Melaka, Negri Sembilan and Sarawak. Although the original planters had come from Bentan (in Riau) to Singapore, now the Singapore *taukehs* were colonizing the other islands of the archipelago. If Riau–Lingga, Singapore and Johor had once been part of the old Johor empire, they were now all part of the same economic zone, whose Chinese were all taxed by the same syndicate of opium farmers in Singapore.

Following Lau Joon Teck's death in 1859, there was another disruption in the revenue-farming system accompanied by a spate of secret society disturbances as a new generation of players emerged. The sons of Cheang Sam Teo, Cheang Hong Lim and Cheang Hong Guan, as contenders for the leadership of the Hokkien faction, battled the Teochew faction under Tan Seng Poh (Seah Eu Chin's brother-in-law). Their struggle lasted throughout the 1860s. In 1870, they created what one observer called the "Grand Opium Syndicate," headed by Hong Lim, Seng Poh and the Johor *taukeh* Tan Hiok Nee. In some respects, this also seems to have signaled an advance in the power of the *taukehs* in general.

Prior to the 1860s, it seems that the lower or middle elements of the secret societies, particularly the Ghee Hin, which was the largest in Singapore, still maintained a certain egalitarian spirit, which has been attributed to the early *kongsi* organizations by Wang Tai Ping (Wang 1995). As Wang has pointed out in his study of the Borneo *kongsis*, by the mid-nineteenth century, the mining *taukehs* of Borneo were allying themselves with the Dutch and the *kongsis* were losing their democratic and self-governing characteristics. The *taukehs* were taking control of the *kongsis* and using them as agencies of labor control and to protect the revenue farms.

It seems obvious that something very similar was happening in Singapore. If we look at the character of secret society disturbances or gang violence in Singapore in the first half-century, it seems clear that there was an element of class struggle in some outbreaks. Particularly in the spate of so-called "gang robberies" that took place in the mid-1830s, violence was directed against the wealthy by the have-nots. Even the Chinese funeral riots of 1846 suggest a struggle by the greater mass of the planters and coolies against a smaller but perhaps better financed group possibly allied with a group of *taukehs*. Clearly, the smaller group, which was attempting to cause a disruption during the funeral procession, seems to have had some sympathy from the policemen on the scene (Trocki 1990: 86–94).

There are clear indications of economic struggle taking place on the gambier plantations. Part of the conflict was between Hokkien and Teochew, but part of it was a conflict between the Quan Teck (or Kien Teck) Hui and the Ghee Hin. The former was thought to be allied with the wealthier Hokkien *taukehs*, who were closely tied to the colonial government, or rather governments, because the fighting extended to Riau as well as throughout Singapore and Johor. Conflicts were reported both in Bentan and on Galang Island. In Bentan, the kapitan of the Hokkien Chinese had been attacked by the Teochew. Galang, once the haunt of *orang laut* "pirates," had been settled by a group of Chinese pepper and gambier planters. In 1847, a large group of secret society men from Singapore, led by one Neo Liang Guan, who had some plantations around Seletar, launched a vicious raid on Galang killing 100 people and destroying twenty-eight plantations (*ibid.*: 91–2).

The ill-feeling and continued economic competition in the gambier plantations between Hokkien, Teochew and newly arrived Roman Catholic planters (who seem to have been Hakka) persisted into the 1850s. In the early 1850s, there were reports of opium smuggling and difficulties faced by the opium farmer. In 1851, the Ghee Hin and the Ghee Hok combined forces to attack Chinese planters who had converted to Roman Catholicism. Comber reports that in a week 500 Christians were killed and twenty-seven plantations were destroyed (*SFP*, 21 February 1851).

All these conflicts came to a head in 1854, when a fleet of twenty-two war junks arrived from China carrying the ousted rebels of the Small Sword Society or Xiao Dao Hui. The uprising in Shanghai had been led by a number of Singapore-born Hokkien, some of whom spoke pretty good English. They had now returned to Singapore with their followers, and their numbers further destabilized an already tense situation there. There was also a rice shortage, and Tan Kim Ching, who controlled the rice trade from Siam, was thought to have been profiteering. The price had risen very high, and when a Hokkien argued with a Teochew over the price of several catties of rice, the entire island erupted on 5 May 1854. The riot lasted for twelve days, and 500 people were killed and 300 houses burned. This conflict was largely between Hokkien and Teochew. The latter had received support from the Cantonese and Cantonese Hakka.

The remarkable level of violence and the fact that most of the activity involved pepper and gambier planters and their coolies suggests that the conflict was rooted in the economic system. However, earlier scholars have tended to explain away these conflicts by commenting that "It was the old feud, brought from China," or pointed to "doctrinal differences," thus ignoring the possibility that the violence was related to specific local conditions (Wynne 1941; Comber 1959; Blythe 1969).

The Hokkien–Teochew conflict was not simply an ethnic or "doctrinal" fight; rather, it was a struggle over control of pepper and gambier agriculture, on the one hand, and the opium farms on the other. The two were intimately linked, since the main source of finance for the planters was the rich opium farmers and people who held shares in their syndicates. On the other hand, the main consumers of opium were the planters and their coolies. It was, in fact, extensive opium sales to coolies, often at inflated prices, that made it possible for investors to increase their profits, since the sales of pepper and gambier alone would not have been very remunerative. It is difficult to trace lines of command and responsibility linking the revenue farmers, who were "respected" members of the urban community and who were well known to the British rulers, to the secret society chiefs who actually controlled the planting communities. These chiefs were the *kangchus* who actually dealt in opium and actually collected the taxes and also the debts due to the shopkeepers. Nevertheless, it is clear that such links existed. Otherwise, it is impossible to see how the economy could have functioned and how power was exercised. There is documentary evidence that such links existed in Johor, and the Johor system was only an extension of Singapore's system, except that in Johor, the lines of control are matters of record (Trocki 1976, 1979).

This failure to consider the vital role that the societies played in the functioning of the pepper and gambier economy is evident in Comber's bewilderment at the behaviour of the government following the 1854 disturbances:

> It is remarkable also, that even after this major riot, no action was taken to suppress secret societies. It is difficult to defend this inaction except on the ground of ignorance, or perhaps it was that Lieutenant-Colonel Butterworth [the Singapore governor] considered it would be impossible to put into practice an order of suppression with the limited forces of law and order available at his disposal.
>
> (Comber 1959: 93)

In a way, his supposition is correct. Butterworth did not have the resources because the secret societies were the resources upon which the finances of the state depended. It is also true that the Singapore authorities felt that such legislation would be impossible to enforce. A few years later, Governor E.A. Blundell reported on a general strike that was launched by the triads in response to a "misunderstood" police order that interfered with their Chinese New Year celebrations. His note also shows the level of power then exercised by the societies. All Chinese shops as well as Indian shops were shut for one day and then were reopened the following day on the orders of the societies.

> This simultaneous movement, in a large and populous Town like Singapore, evinces a power and spirit of organization among the Chinese which has excited a considerable degree of alarm and apprehension. It is not, I think, to be denied that the Secret Associations existing among the Chinese are the framework of this organization, and the leaders of these Associations may have objects in view far beyond a mere redress of Police grievances; but their power and influence among their own people cannot be successfully contended against with the means now at our disposal. Much dissatisfaction is felt by the European community of Singapore that no Legislative Enactment has yet been brought forward aimed at these Secret Associations, but with every respect for the opinions of gentlemen equal and superior to myself in experience of the Chinese character, I retain my firm belief that no mere Legislative Enactment, aimed at putting down Secret Associations, and at destroying the influence of its leaders, can ever prove successful. ... Associations of all kinds are natural with the Chinese. They form a part of their existence; Labour and Trade are mostly carried on by them, and in every Tribe or Class there is an

Association for mutual assistance and protection. These latter have become dangerous.

(IOR V/10/4, Blundell to Sec. of Govt India, 10/1/1857)

Blundell claimed that there were some Chinese who were "devoted" to the British but who were intimidated by the societies. This was clearly a high point of the societies' power, and within the next twenty years their influence was gradually reduced, but this did not happen until it was possible to unify the revenue-farming syndicates under *taukeh* control.

The merger of the farming syndicates marked the crystallization of power in the Chinese community under a coalition of Hokkien and Teochew *taukehs*. The first effective anti-secret society legislation, which registered them and classified them into "dangerous" and "friendly" societies, was passed in 1869. In the same year, the revenue-farming syndicates were brought together in the so-called "Grand Syndicate" led by Teochew leader Tan Seng Poh with Cheang Hong Lim, leader of the Hokkien Chang Tai faction, and Tan Hiok Nee, the Major China of Johor. The syndicate took control of the farms in 1870, but the coalition was formed in 1869, when they bid for the farms. An important aspect of this coalition was that Tan Seng Poh created a group of revenue police out of the members of his own surname association, the "Seh Tan." Having consolidated the farms, there was no longer a need for the involvement of other secret societies or strong-arm gangs in the revenue-farming business, or for that matter in the coolie-broking or labor-control businesses.[22]

The problem for the government following the formation of this coalition was wresting power from the *taukehs*. The "Grand Syndicate" clique held unchallenged power in Singapore for the next decade. A mark of its control is seen in the fact that the annual rent for the revenue farms increased only minimally during that period. Tan Seng Poh was also a legislative councillor and a partner in the Alexandra Gun Powder Magazine and the Tanjong Pagar Dock Company. With his family links to the Seah clan (whose business interests he then controlled), he dominated the pepper and gambier industry. He also controlled the Kongkek, or Pepper and Gambier Association, the group of *taukehs* who controlled the trade. Hong Lim dominated the Hokkien community. Tan Hiok Nee controlled the Johor side of things, and all three were very wealthy and had large property holdings in Singapore. For all practical purposes, the three of them ran the Chinese communities of Singapore and Johor. The 1870s was the epitome of the *laissez-faire* state, but the 1880s brought many changes that sharply curtailed the power of Chinese merchants in British Singapore.

The great showdown between government and the opium farmers came in 1883, when Governor Frederick Weld was able to break a conspiracy led by Hong Lim and Tan Keng Swee (Seng Poh's son). In order to increase the tax in 1879, Archibald Anson had taken the unprecedented step of going outside the Singapore syndicate and asking for bids from Penang.[23] Weld (who became governor in 1880) obtained a large increase in rent when Penang merchant Koh Saeng Tat took the Singapore farm. Unfortunately, both Sir John Pope Hennessy and Weld were disappointed when the outsiders lost money because of smuggling conspiracies by the locally based syndicates and their henchmen.

Although Seng Poh had died in 1879, it appears that control of his secret society forces, the Seh Tan, passed to his son. In 1883, Weld was successful in enticing yet another bidder from Penang, Chiu Sin Yong. He too faced a determined group of local smugglers and nearly went bankrupt before he had held the farms for a year. It was only with decisive and somewhat draconian actions by Weld that the smuggling conspiracy was crushed. Three secret society leaders were banished, and William Pickering, the protector of Chinese, was finally successful in piercing the cloak of silence that hid the machinery of the secret societies and the revenue-farming system. Tan Kim Ching, the powerful Hokkien *taukeh* and rival of Cheang Hong Lim and his Teochew allies, was persuaded to give evidence against the conspirators. In addition, they were able to get further testimony from Koh Sun Chai, an inside member of the clique.

This was a rare breakthrough and did much to crack the power constellation within the Chinese community. The old pepper and gambier and opium clique had been broken. It had also been weakened by the fact that new sources of wealth were then being created, and a new generation of ambitious Chinese entrepreneurs was coming of age. Within a few years, individuals such as Lim Nee Soon who were newcomers to Singapore would directly challenge the Seah clan for control of the Ngee Ann Kongsi. Lim was also a member of the group of *taukehs* that created the Singapore Chinese Chamber of Commerce (SCCC) in 1889.

From this point until the coming of the Japanese, the power structure of the Chinese community would be founded in the hierarchy of clan, place of origin, temple and other regional groups that were organized under the *bang* structure. Also in 1889, the government created the Chinese Advisory Board (CAB), whose membership largely duplicated that of the management committee of the SCCC. Singapore's Chinese community remained under the control of the *taukeh* elite, but it lacked the police power and official status that the old revenue farmers had enjoyed. Overall, this was a relatively tame elite. They were businessmen who did not strive for political power, but they did have prestige and status within their communities, and they supported schools, temples and ultimately newspapers. When political waves began to sweep out of China, these men were among the first to respond.

While it is true that secret societies still existed, they no longer resembled those that existed before the 1870s. The formation of the Great Syndicate had made it possible to detach most of the secret societies from the mainstream elements of the local economy: pepper and gambier, opium, and the coolie trade. When Tan Seng Poh employed his own personal gang, the Seh

Figure 3.1 Governor Weld and his family together with the Maharaja of Johor at Government House in Singapore, 1882. Standing, from the the left: Capt. Lord C. Scott, RN; W.E. Maxwell; Capt. H.S. Townsend, ABC; Sir Fredrick Weld (governor), HRH Prince Edward; HH Maharaja Abu Bakar of Johor; HRH Prince George, Prince of Wales; George Brown. Seated, from the left: Col. H. Parnell, CB; Minnie Weld; Miss Weld; Lady Weld; Cecilly Weld; Eddy Weld; Rev. J. Dalton; (on ground) Capt. Martear, RN; (Lying) Capt. Durrand, R.N.

Tan, as his own revenue police, he had pushed the other societies out of the mainstream of the economy. The secret societies that emerged after 1870 were largely made up of outsiders and could only manage to subsist by petty extortion, gambling, prostitution and minor smuggling. They were no longer part of the power structure. After Tan Seng Poh, it was only necessary for the British to eliminate the Seh Tan and his allies in the Kongkek. This was accomplished by Weld and Pickering with the assistance of Tan Kim Ching in 1883 so far as Singapore was concerned. The other supports of that power group were curtailed by Sultan Abu Bakar in Johor, who pushed aside the Kongkek and, with the assistance of Wong Ah Fook, took control of his own revenue farms in 1886 (Lim 2002: 82–5).

This shift was part of a number of major changes taking place in Singapore in the last two decades of the nineteenth century. The expansion of the colonial state, including the creation of a larger and more effective police force, was also part of the change. Weld was one of the first governors to select educated Englishmen with public school backgrounds in an attempt to create a more professional colonial service. He put them through a systematic in-country training program where they learned Malay, and some (the unlucky ones, according to Victor Purcell) even learned Chinese (Purcell 1965). This was the end of the *laissez-faire* colonial state and the beginning of a much more autocratic and intrusive form of imperial governance. It meant a radical change in the manner in which the peoples of Singapore were governed, and it also led to unexpected reactions from the Asian population. Beyond colonial policies, however, other changes taking place in Asia came to affect Singapore, including the rise of national consciousness in China, India, Malaya and the Dutch East Indies, and even among the English-educated peoples of Singapore itself.

Contesting territory

The difficulty that the colonial government experienced in gaining control of its revenue reflected their general lack of influence in the day-to-day lives of the ordinary people of Singapore town. For most Europeans, the tightly packed and teeming shophouses of Chinatown and Kampong Glam were an unknown world, and it remained that way through most of the colonial era. The first truly detailed description of an area of Singapore's Chinatown was Barrington Kaye's *Upper Nankin Street*, which was researched in the mid-1950s (Kaye 1960). During the colonial era, Chinatown and most of the "native" areas of the island were, to Eurpoeans, oceans of darkness, crime, squalor and filth.

Brenda Yeoh has described the attempts by the colonial government during the 1890s and early 1900s as a power struggle between the government and the people of Singapore. She presents "the colonial landscape as contested terrain [that] not only 'articulates the ideological intent of the powerful who plan and shape the landscape in particular ways' but also 'reflects the everyday meanings implicit in the daily routines of ordinary people associated with the landscape" (Yeoh 1996 :10).

The colonial authorities sought to exercise power so as to regulate space, to construct social and racial categories, and to "define what constitutes health as opposed to disease, science as opposed to 'quackery', order as opposed to disorder, or public 'good' as opposed to public 'nuisances.'" This need to impose their own "order" on the Asian population of Singapore was hindered by a mutual and almost deliberate ignorance on both sides. The struggle for control over public space and the built environment in urban Singapore during the late nineteenth and early twentieth century shows the depths of this mutual ignorance (*ibid.*). Both Europeans and Asians, particularly the Chinese, had their own sets of names for the various streets, districts and other landmarks of the city (Firmstone 1905). These separate nomenclatures represented separate worlds that only intersected at random and infrequent points. The separate systems also led to endless conflict, confusion and misunderstanding between the government and the Asian communities of Singapore throughout the colonial period (Yeoh 1996: 219–35).

After nearly a century of living cheek by jowl with the Chinese and other natives of the region in Singapore, the Europeans sought to "open up" the areas of "darkness" by essentially bulldozing their way into the heart of their buildings. The state wanted to "see" what was happening in the world that had been closed to them. The aim of the project was to carry out the sanitation agenda of nineteenth-century urban planners by opening up the shophouse world. Yeoh provides maps of the blocks of Chinese shophouses (actually, most of them were residences as well as businesses) showing that each block was a virtual fortress. Each possessed a solid façade composed of 6- or 7-meter wide shop fronts that provided the only access to the remainder of the building. The typical shophouse was three stories high and often extended back as much as 30 or 40 meters until it met the back of the shophouse on the other side of the block. In the years 1906–17, "Block densities varied between 635 and 1,304 persons per acre while house densities ranged from 18.7 to 44.5 persons per house" (Yeoh 1996: 138).

It took the municipal authorities nearly three decades to penetrate these blocks to provide "back lanes" in these "fortresses" in order to lay sewer lines and to provide drainage systems for the blocks. The authorities saw the "dark and fetid" interiors of the houses as breeding grounds for disease, immorality and crime. They aimed to bring in light, air and surveillance. For the Asians, these were seen as moves to confiscate their property, reduce their living space and threaten their security.

In addition to the rear of the shophouse buildings, there were continual struggles over the frontages that went back to the middle of the nineteenth century. In the early 1870s, the "Verandah Riots" erupted over attempts to prevent hawkers and shop owners from using the "five-foot ways" or covered sidewalks that fronted the shophouses as additional retail, storage and even living space. Cultural and economic priorities on the part of the Asians conflicted with European intentions to improve traffic circulation and prevent "congestion." Similar rationalistic priorities led the colonial state to take control of the streets, ultimately developing policies that favored horses, while Europeans rode them and, later, motor cars. This was usually felt to be to the detriment of Asian pedestrians, rickshaws and other forms of transport.

Likewise, the expulsion of hawkers from the five-foot ways was a great inconvenience to the people who lived in the area. Not only did it deprive many of them of their livelihoods, but it was felt that it would be a great inconvenience to those who depended on these hawkers for their food and everyday purchases. In fact, there were several misunderstandings, and the government later claimed that it only wanted to remove the stalls of vegetable sellers, who should have been in the marketplace, and that the order did not apply to the food hawkers.

A major step in enlisting at least some sectors of the Asian communities to support these "enlightened" policies was the organization of a municipal commission to deal with the everyday affairs of the city, as opposed to the broader areas of political life. During the Verandah Riots, individuals such as Tan Seng Poh, Tan Beng Swee and Whampoa were enlisted to go out into the streets and explain the policy to the people. Tan Seng Poh was in fact stoned by a group of people whom he identified as *samsengs* or simply thugs. He claimed that the actual hawkers, who made up some of the initial crowd, were amenable to reason, but that the *samsengs* were incorrigible and should be shot. These events highlighted the irony of the situation. Once the headmen had broken their links with the secret societies, they could no longer control them.

In order to deal with the "sanitation" problems, the government organized a reformed municipal commission in 1887. It was clearly intended to carry out the government's agenda of municipal "reform":[24]

> The editor of *The Straits Times* welcomed the "ample provisions" in the bill to enforce stringent sanitary rules and expressed hope that "the reformed Municipality [would] with the proverbial thoroughness of new brooms sweep away the hindrances in the way of sanitary reform to the fullest extent." The elastic powers invested in the commissioners "to act promptly and effectively in the cause of public health or in the interest of public morality" were redeeming features of the bill which "alone contributed largely to counterbalance, in the public view, many of its objectionable clauses and modify the acrimony which they gave rise to." To press on with sanitary reform "with unswerving tenacity," alleged the press, was a vital municipal task given the "utter indifference [of the Asiatic population] to any conditions of sanitation, and the filth in which they [were] accustomed to revel."

(Yeoh 1996: 50)

There was obviously very little faith among the Europeans, both official and otherwise, that Asians were capable of creating and maintaining a sanitary environment. Nonetheless, the municipal authority was intended to coopt Asian leadership in support of the reform agenda. The Asians who did serve were almost all from the English-educated, pro-British elite, and none were leaders of *huiguans* or possessed strong links to the Chinese masses. Although they could do little to influence the majority of the population, they could present, in a civil format, the objections and concerns of the Asians regarding a number of the reforms.

Asian nationalism and labor

The beginning of the twentieth century saw two essentially separate movements begin to mobilize the masses of Singapore in ways that struck at the heart of the colonial project. One of these was the appearance of Asian nationalist movements, which were often sparked by anti-colonial or anti-Western movements in the home countries. Thus the rise of Gandhi's movement to drive the British out of India resonated with Singapore's Indian community, and while relatively little anti-British sentiment was expressed by these groups, the movement did raise their consciousness. More threatening to the British in the long run were the anti-Manchu, reformist and revolutionary movements of the Chinese. A number of Singapore Malays also responded to the call for an Indonesian nation in the Dutch East Indies and to pan-Islamic movements. What was also troubling was the fact that Singapore often became a refuge for fleeing reformers and revolutionaries. Thus individuals such as Sun Yat-sen and, later, Tan Malaka were able to escape their pursuers in the teeming port city.

The other movement was the beginning of labor organization and the formation of unions in Singapore. Singapore had a history of labor exploitation, which as we have seen was at the very heart of the local economy throughout the nineteenth century. Since the banning of secret societies, Chinese coolies and workers had few vehicles where they could legitimately find solidarity. Those that existed were usually dominated by merchants. The *huiguans*, the place-of-origin, surname and occupational groups were all vertically organized and led by the very merchants who exploited the coolies. Later, when mass action by laborers did occur, it was often mixed with political motivations and even directed by the merchants or *taukehs*. As nationalist sentiments began to manifest themselves in Singapore, they brought the incipient labor movement with them, and to some extent nationalists and others with "political" agendas managed to control the labor movement for a time.

It should also be understood that as various ethnic groups responded to nationalist movements in their home countries, mobilization around these agendas often separated them from other groups in Singapore. This consciousness of kind also extended to the labor movement. That is to say that when unions were formed, they tended to be Chinese unions, Indian unions, unions of the English-educated, etc. This deprived them of broader action that would transcend ethnic lines (Trocki 2001).

The first stirrings of modern nationalist sentiment became evident among the Singapore Chinese during the late nineteenth century. Supporters of the Qing dynasty, reformers such as Liang Qichao and Kang Youwei, and revolutionaries like Sun Yat-sen all sought allies among the Singapore Chinese. At first, it was the more educated or wealthier elements of Singapore's Chinese society who were attracted to China-oriented political issues, and most but not all of these tended to support more conservative groups. Initially, events such as the defeat of China in the Sino-Japanese War in 1894 and the thwarted reforms of the Hundred Days in 1898 gained the attention of individuals such as Lim Boon Keng and Khoo Seok Wan and those involved in the *Straits Chinese Magazine*. Khoo hosted Kang Youwei when he visited Singapore in 1900 (Chui and Hara 1991: 68). Even Sun Yat-sen and the Tung Meng Hui were initially supported by prominent merchants, Tan Chorn Nam and Teo Eng Hock. They led the first branch of the Tung Meng Hui in Singapore and spread the revolutionary organization to other parts of Malaya. In the years between 1906 and 1911, these two factions, reformers and revolutionaries, both dominated by merchants, struggled for control of other Chinese organizations, newspapers and schools. By 1911, the revolutionaries had been outspent and were less successful in gaining popular support than the reformists. However, when the Qing dynasty was finally overthrown, the reformists were left with no alternative but to support the GMD, or more conservative moments within China. Also, by this time, the colonial government had taken steps to ban the GMD and other Chinese political parties in Singapore, so many withdrew from politics or aligned themselves with the authorities (*ibid.*: 70).

One of the reasons for British action against the GMD was the support the revolutionary cause gained among the coolies and other working-class Chinese. While these groups may have had little in common with the class interests and political goals of the merchants, they found themselves pulled into political issues. The coolies were initially mobilized by the merchants in support of what might have been seen as joint economic interests. Later, when they were mobilized as *Chinese*, they became conscious of their own strength and the value of solidarity. Warren has noted that the first "strike" action by rickshaw pullers was instigated by the owners to protest against government attempts to tax and register the rickshaw trade. Pullers participated in a series of rickshaw strikes between 1897 and 1903, stopping work and harassing, stoning and intimidating pedestrians, cyclists, people in horse-drawn carts and other coolies who sought to break the strike. The pullers realized their own power.

> Rickshaws were indispensable. The public and authorities recognized this as a fact after the strike ... there was veiled strength in numbers.

Solidarity emerged among the pullers. The collective act of putting down the shafts had seriously upset the tenor of Singapore's economy and society. A legacy of the week-long strike [in 1903] was a strengthening of the pullers' sense of independence and injustice.

(Warren 1986: 113–14)

It was not until the laborers and the revolutionary leaders joined together in the same struggle that the nationalist/labor movement gained real power. From 1912 to 1919, the GMD languished under British repression, but following the May Fourth Movement in China in 1919, there was an outpouring of Chinese nationalist sentiment in Singapore. In the anti-Japanese boycotts in Singapore, rickshaw pullers and other laborers took protest action, some of which was aimed at signs of the Japanese presence in Singapore and included smashing Japanese shops and brothels, looting shops that sold Japanese goods and even breaking into the houses of Chinese where Japanese goods were thought to be present. Organization and experience of street action now emboldened the pullers to take action on their own behalf.

In February 1920, the pullers staged another strike, this time for a fare increase. When the government refused their demands, they struck for three days and brought the city to a halt. The government was forced to accept their demands but refused to acknowledge it publicly, so they stayed out until they had forced the government to yield. From this time on, the government was determined to break the community's dependence on the pullers and began moves to develop other means of transportation, including trams, buses and roads for automobiles. As a result, the pullers gradually ceased to be a force in Singapore, despite their solidarity. Likewise, because of unified government and business action, no other labor unions were able to establish themselves in prewar Singapore. With both Governor Cecil Clementi and the business community against them, there was strong official and unofficial opposition to any mass organization among workers.

In addition to revitalizing Chinese nationalist sentiment, the 1920s also saw the founding of the Chinese Communist Party (CCP) and the alliance between the CCP and the GMD. Both groups sought supporters in Singapore and began to organize their own branches. The first communist organizers to reach Singapore were a different sort of individual to those who had previously migrated to Singapore. When once most were merchants or coolies, now for the first time intellectuals began to seek a living in Singapore. Many of these were refugees fleeing repression in China. In Singapore, they found work as school teachers, journalists and labor organizers.

The large numbers of Chinese workers and the growing number of Chinese-medium schools offered these individuals fertile fields for political and social action. One of the first labor unions in Singapore was the South Seas General Trade Union (SSGTU), which was organized in 1926 by CCP members who were working in the United Front with the GMD. With the split between the two parties in 1927, the labor movement was also affected (Chui 1991).

If the association with political movements was a boost for labor organization in Singapore, it also complicated matters. Workers' economic issues were always combined with a political agenda, and political issues usually came first. At this time, both the CCP and the GMD were largely concerned with what was happening in China and considered the Straits as merely a base from which to raise funds and supporters for some final impact in China. Also, when the political tide turned, the labor unions associated with specific political movements were also affected.

It was in this atmosphere of increasing restlessness among the Asian masses that the British government moved to create a much more intrusive and calculated system of control and surveillance. Following the mutiny by Indian troops in 1915 (a movement largely provoked by German agents during World War I), Sir David Petrie was appointed as Indian intelligence officer for the Far East. He recommended the formation of a special intelligence department within the police force. Initially called the Criminal Intelligence Division, it was later renamed Special Branch and from 1918 onward developed into a secret agency concerned only with political security. According to Rene Onraet, one of the key leaders of the agency during its formative years in the 1920s and 1930s, "In addition to security work against political movements and suspects, the Special Branch concentrated on all racial, religious and social activities, and kept an eye on the trend in neighbouring countries" (cited in Ban 2001: 75).

Ban Kah Choon, who has written a history of Special Branch during its early years, gives Onraet credit for developing the central doctrine of the department in these years:

> The Branch's fundamental task was to defend the peninsula from the infection of radical ideas that would stir up the population. He argued that the local population would not be likely to give trouble if left to themselves. To him sedition and insurrection always had a hidden foreign hand. The revolutionary impulses that came from overseas (first Germany, then the Middle East and India and then Russia and China followed by Japan) had to be identified and erased. ... Above all else, Onraet felt – and this gave the necessary muscularity and conviction to his work – that untoward events in the Straits Settlements nearly always had an external influence.
>
> (*ibid.*)

It is of interest that this attitude among the colonial security forces was adopted in the post-independence years and came to characterize the mindset, not only of the postwar Special Branch but also of the Singapore security forces as they developed under Lee Kuan Yew in the 1960s. Ban's book contains a foreword written by Lim Chye Heng, Director of Internal

Security from 1975 to 2001, who worked in Special Branch during the 1950s and 1960s. Lim frankly stated his own belief that Onraet's statement about external influences continued to be true. Thus there was always the conviction among the security forces that there was nothing intrinsically wrong with either the colonial system of domination, or with its successor. That was that all opposition to it came from "sinister" outside influences (*ibid.*: vii–ix).

The key target for Special Branch during the 1930s was the Malayan Communist Party. In fact, because it was so concerned with the Chinese and the communists, Special Branch paid far less attention to the Japanese threat. It is difficult to say how solid a network the Communist Party had created in Singapore by the late 1930s since it was almost continually under pressure as an organization. The British Special Branch regularly arrested its members and nipped most efforts in the bud. It had also succeeded in infiltrating at least one of its agents into the organization. This was the man known as Lai Tek, apparently a Sino-Vietnamese or a Chinese from Vietnam who had worked as a spy for the French. He had been passed from the French to the British. In the mid-1930s, he was successful in passing himself off to the local party organization as a representative of the Vietnamese party, which at the time had close links to the CCP. In a short period of time, he rose to be secretary-general of the Malayan Communist Party. Throughout the key period of the 1930s, the MCP was completely under the control of Special Branch.

The political awakening of the Singapore Chinese was largely focused on events in China in the first instance. While it was useful in mobilizing thousands of Chinese, the tactic had the effect of dividing them from the Indians, Malays and other races and cultural groups of Singapore. It also focused their attention on events in China, and in so doing, galvanized opposition to the Japanese. This would make them targets for even more brutal repression when the Japanese invaded. Despite the infiltration (and the fact that Lai Tek also betrayed many leaders of the MCP, first to the British and later to the Japanese), the organization was the only one that mounted an effective armed opposition to the Japanese and came out of the war better organized than before. It might be that the resilience of the party had more to do with grassroots dissatisfaction and radical sentiment than with any genius within the party.

The British and the English-educated

The other group that would be a contender for political power in the postwar era were the English-educated. The ability to speak English was always an economic and social advantage in Singapore. Because of this, it also translated into a political advantage. As the language of the ruling class, it was the language of power and the language of more prestigious and profitable employment. It was thus to be expected that those who sought power and wealth would gravitate to things English. Although the emergence of schools, in any language, was a slow process in Singapore, by the last quarter of the nineteenth century there was a growing demand for education. Straits Chinese families, English-educated Indians from the subcontinent and Ceylon, Eurasians and other Christians all formed a constituency for English schools. The government, too, seeing a need for an educated but cheap labor force for government and business, was eager to sponsor the expansion of English education.

By the beginning of the twentieth century, there was a definite class of English-speaking Asian Singaporeans. They included relatively prosperous and respected businessmen, lawyers, doctors and government officials, as well as clerks and employees of the post office, the railway and numerous other enterprises. They were, for the most part, the allies, or perhaps more exactly, the apprentices of the British, although the British certainly did not see them in that way at the time. Nonetheless, it seems that some of them were beginning to see themselves as such. Clearly, many could see, after having been educated in British universities, that they were as proficient as or better at their jobs than many Englishmen. Their businessmen were as wealthy, if not wealthier, than most Europeans. Much of the mystification of power had worn thin, and they had come to understand that Malaya (including Singapore) was their country. Certainly, many of them belonged nowhere else, and their families had been there for generations.

They saw themselves, then, in the 1930s, as loyal subjects of the empire. They included the Straits Chinese British Association. They organized the Singapore Volunteers and sent soldiers and donations to support England in World War I. Many of them were, in fact, British subjects. They did not yet see themselves as rulers of an independent Singapore, but they did see that now the British administrators were coming and going with greater frequency. Proportionately fewer were mastering the local languages, and most striking of all were the color bars and systematic double standards in terms of pay, benefits and simple respect.

However, they were yet to learn some very harsh lessons about power and respect. For the English-speaking domiciled community, the fall of the empire, for that is what the Japanese conquest of Southeast Asia constituted in 1942, was a true disaster. In the space of two and a half years, not only was their world shattered but so too was the one to which they had aspired. The Anglophone dream of a comfortable yet exciting modernity had been snatched away and crushed under Japanese boots. English power, once seen as so firm and unshakeable, had been swept aside in a few short months. Under the Japanese, the ability to speak English counted for little. Their many accomplishments, their Westernized lifestyle, their table manners and their language skills were no longer an advantage.

What was perhaps worse was that they were not particularly singled out as enemies. True, they were not trusted, but they were not systematically hunted down and killed for what they were. To a great extent, they were ignored. To the Japanese, the real enemies were the Chinese-educated. These had been the hard core of the anti-Japanese movement before the war, and they were the ones who were now in the jungles of Malaya fighting a guerrilla war against the Japanese.

To make matters worse for the English-educated, the postwar era would see that the ground had shifted under them. No longer were they the main contenders for power in Singapore, because the other Asian masses were now asserting themselves. On the peninsula, the Malays had stepped forward to claim their birthright, and in Singapore the Chinese-educated represented the most powerful political force.

Singapore in the greater East Asia co-prosperity sphere

The Japanese conquest of Malaya reminds one of a scene in those old Japanese samurai movies, where Zatoichi, the blind samurai, masquerading as an itinerant masseur, is wandering along a forest path at dusk. He suddenly finds himself surrounded by eight or ten hostile enemies. A twig snaps, and there is a flash of slashing blades and flying bodies, followed by an abrupt silence. All the bad guys lie dead except for one who is still standing, until his head falls off, then he too collapses. Although the Japanese were by no means inoffensive, the British, like the other imperial powers in Southeast Asia, clearly had no realistic sense of the power of their opponent. The Japanese victory was as rapid and as unexpected as Zatoichi's swordsmanship.

It is not clear that *every* British military planner had woefully underestimated the Japanese military capability, but certainly no one in authority seems to have had a clear idea of what they faced in 1941. Japanese forces landed in Kelantan on 8 December and rapidly swept down the Malayan Peninsula, deftly outflanking the ill-prepared British and Australian troops that had been sent to stop them. Not a single line held, and the Japanese were charging through Johor by the middle of January. In the meantime, on 9 December, the British had sent their ultimate weapon, the battleship *Prince of Wales*, accompanied by the cruiser *Repulse*, to interdict the landings on the east coast. Japanese planes based in southern Vietnam sent both ships to the bottom on 10 December. From then on, the Japanese had virtual control of the skies and the seas around Singapore and Malaya and could bomb Singapore more or less at will. Allied shipping was at the mercy of Japanese submarines and air patrols. Quickly, the noose around Singapore tightened. The British dithered until panic set in. On 15 February, Lieutenant-General A.E. Percival surrendered to the Japanese General Yamashita Tomoyuki.

The British defeat was not only an unprecedented disaster, it was a humiliation. The Japanese took 60,000 prisoners. Never again would the British enjoy the respect and awe they had had before. The spectacle of European prisoners being marched through the main streets of Singapore by short, illclad Japanese troopers before stunned Asian crowds left an indelible mark.

The scene was the same all over Southeast Asia, except in the Philippines, and only a handful of Europeans escaped internment, because most found no refuge with their former colonial subjects. All were delivered up to the new Asian conquerors without question.

Only one group of Asian natives was prepared to resist the Japanese from the beginning, and those were the Chinese, particularly the Chinese-educated of Singapore and Malaya. Of these Chinese, only the communists were organized and determined enough to flee from the cities and establish bases in the jungle. A few weeks before Singapore fell, the British decided that they might train them in case guerrilla troops were needed following a possible Japanese victory. The few British soldiers who escaped capture were those who were able to make common cause with the Malayan People's Anti-Japanese Army (MPAJA). But because the Japanese knew that Chinese nationalists were their enemy, and because British intelligence operatives had foolishly not destroyed their records, the Kempeitai was able to identify large numbers of such "dangerous individuals" in Singapore and Malaya. In the *sook ching* or "purification" that followed the Japanese victory, tens of thousands of Malayan and Singaporean Chinese were rounded up and summarily massacred.

The worst-hit areas seem to have been Singapore and Johor. Estimates range up to about 20,000 for Singapore alone, and for Johor, the numbers may have been even higher, but there is far less available data on which to form a realistic figure. It is clear from fairly recent research that Japanese soldiers moving through rural Johor (where large numbers of Chinese pepper planters, rubber smallholders, market gardeners and agricultural coolies lived) wiped out entire villages on relatively slight pretexts. In Singapore, victims were not limited to communists but included school teachers, journalists, government servants, union members, nationalist activists and hundreds of others who just happened to be in the wrong place at the wrong time. Virtually all of them were young men between the ages of about 15 and 40.

Despite this, a resistance was mounted in the jungles, and the MCP established a united front that maintained a clandestine presence in the towns, particularly Singapore. By the end of the war, the MCP was the strongest political force in all of British Malaya. In addition to a battle-hardened guerrilla army that marched out of the jungle to pre-empt the Japanese surrender before the British could arrive in the country, there were active party cells that immediately sprung to life, mobilizing students, workers and the masses of the Chinese-speaking population in an anti-imperialist front. They would take nothing less than independence.

4   The politics of independence

The period between 1945 and 2000 can be divided into three more or less equal segments. The years between 1945 and 1965 saw the transition from colonial status to full independence for the republic of Singapore. From 1965 to 1985, Singapore boomed economically and was transformed from a seedy Asian port to a gleaming metropolis and major manufacturing center. Politically, the People's Action Party (PAP), under Prime Minister Lee Kuan Yew, defeated all its rivals and eliminated almost all visible forms of civil society in the republic to create a system of one-party dominance. The most recent period, for the leading party, has been one of "managing" its success and attempting to institutionalize the political gains of the previous four decades. This has meant significant changes in the manner in which the party/state (for, indeed, they are virtually inseparable) itself operates, particularly in the manner in which the process of leadership transition occurs.

It is worth asking exactly who the PAP represents as well as who its opponents really were, or are. One of the things that has kept the PAP in power all these years has been the sense of crisis and threat that has regularly been manufactured by the party's propaganda machine. Who are these enemies whose possible victory would be so dangerous for Singapore? A look at Singapore in the years immediately after World War II can provide some answers.

In the decades immediately following the war, there was an atmosphere of almost complete political plurality in Singapore. Political movements of virtually every possible stripe arose in the wake of the double shocks of the British defeat and the trauma of the Japanese occupation. Nationalism, racism, communism, capitalism, anti-colonialism and colonialism all appeared as important movements. They affected waterfronts, the streets and slums; the schools, work places and *kampongs* of the colony. The proponents of each sought to dominate the outcome of the political struggle.

This period of plurality and relatively open politics ended with the PAP's victory. In the early 1960s, the party launched its final offensives against what remained of a viable opposition. In February 1963, it detained without trial nearly 150 opposition and labor union leaders in a series of sweeps beginning with "Operation Cold Store." They were kept in jail for many years under inhumane conditions, and a number of them were subjected to torture as well as general mistreatment. At the same time, the PAP worked to marginalize the Singapore Chinese Chamber of Commerce (SCCC) and weaken or coopt all other forms of civil society. Finally, with its separation from Malaysia in 1965, Singapore won complete independence and found itself completely dominated by the PAP.

In the years between 1965 and 1983, there were no opposition members in Parliament, and those opposing voices that persisted were ruthlessly marginalized, intimidated and ultimately coerced into silence. The formation of any alternative political organization was hindered by patterns of legislation and enforcement that systematically crippled and ostracized these groups. The local media were rigorously controlled. The international media found offending stories blacked out in local editions, while their reporters were expelled.

Official political discourse became one of self-congratulation, petty defensiveness and endless advertising campaigns to rectify social habits; to promote the government's myriad programs; to support its elitist ideas; to galvanize the population against foreign and domestic dangers (both real and imagined); and to instil a sense of loyalty and gratitude to the government.

Realizing that fairly high levels of dissatisfaction had built up among the population in the previous decades, the years since 1985 have seen the PAP seeking ways to release some of these pent-up pressures while retaining its monopoly on power. These measures included appointing non-constituency, non-PAP MPs and organizing feedback sessions with citizens. At the same time, the party began to realize the need to find ways of renewing its leadership while keeping the Lee dynasty in power.

How had Lee and the PAP, a party led by English-speaking Chinese, whom Chinese Premier Zhou Enlai had dismissively called "bananas" (yellow on the outside, but white on the inside) and a few Indians been able to gain the electoral support of the mass of Chinese-speaking citizens? This is one of the important questions of Singapore politics; indeed, the story of the last half-century is deeply intertwined with the story of the PAP's rise to power. On another level, however, it is essential to understand that the party's opponents were more than a rabble of flawed also-rans. The PAP's victory was not inevitable. Even in 1955, few would have predicted that the PAP would gain power let alone develop the capacity to totally dominate society. However, the history of Singapore is more than rise of one party.

The city's history is the story of a very dynamic and extensively mobilized society and of its popular efforts to find freedom and self-expression. It is also the story of what might be seen as an ethnic conflict – a struggle between an Anglophone, mestizo/creole *peranakan* Chinese elite that had a history of collaboration with the colonial powers against a newly mobilized Chinese working-class movement that had emerged from the struggle against the Japanese. This was not simply a class division. Also in the "enemy" camp, so far as the PAP was concerned, were the ethnic Chinese represented in the SCCC. This division, seen perhaps as one between the Chinese-educated and the English-educated, lies at the heart of Singapore's social fabric and has been one of the dynamic themes that binds the nineteenth-century history of the place to the twentieth.

Withdrawal from empire

To understand the situation after the Japanese occupation and the lead-up to Singapore's independence, it is worth looking at the various parties involved. They included all of those who were seeking to take power themselves, or maintain power, or at least ensure that their interests were guaranteed by whoever took over when Singapore became independent. The parties included both international and domestic players.

The most significant of the international actors were the British. Even though they were the ruling colonial power, the postwar situation had left their position so compromised that there was no longer any question that they would continue as such. It was only a matter of when and on what terms they would leave.

Although they could exercise influence domestically in the short term, they had no long-term future as rulers, and thus their aim was to leave behind a government that they could continue to influence and that would defend their economic interests in the region. British banks, trading companies, agencies, insurance companies and industrial concerns owned or were deeply involved in the plantation, mining and shipping industries of Malaya, all of which were centered in Singapore.

Singapore was a major naval base supporting Britain's global strategic position, and it also housed a large army base. Despite the fact that the empire was collapsing around its ears, the realization that Britain was no longer a world power had yet to penetrate fully. There was, in fact, a certain ambivalence about leaving Singapore on Britain's part. During the war, the Colonial Office and Whitehall had taken the unprecedented step of separating Singapore from Malaya. It was decided that following Japan's defeat, Malaya would be given independence under the Malayan Union scheme, while Singapore would remain a crown colony for some indefinite period.[25] Thus the giving of independence to Singapore was a far less straightforward operation.

Ironically, the Malayan Union scheme failed because of Malay opposition despite the separation of Singapore. The British government retreated before Malay protests and restored the sultans to their former positions, reinstated special privileges for Malays and created the Federation of Malaya. The thought of giving Malayan Chinese equal status with the Malays was abandoned, and Malaya was set on the path of independence under a frankly racist Malay-dominated political party. It would do so without Singapore and in the midst of a communist insurgency led by veterans of the MPAJA. In 1948, Britain declared a state of emergency in both Malaya and Singapore and together with Australia and New Zealand committed troops to the suppression of this movement.

In the United States, Cold War fever was spurred by the erection of the Iron Curtain in Europe and the communist victory in China. With the outbreak of the Korean War in 1950, American policy became focused on preventing any left-wing or even neutralist governments from gaining power in the former colonies of Southeast Asia. While US attention focused primarily on Thailand, Vietnam and the Philippines, the US consuls in Kuala Lumpur and Singapore took an active interest in local events and were particularly interested in promoting anti-communism among the Chinese. They also attempted to support groups linked to the Nationalist government in Taiwan, such as certain trade unions, newspapers, schools and groups of businessmen in the SCCC. US agents were also engaged in a coordinated effort to spread anti-communist propaganda throughout the British colonies in Asia. They planted bogus articles in the Asian press aimed at supporting anti-communist movements in Singapore, spread disinformation about the communists and pressed the British to take action against "pro-Peiping towkays" such as Tan Lark Sye and Lee Kong Chian

Figure 4.1 Memorial to Lim Bo Seng, a Chinese resistance fighter killed by the Japanese. The memorial service, held in Raffles Square in 1945, was attended by thousands from Singapore's Chinese community, including members of the communist-led Malayan People's Anti-Japanese Army, leading merchants of the Chinese community and leaders of the British Military Authority.

(USCR, 611.46F3–558, SCG to SOS, "Progress report on OCB Courses of Action, 1 August 1957 – 31 December 1957").[26]

It is difficult to document clear actions being undertaken by the USSR and China at this point, since the examination of their internal documents is not part of this study, and Chinese documents are not available. However, British and American officials were convinced that they were combating a determined "cultural offensive" by China and the USSR, not to mention political and possible material assistance for the communist movements in Singapore and Malaya. Most of the evidence for these activities comes from US and British sources. Obviously, there was strong sympathy for China among the Singapore Chinese, and many Chinese students were still returning to China for schooling at this time. The USA saw China as promoting a policy of "popular diplomacy" by sending cultural films, music and publications in a similar vein to Chinese communities in Southeast Asia.

The other, and perhaps more significant, outside interests were the neighboring states of Malaya and Indonesia. Even though Singapore was separated from Malaya, there were powerful popular movements in both countries to rejoin the two. At the time, most Singaporeans believed that the island's economy depended on Malaya. Chinese in Malaya, who made up over 40 percent of the population in the immediate postwar period, felt the need for Singapore to be part of their country. The United Malays National Organization (UMNO), which came to dominate the political scene in Malaya at the head of the anti-Malayan Union movement, was reluctant to allow Singapore's Chinese majority to become a major force in federation politics. At the same time, if Singapore were to join Malaya, then UMNO hoped to be the major party representing the Malays of Singapore, who made up about 10 percent of the island's population.

Indonesia, which had won its independence from the Dutch in 1949 after a bloody popular uprising, was under the leadership of the charismatic nationalist leader Achmed Sukarno. Sukarno's ambition to dominate British territories in Borneo and his concern about the economic role of Singapore in Southeast Asia led him to oppose the merger of Singapore with Malaya and the Borneo territories, the formula for the "Malaysian" solution for the independence of the British territories. His policy was called "Konfrontasi," and it involved military as well as diplomatic efforts to oppose the merger. Economically, Singapore's free-trade policies made it the focus for the illegal export of rubber, tin, tobacco and other products of Sumatra and other Indonesian territories in violation of Sukarno's nationalist trade policies.

Naturally, those most interested in the structure of an independent Singapore were the Singaporeans themselves. The war had been a traumatic experience for Singapore's culturally diverse population. The English-educated saw themselves deserted and betrayed by those whom they had assumed would protect them. Likewise, their faith in the universal validity of English culture was badly shaken. The Chinese-educated had suffered the massacres of the *sook ching* and were the only group to systematically and effectively resist the Japanese. The MPAJA was staffed by numerous young people who had fled Singapore and the towns of Malaya for the jungles. Their attachment to their Chinese identity was strengthened, and there was a feeling of self-confidence and entitlement among the ethnic Chinese.

However, the Chinese were not a single group. Aside from the distinctions of dialect and region, there were important differences in class and occupational outlook. The merchants and the membership of the SCCC had interests that separated them from the labor unions. The unions, in their turn, were often divided by race and language. The Malayan Communist Party (MCP), because of its role in fighting the Japanese, had an organizational edge over all others, and it also possessed an armed force, but that was to prove more of a liability than an asset in the long run. Despite such differences, it was possible on occasion for the Chinese-educated to come together around issues of Chinese nationalism and the future of Chinese schools. It was a movement seen by the British, the English-educated and others as "Chinese chauvinism."

The "rebels" in Singapore in the 1940s and 1950s were often angry young men of talent and education. Because of their race, whether Chinese, Indian, Arab, Jewish, Malay or Eurasian, they were denied access to the careers and positions that Europeans held. Frustrated in their aspirations, the English-educated turned to politics and the law in search of justice and to bring about change. Some of these individuals already worked in government, and many of them were British subjects, thus when the first elections were held under the colonial government, it was they who were eligible to vote, and they who sought elected positions. They formed the first political parties and felt that they had some idea of democratic processes.

While some of these were quite radical and joined the MCP or were active in the Anti-British League (ABL) and the Malayan Democratic Union (MDU) immediately after the war, many more were quite conservative. Most, however, even those who might have been socially conservative, were strongly anti-colonial. Those who attended universities in the late 1940s and early 1950s were often influenced by socialist ideals, and while they were anti-colonial, few actually joined the MCP, which many felt was dominated by the Chinese-educated. The English-educated were active across Singapore's political spectrum. Individuals such as C.C. Tan, David Marshall, Goh Keng Swee, Lee Kuan Yew, Devan Nair and Sidney Woodhull all came from the "English stream." Those English-educated individuals who were less ambitious found positions in the bureaucracy, where they formed an important force steeped in the rationalist paternalism of the British civil service, but they too chafed under the double standard that separated the expatriates from the locals.

The attraction of the left, especially the MCP, had much to do with the fact that it was they who opposed the Japanese most effectively. In the immediate postwar years, the MDU and the MCP commanded the support of large segments of the population regardless of ethnic background. Because the party had been allied with the British during the war, it was able

to remain a legitimate political force for a brief period of time in the immediate postwar years.

However, there was only an uneasy truce between the MCP and the BMA
and later with the returned Malayan civil service. The MCP quickly adopted
an anti-colonial stance, and the colonial government, after disarming the
MPAJA and passing out a few medals, looked for ways to undermine and
ultimately outlaw the MCP. Such ceremonies as the Lim Poh Seng memorial
service held in Raffles Square in 1945, which was attended by members of
the civil service, the BMA, the SCCC and the MPAJA, were fleeting
moments in an uneasy truce.

The British offered their erstwhile allies no significant political concessions. As both T.N. Harper and Cheah Boon Keng have shown, the years
between 1945 and 1947 were very tense. The colonial government persis-
tently limited the freedom of action of the left. At the same time, workers on
the mines and plantations steadfastly refused to be bullied back into
accepting prewar pay scales and working conditions. The outbreak of hostil-
ities between the Chinese-dominated left and the colonial government was a
major setback for the evolution of democracy in Malaya and Singapore
(Cheah 1983; Harper 1999). In Malaya, the Malays and the UMNO were
able to find favour with the colonial power and ultimately take over the
government as colonial surrogates, while Singapore was left in political
limbo until the mid-1950s.

The other important English-educated group in Singapore was the very
wealthy *taukehs*, who controlled the governing council of the SCCC and the
major banks and financial groups of Singapore. These were almost invari-
ably conservative and pro-British. Individuals such as Tan Chin Tuan of the
Overseas Chinese Banking Corporation (OCBC), Lien Ying Chow of the
United Overseas Bank (UOB), Tan Siak Kew of the Four Seas Corporation
and Yap Pheng Geck were the major figures in Singapore's economy, but
they found themselves almost paralysed when confronted with the prospect
of independence and the need to involve themselves in politics (Visscher
2002). Although they dominated the SCCC, these men had little in common
with the majority of their constituents, most of whom were small to
medium-sized traders and predominantly Chinese-educated.

However, the Chinese-educated were a varied group. They included
wealthy *taukehs* such as Lee Kong Chian, Tan Lark Sye and Tan Kah Kee,
self-made millionaires, mostly in rubber, who felt a strong bond with China
and a deep commitment to Chinese education and culture. They found a
ready constituency in the many smaller merchants and shopkeepers who
made up the vast bulk of the membership of the SCCC. Because of their
poor English-language skills and their commitment to things Chinese, they
were distrusted by the British and Americans.

The so-called "Middle Road" labor unions[27] and the Chinese high school
and middle school students were the most formidable popular force in
Singapore during the 1950s and early 1960s. With the outlawing of the

MCP, they remained the voice of the greater number of the people, and through them, the party continued to exercise a level of influence in Singapore. These students were younger and even angrier than the privileged, English-educated university students and graduates. Under the United Front, which operated for about a decade from the early 1950s to the early 1960s, the student unions and the labor unions were a major political force in Singapore. With the charismatic leadership of people like Lim Chin Siong and Fong Swee Suan, it was thought that they could bring Singapore to a halt on virtually any day they chose. True, they could be halted by brute force, but they could never be completely destroyed. Ultimately, in order to win elections, it would be necessary to gain their cooperation and support. They had the support and sympathy of the masses of the Chinese-educated of Singapore. They were the "tiger" that had to be mastered (Bloodworth 1986).

The MCP itself was a shadowy, almost mythic, entity that often seems to have been more a figment of the imagination of the Americans, the British Special Branch and the right-wing forces in Singapore. Its "ghost" may have lived a much longer and more active life than the real one ever did. While the party and the MDU attracted idealistic recruits from Singapore and persisted during the late 1940s and early 1950s, we may question the extent of its organization and power in Singapore, particularly during the United Front period of 1952–63. Repeated waves of arrests, banishments and defections between 1948 and 1963 severely limited its ability to launch an effective organization. Many were accused of membership of the party, but few admitted it, even many years later after their release from prison.[28]

The Malays of Singapore constituted a force beyond their numbers so long as the possibility of a merger with the Federation existed. Seeing Singapore as a component of Malaysia, the political leaders of the colony placed considerable stress on the role of Malay language and culture. The advancement of Malay interests would certainly have been promoted by the federal government. On the other hand, there was considerable diversity among Singapore's Malays. Not all blindly followed the UMNO. Some joined the MCP, and others sought union within a greater Indonesia. During the 1940s through the 1950s, the *Utusan Melayu* sought to mobilize and raise Malay consciousness, and for a time it seemed that it would persist as one of the independent voices in a plural society. With Malayan independence, however, the *Utusan* was pressured into becoming a mouthpiece for the UMNO, and its more independent voices such as Said Zahari, Samad Ismail and Yusof Ishak (all of whom were Singapore-born) returned to Singapore (Said Zahari 2001: 58–63).

These were the players, the contenders for power and influence in Singapore, during the two postwar decades. The British were concerned with the "end game" of empire, while the Americans and communist powers were more interested in the place that Singapore would occupy in their global strategies. In the years before 1965, both Malaya and Indonesia sought to dominate the outcome of Singapore's power struggle. Internal groups sought alliances among themselves and with the global powers as they tested each other's mettle. The major domestic forces were the English-educated elite, whether conservative, liberal, or socialist, and whether Chinese, Indian or Eurasian on the one hand; and the Chinese-educated (or uneducated) merchants, shopkeepers and small businessmen, together with the radical Chinese-educated intellectuals, students and workers. In the end, Lee Kuan Yew and the PAP, led by members of the English-educated, would exploit the power of the Chinese radicals while maintaining the tolerance of the imperialists and seize power.

Priorities and issues

There were a range of issues and priorities that motivated the various groups in these years. Some were shared by all, or most, but others were contradictory. For almost all Singaporeans, the primary unifying priority was independence, which meant an end to colonialism and the establishment of self-government. The main conflict here was over who would rule and on what terms. Related to that issue was the question of a merger with the Federation of Malaya. Virtually every domestic party in Singapore saw the separation that the British had surreptitiously foisted upon their Malayan possessions as a violation of the natural and historical order of things. Because Singapore's economy depended on the federation, separation was a threat to the island's survival.

In the aftermath of the Malayan Union debacle, Malaya came under the control of conservative Malay aristocrats who dominated the UMNO. Ultimately, these Malays were able to make common cause with the wealthiest Malayan Chinese *taukehs*, who created a Chinese political party, the Malayan Chinese Association (MCA). Thus the Malayan political order was socially and economically conservative, if not absolutely reactionary, and was structured around racial parties. Singapore was a dilemma. If left alone, it might come under the control of communists or radical socialists, and Chinese chauvinists. All of these constituted a threat to the neo-feudalist society of Malaya and its *taukeh*-dominated economy with its own large Chinese underclass. If encouraged, the latter might respond positively to the example of Singapore. On the other hand, if Singapore was a part of Malaya, perhaps the radical tendencies could be controlled.

In the 1950s and 1960s, it seemed almost certain that Singapore would adopt a socialist if not a communist form of government. Except for a small group of conservative lawyers and businessmen backed by British firepower, there seemed to be no serious obstacle to such an outcome. The SCCC, while somewhat unhappy at such a prospect, was paralysed by internal disputes about involvement in popular politics. There were those who remained close to the British and even as late as 1955 saw independence as only a distant possibility. Sikko Visscher has styled them the "ambiguous" group. Others were "ambitious" and hoped to use the SCCC as a vehicle to gain political power. Likewise, there was considerable sympathy in the SCCC for the more radical students and intellectuals, particularly on issues regarding Chinese education and culture in Singapore (Visscher 2002). Singapore was, after all, a city of propertyless workers, a virtual proletarian metropolis. The full extension of the democratic franchise to such an electorate could have only one result. Thus, following the early initiatives of the MDU and the Singapore Factory and Shopworkers Union (SFSWU), the first electoral political parties of the 1950s, with few exceptions, proclaimed a progressive social vision.

We see this vision in one of the 1957 speeches of David Marshall, an English-educated Jewish barrister who became Singapore's first elected chief minister in 1955:

> I believe the Socialist road is the only road for our people. Our unique position as a heavily populated entrepot port without natural resources calls for considerable adaptation of socialist methods while maintaining socialist ideals. I believe we should nationalise transport and the tobacco and liquor trades; that Government should go into active partnership with private capital in the fields of industry and agriculture, and that we should create a research and propaganda department for our entrepot trade.
>
> I believe that social security measures for the aged, the sick, the widowed and the unemployed should be pressed on with at top speed and free medical attention and free legal aid should be a reality for all.
>
> (DM44.4, 24 January 1957)

The more conservative groups, often in alliance with the British, or at least hoping for their support, were anti-communist. They had the support not only of the British and Americans (who had shown they were eager to offer clandestine aid) but also of some Malays, particularly those around UMNO. In the anti-colonial atmosphere of the times, however, anti-communists looked as though they would accept some sort of semi-colonial status for Singapore. The fact that the MCP was waging a guerrilla war in the Malayan jungles, and that most of Singapore and the federation were under the Emergency Regulations throughout this period, made it difficult for the party to operate openly, and it is not clear that its clandestine organization, the so-called "Town Committee," was a very substantial body after 1948.

For most Singaporeans, the lifting of the Emergency Regulations, particularly the Internal Security Act (ISA) and the Protection of Public Security Ordinance (PPSO), were perennial priorities. Those seeking political office campaigned for their repeal, but once in office, most found them useful tools. These acts, which had existed in Singapore and Malaya in some form since the nineteenth century, reached their final form during the Emergency. Ostensibly aimed at "communist terrorists" (CTs, as the guerrillas were called) as well as secret societies, they allowed for the detention of any citizen/subject (and the deportation of non-citizens) without charges and without trial. Individuals could be held almost indefinitely in this condition without recourse to law and without a need for their detention to be acknowledged by the state. They also forbade the creation of organizations without registration as well as the conduct of meetings. They were thus clear blocks to any form of public social action.

The other issue that again placed Singapore in contrast to Malaya was the idea of a multiracial social order. Malaya had opted for a politics of ethnicity that saw the Malays as the "true" owners of the country and all others (Chinese, Indians and other non-Muslims) as sojourners and aliens. UMNO's aim was to protect the rights and privileges of Malays. Singapore's politicians have, despite its Chinese majority, generally refrained from appealing to the electorate as Chinese. For the PAP, led as it was by English-educated individuals, the prospect of ethnic Chinese domination of society was a threat, and they have systematically used charges of racialism or chauvinism against any who opposed their particular brand of multiracialism.[29]

Racial politics in a plural society was recognized as a dangerous practice in Singapore. There had been outbreaks of racial violence, primarily between Malays and Chinese, on the peninsula in the immediate aftermath of the Japanese surrender. In 1946, Malays had reacted with violence in protest against the Malayan Union. The Maria Hertog issue caused riots between Christians and Malays in Singapore in 1951.[30] The prospect of further outbreaks, either in Singapore or in the Federation, was always just beneath the surface of the political life of both countries. For Singapore, the policy of multiracialism would put it at odds with Kuala Lumpur once it joined the Federation, since it cut at the very heart of UMNO's political structure.

The other important aspect of political life during this period was the issue of the Malayanization of the workforce, particularly in the civil service, the educational system and the international corporations. This was an important issue for the English-educated, since many of them found themselves passed over for promotion and saw jobs for which they were better qualified given to newly arrived Britons. In fact, as late as 1954, David Marshall could report that the British governor of Singapore, Sir John Nicoll, would not hire an equally qualified Asian over a European.[31] The racist policies of the colonial regime, which persisted until independence, were an unacceptable aspect of their situation. Every educated Singaporean could sympathize with the policy that the government and the economy should be staffed by competent Asians as quickly as possible.

Strategies

As it came down to the wire in the mid-1950s, no one group was in a position to take power without opposition. It was thus necessary to find suitable partners from the other groups or with the British. The English-educated groups lacked the numbers to win elections, but they had the leadership and administrative skills, and they could count on the support of the British. The Chinese-educated, on the other hand, had the numbers and the organization, but they were short on individuals with leadership and administrative experience, and they did not have the trust of either the British or the Malays.

In 1954, the British government organized a commission under Sir George Rendel to study the issue of constitutional reform in Singapore and its continuing relationship with Britain. The MCP in the Malayan jungles had been largely defeated, and the Federation of Malaya held its first election in that year and was to be fully independent in 1957. Likewise, following the Suez crisis in 1956, the British had begun to rethink their global position. It was clear that without Suez, Singapore would be difficult to maintain as a colony. Rendel recommended a constitution giving Singapore limited self-government, elections under a broader franchise and control of most of the functions of domestic rule, while the British continued to control the military, foreign affairs and internal security. In fact, it did little more than give Singapore what David Marshall later called a municipal government.

Three or perhaps four major groups contested the 1954 elections. The most prominent was the Progressive Party, led by C.C. Tan. It was made up largely of English-educated lawyers and bureaucrats, and it also had links to the SCCC. The leaders were known to the British and were people they trusted. The Progressives, the British and the English press all expected that they would have an easy time at the polls. They apparently lacked any social vision, they had no idea that Singapore should speedily gain independence, and they appeared completely ignorant of the popular will of Singapore. They were committed to not rocking the boat.

Opposing them with a more radical program was the Labour Front, led by David Marshall. Here too, however, the social background of the leadership was very similar to that of the Progressives. The only real difference was that the Labour Front had support from some of the unions. Marshall had previously been a part of the Progressive Party, but he had become disillusioned with Tan and had become somewhat radicalized. He had come into contact with individuals such as the men who were establishing the People's Action Party whom he met through his relationship with the Sino-European novelist Han Suyin.[32]

Marshall had trained as a lawyer in England in the 1930s and had fought with the Singapore Volunteers and been interned by the Japanese. In the postwar period, he came into his own and by the early 1950s was an extremely successful barrister earning about $300,000 annually. His experiences, both with the Japanese and in postwar Jewish welfare activities, had apparently given him a broader social conscience than many of his contemporaries. When he first encountered socialist ideas and their application to Singapore, he seems to have undergone a sort of conversion. He wrote a manifesto, "I Believe," and published it in the University of Singapore's student magazine, *Fajar*. The statement earned him the ire of Sir John Nicoll, who felt the need to call him in for a lecture, but it also impressed another group of labor leaders and English-educated administrators who were forming the Labour Front. Seeing the popularity that Marshall had gained from his forthright stance, they approached Marshall to join them. Among them were Lim Yew Hock, a labor leader who proved later to have strong secret society connections, and Francis Thomas, a senior civil servant in the Education Ministry. The group quickly gathered a slate of candidates and put itself forward for the election, contesting all seats.

Socialism, socialists and the PAP

The other major group was the PAP, which was led by a group of men who had taken to gathering together over beers for long evenings at Lee Kuan Yew's house on Oxley Rise. They included Sinnathamby Rajaratnam, a journalist; Goh Keng Swee, an economist and a senior civil servant in the Social Welfare Ministry, and Dr Toh Chin Chye, a physiologist (Turnbull 1989: 252). Like the others, they too were English-educated, but they were far more cautious and deliberate. At the time, they too expected C.C. Tan to win the election and decided to use this round for practice, fielding only five candidates. They had adopted a much more radical stance than the other parties, calling for immediate independence, a socialist system and an immediate end to the Emergency Regulations in Singapore. They appeared to be almost as far left as the communists, who were not allowed to run but who were, at this time, giving a certain measure of support to the PAP.

Despite the party's left-wing position, Lee Kuan Yew himself was well connected to the more conservative side of Singapore's social order. His education at Raffles College and later at Cambridge was not that of a poor boy. His wife was a niece of Tan Chin Tuan, the controlling figure behind the OCBC. His relations with key British administrators and intelligence operatives, particularly in the late 1950s and early 1960s, seem to have been quite intimate. Despite his occasional radical postures, it seems that Lee was never in danger of being arrested or otherwise sanctioned for his criticism of the colonial order.

The PAP began to develop alliances with the left. Lee Kuan Yew emerged as a successful defender of workers' and students' rights in the courtrooms. He had also developed contacts with the former student leaders of the late 1940s who had been arrested as communists at the beginning of the Emergency. These included Devan Nair, James Puthucheary and Samad Ismail, whom Lee had visited in 1955 and whose release he had helped to secure. In the years between 1955 and 1959, there were many who suspected that Lee and his party were communists. Certainly the presence in the PAP of charismatic leaders of the Chinese labor unions such as Lim Chin Siong and Fong Swee Suan raised suspicions in many quarters. Later, after he had arrested them, Lee would boast that they were the ones who helped him "ride the tiger" (Bloodworth 1986; Lee 1998).

It is difficult to determine whether Lee's socialism, egalitarianism, multiracialism and support for a merger with Malaysia in the early 1960s were real or simply part of the grand scheme to gain power. There are those such as Thomas Bellows and James Minchin who suggest that he was less than sincere; however, they offer no solid proof (Bellows 1968; Minchin 1990). Circumstantial evidence and the knowledge of subsequent events shows clearly that the Lee and his immediate lieutenants (i.e. Goh, Raja, Chin Chye and a few others) had from the beginning mapped out a careful strategy for taking power, and that neither ideology nor personal relationships restricted them. Once in power, they never let go and they, as David Marshall attested, were utterly ruthless with their opponents.

The "sensation" of independence

During 1955 and 1956, the PAP had a plan and followed it carefully. It gained the support of the communists and other left-wing forces among the unions and students. With the aid of the left, it helped David Marshall to win a surprise victory in the first election. Thereafter, they worked just as hard to undermine his government, to embarrass him and to discredit him. On the other hand, Marshall was not very effective as a politician. Although a charismatic speaker, he was a newcomer to his own party and had little control over the organization of the Labour Front, not that there was very much to begin with. The party had virtually no grassroots organization, no clear policies and very little cohesion among its leading members. At the same time, some of its leaders were people of questionable ethics. It had been catapulted into power by circumstances that the party did not control, and it just as quickly lost power.

Nonetheless, Marshall played a crucial role in leading Singapore through its first steps toward independence. In particular, he forced the British to take Singaporeans seriously. When Marshall met Sir John Nicoll to assume office after his election, he expected some words acknowledging the significance of this first step toward independence. Instead, they sat at a table and Nicoll simply said, "I use red ink." The colonial administrators had not even thought that Marshall might need an office from which to carry on the people's business. It was only after an emotional outburst and a threat to set up a table on the *padang* that Marshall was given a tiny office under the stairway in the Secretariat. Marshall faced this sort of petty obstructionism from the colonial authorities at every step. Once he stood outside the door of an official reception organized by Runme Shaw, the movie mogul, for an hour before the seating arrangement was changed to acknowledge his status. It was perhaps no wonder that he developed a reputation for being emotional.

On the other side, the PAP and its left-wing allies were busy stirring up trouble with the unions and the students. Within a couple of months,

Marshall had to quell the outbreaks of violence as a result of the Hock Lee bus strike and at the same time to try to get the Chinese middle school students back to their classes. He was forced into a position of allowing the British to reinstitute a number of the Emergency Regulations and thus found himself caught between two very unsympathetic forces. The weakness of his position was exposed when he traveled to London in 1956 for talks with the Colonial Office on revising the constitution and expanding the powers of the elected government.

At that point, Her Majesty's government had no intention of loosening the controls it then held over Singapore's affairs, and it had little confidence in the ability of Marshall's government to deal with the students and the unions. The negotiations went badly, and Marshall was again caught between the hard line of Lee Kuan Yew (who accompanied him) and the British. Nonetheless, Marshall did have an impact. When the constitution was revised in 1959, it contained virtually all of Marshall's key demands. This was the constitution under which Lee Kuan Yew first assumed power. While Singapore was still dependent on Britain for defense and foreign affairs, Lee's government had much broader control of the domestic situation than had Marshall.

The 1959 elections

Marshall had resigned after his apparent failure to achieve his objectives in London. His resignation left the government in the hands of his deputy Lim Yew Hock, a man who had also schemed to unseat him. Fed up with politics, Marshall claimed he was finished, but he soon found himself back in action as a member of the opposition. In the meantime, Lim Yew Hock, as the new chief minister, was only too willing to work with the British. He took quick steps to cripple the labor unions and to quell the Chinese students. A new wave of arrests and detentions followed, and the scope for open political action was again decreased. Things remained this way until the new constitution came into effect, and a second round of elections was held in 1959. This time, the PAP was ready. It had established firm links, according to Lee and Bloodworth, with the communists and their "open united front." They were able to count on the left's grassroots organizations to get out the vote of the Chinese masses. Lee had also established personal links with a number of key British officials. He thus had the confidence of both the left wing and the colonialists and was in a position to make a serious grab for power. The PAP appealed to the people and promoted workers' rights, a policy of democratic socialism, abolition of the Emergency Regulations and an end to colonialist exploitation.

Once in office, the PAP's plans had no place for the political left or for an independent labor movement. At the beginning of 1959, just months before it won the general election and took over the government, the PAP was beginning to develop a more conservative economic policy. A series of papers published in *Petir*, the party journal, addressed such issues as the flight of capital, the level of industrial strife and the means of developing pools of investment capital within Singapore. These papers suggested a drift away from more radical versions of democratic socialism and workers' rights and toward the creation of a favorable investment climate (*Straits Times*, 16 January and 3 February 1959). Nonetheless, on the eve of its election victory on 1 June 1959, the PAP reasserted its support for a united and powerful labor movement to ensure that "workers can be assured of a fair return for their labour and so improve their material welfare."

The PAP victory on 30 May 1959 was solid and convincing. The party swept the polls, winning forty-three of the fifty-one seats. As things stood, however, Lee and his clique of English-educated leaders were still in a very weak position, even within their own party. Nearly half of the elected MPs were Chinese-educated left-wingers, labor leaders or others who would come to be considered too radical for the party. Lee's clique did not fully control the party's central committee, and most of the grassroots organizations were dominated by the left under the leadership of Lim Chin Siong and Fong Swee Suan. Over the next three years, Lee and his group carefully maneuvered the left out of power. Using the threat of British force, the powers of the ISA and the ability to dominate the legislative agenda they gradually broke the power of the unions and isolated the left.

New laws were introduced to break the left-wing forces that had gotten the PAP into office. The Trade Union Bill, which provided "for the re-registration of federations of trade unions" and which made important changes in the conditions for trade union registration, now made it possible for the PAP government to de-register many of the left-wing unions. By September 1960, the PAP leadership was beginning to criticize "slogan-shouting" labor leaders and stressing the need for "industrial peace" if Singapore was to carry out its policy of industrial expansion (*Straits Times*, 8 September 1960). The PAP, which had begun its career as the champion of a free labor movement and democratic socialism, had begun to swing around. The other shoe hit the floor with the *Petir* editorial defending the party's new industrial policy. The policy was described in a *Straits Times* article:

> The editorial said that the industrialisation of the State – one of the paramount goals of the PAP – could only be carried out by a vigorous and concerted campaign on three fronts, mass front, trade union front and the government front.
>
> "The essential conditions for industrialisation," it said "will only be realised if there is close co-operation and understanding between Government, the trade unions and the industrialists."
>
> "Industrial peace with justice for the workers is the most essential condition, and the party has taken steps to ensure that industrial relations are established on the basis of peace and justice."[33]

The trade unions were gradually shepherded under the iron wing of the NTUC, and strike action, confrontation and worker militancy became things of the past. The government began to exercise complete control over the workers' movement, and unions became instruments of government policy (Trocki 2001).

The next big step was to eliminate the so-called radical leaders of the unions and student groups. Individuals such as Jamit Singh, a man of Sikh background from Ipoh in Malaya, who had left university to help Lee Kuan Yew to organize the workers at the Singapore Harbour Board (SHB), were quickly neutralized. Singh, who had helped to carry Lee through the streets during the victory celebrations in May 1959, found himself under investigation for misuse of union funds.[34] He was convicted and banished to the Federation (Liew 2003).

In 1961, matters within the PAP came to a head and the left wing split from the party and formed the Barisan Socialis (BS) or Socialist Front. Lee Kuan Yew's initial tolerance of socialist "radicalism" and democratic dissent declined significantly. After 1959, Jamit Singh noted that the PAP government had developed a mentality along the lines of "those who are not with us are against us." This led to the historic rift between the fragile PAP government and its supporters in the labour unions. Two opposing groups came to dominate the political scene, with the PAP and the pro-government National Trade Unions Congress (NTUC) on the one side, and the Barisan Socialis, consisting of former PAP activists, and its affiliate body, the Singapore Association of Trade Unions (SATU), on the other. The PAP controlled the government ministries and statutory boards, including the SHB and other public sector trade unions. The support base of the BS lay in the six major Middle Road unions, led by Lim Chin Siong and Fong Swee Suan; Dominic Puthucheary of the white collar unions; S.T. Bani from the Business and House Employees Union; and from the waterfront, Sidney Woodhull from the naval base and Jamit Singh from the SHB. They were collectively known as the "Big Six" and were also founders of SATU. Liew Kai Khiun, who has written about Singh and the Singapore Harbour Board Staff Association (SHBSA), has argued that although all the SATU unions were on the left, the Indians and Malays of the harbor unions were suspicious of "Middle Road" unions, which were largely Chinese. They also distrusted the BS, which appeared to be dominated by a Chinese-educated leadership (*ibid.*). The PAP propaganda machine did its best to stimulate these fears.

As it moved against one group after another, the PAP was able to play the racial card, accusing the Chinese-educated groups of "Chinese chauvinism" when they championed the cause of Chinese education. Since the Malays and those in the English-speaking unions were outnumbered by the Chinese, there was room to drive the wedge of distrust. Nevertheless, the PAP had lost a great deal of popular support, and by 1961 Lee and his clique found themselves clinging to power by a very narrow margin. In 1961, the PAP candidate was defeated by Ong Eng Guan, a PAP defector, in the Hong Lim by-election. The BS and its supporters had thrown their weight behind Ong in a test of strength with the PAP and had won. At the same time, David Marshall had been elected to the Assembly as the member from Anson, also defeating a PAP candidate, again with Barisan support.

Cold storage

It was possibly around this time that the PAP began to plan its *coup d'état*, known as "Operation Cold Store." The major security agency was the Internal Security Committee, which was composed of three members: one from the Singapore government, one colonial official and one from Malaysia. The last member had been proposed as a measure to woo the Malays into accepting a merger with Singapore by giving them a voice in Singapore's affairs. It had the power, under the ISA, to detain and to deport anyone who could be deemed a threat to national security. By the beginning of 1963, the BS was gaining strength and appeared to be moving toward a coalition with the Partai Rakyat, a largely Malay party led by Said Zahari. He was a Singapore-born Malay journalist who had formerly worked with the *Utusan Melayu* and *Berita Harian*. As it would soon be necessary for the government to call an election, an alliance between popular and progressive parties that could call upon the support of large numbers of the Chinese-educated and Malays could form a powerful opponent for the PAP.

On 3 February 1963, the security forces struck. In one night, nearly 150 journalists, student leaders, labor activists, and opposition politicians were arbitrarily detained. There were no trials. No charges were filed and, in many cases, the detention was not even acknowledged by the government. The top rank of BS and PR leaders was effectively neutralized, and the way was now clear for PAP domination of legitimate politics. The detainees were held in grim conditions at the Outram Road Prison in Singapore for over three months until David Marshall, acting in his capacity as an MP, visited the detainees and publicized their situation.[34]

Malaysia

The arrests gave Lee and his group the breathing space they thought they needed to call for a plebiscite on the Malaysia question. Lee and the PAP gained a measure of credibility with the conservative Malayan government that they would be tough on left-wing radicalism. A series of negotiations were carried out with Federation officials. These talks were also fostered by the British and the Australians. The British, who were by this time enthusiastic supporters of the project, offered to add the Borneo territories of Sarawak, North Borneo and Brunei to the proposed federation. Brunei, which was a protectorate, refused to give up its independence (and its oil profits) and managed to maintain its sovereignty. Sarawak and North Borneo (later Sabah) were polled by a United Nations representative and deemed to favor joining Malaysia. Although questions were later raised about the conduct of this poll, objections were brushed aside, and the UN agreed to accept the contention that the peoples of the Borneo states would favour joining the Malaysian Federation, although the exact terms of their membership were not made public at the time.

The PAP government organized a poll in Singapore that brought objections from a number of quarters. The ballot offered only three choices, all of which were "yes." All offered membership in the Federation, only on slightly different terms. It was impossible to vote "no," and people were led to believe that blank ballots would be counted as "yes"; moreover, they were told that there would be no report on how many blank votes were cast. Singapore voters, in fact, received no real choice in the matter and believed they had no way in which to register a negative ballot. In addition to the Barisan, David Marshall and a number of others led a campaign against Singapore joining the Federation on the proposed terms.

In July 1962, Marshall led a delegation of opposition MPs known as the Committee of Seventeen to petition the United Nations Committee on Colonialism, which was overseeing the merger. He asked that the committee require that a fourth item be added to the ballot that would allow Singapore voters to express a desire for immediate independence.[35] The request was refused, and the referendum went ahead as the PAP had structured it. In the meantime, the PAP had launched a massive propaganda campaign to support its preferred option. This ran for nearly a year before the actual vote. In the end, Singaporeans voted to join Sabah, Sarawak and the Federation of Malaya to form the Federation of Malaysia. The PAP claimed a victory of over 70 percent of the vote for its recommended option and noted that less than 30 percent had turned in blank ballots as the Barisan had recommended (Yeo and Lau 1991: 142). With this mandate, PAP leaders now felt strong enough to challenge the Barisan and the Chinese-educated masses on their own ground. Despite objections from the Philippines and armed opposition from Indonesia in the form of Sukarno's policy of "Konfrontasi," the Federation of Malaysia was formed on 31 August 1963.

By 9 August 1965, Singapore had separated from Malaysia and had become independent. Albert Lau has written the best history of Singapore's brief spell as a member of the Malaysian Federation (Lau 1998). He has highlighted four pivotal events that led to Singapore's separation from Malaysia. The first was the snap election for the Singapore state assembly that Lee Kuan Yew called immediately following the formation of Malaysia in September 1963, in which the PAP thoroughly trounced candidates fielded by the Malaysian Alliance parties. Both the Barisan and UMNO were caught unprepared. The Barisan, with half of its leadership incarcerated, fared poorly, winning only thirteen seats and 32.1 percent of the vote, against the PAP's thirty-seven seats and 47.4 percent (Yeo and Lau 1991: 143). The UMNO did even worse, winning no seats. This experience immediately soured relations between Kuala Lumpur and Singapore.

The next issue was the decision by the PAP to contest seats in Malaya in the first Malaysian national elections, in April 1964. This was contrary to a "gentleman's agreement" between Lee and Tunku Abdul Rahman made at the time that Malaysia was formed. Despite aggressive campaigning and apparent widespread popularity, the PAP won only one seat outside Singapore. The third issue was the racial riot that broke out in Singapore during Muhammad's birthday celebration on 21 July 1964. Lau lays much of the blame for this disturbance on the activities of Syed Ja'afar Albar, UMNO secretary-general and editor of the *Utusan Melayu*. This led to further bad blood between Singapore and Kuala Lumpur.

The fourth development arose as relations between Singapore and Kuala Lumpur worsened in the second half of 1964. Lee and the hardliners in the PAP, particularly Rajaratnam and Toh Chin Chye, began to organize an opposition coalition, the Malaysian Solidarity Convention, which would have included other "democratic," multiracial and socialist parties in the Malay states, Penang, and particularly in Sabah and Sarawak. PAP rhetoric about a "Malaysian Malaysia" struck at the heart of the UMNO-dominated Alliance, which stood for Malay privileges, racial politics and a conservative social order. Continued PAP attacks on the "feudalist" Malay leadership and their "reactionary" *taukeh* partners in the Malaysian Chinese Association (MCA) raised temperatures in Kuala Lumpur exacerbating already strained relations between the leaders in the Alliance and the PAP.

These developments, together with conflicts over taxes and the budget, drove the final wedge between the two political orders. Negotiations for some sort of "disengagement" were underway from August 1964. It ultimately became clear that there was virtually no common ground. Finally, after delicate negotiations between Malaysian Deputy Premier Tun Abdul Razak and his old school chum, Goh Keng Swee, the deal to separate was struck as both Lee and the Tunku sat on the sidelines.

Despite reports of Lee Kuan Yew's "anguish" on learning of the decision to separate, it seems that few would argue today that the government of either Singapore or Malaysia has suffered as a result of the separation. Singapore has been able to turn what appeared to be a rather nasty setback into an opportunity to emerge as a prosperous industrialized city-state, while Malaysia too has developed economically and at the same time maintained the Malay-dominated political order. As it has turned out, Singapore has been able to do quite well despite fears about access to Malaysian markets and raw materials to sustain its economy. When separation came, there were few in Singapore who mourned the failed attempt at merger.

The rugged society

It was perhaps a very gutsy move for Lee and his fellows to step out onto the world stage in 1965 as leaders of a fully independent city-state in the middle of Southeast Asia. It was but a single small island with a population of less than two million, high unemployment and no natural resources. Admittedly, they had little choice, and it must have seemed that their backs were to the wall. They may have been comforted that Britain still maintained naval and army bases there, but that last scrap of colonial carpet was whipped out from under their feet a few years later when Britain announced its plans to close the bases. Economically and politically separate from Malaysia, militarily separate from the UK, not many would have predicted the economic success and political stability that characterized the ensuing years.

The party's able triumvirate – Lee, Goh Keng Swee and Rajaratnam – now came into their own. If Lee was the great leader, it was Rajaratnam, whom David Marshall claims was the foreign policy genius, who charted Singapore's course in the next two decades.[36] Goh was the economic and bureaucratic mastermind who promoted the policy of export-oriented industrialization (EOI) backed by large doses of foreign investment. He also acted to win the loyalty of Singapore's civil service as the state came under its new masters. With the threat of further arrests, constant surveillance and continuous pressure on the left and any other non-governmental organizations, the PAP was able to disable any possible opposition permanently.

The three saw themselves in a dangerous world, but one that was also pregnant with opportunity. Singapore might have talked solidarity with the Afro-Asian nations at the time, but it also sought alliances with the United States and Japan while maintaining close relations with Britain, Australia

Figure 4.2 Singapore Armed Forces women marching in a National Day parade (*c*. 1971) in uniform with Uzis.

and the Commonwealth. It was aware that its future depended on US capital and a US guarantee of security in the region. This was particularly true so long as the Americans were committed to the conflict in Vietnam. The PAP also quickly normalized relations with Japan and, despite lingering memories of Japanese wartime atrocities, aggressively began to woo Japanese capital.

Singapore also opened cordial relations with Indonesia when it was clear that Suharto and the military had abandoned Konfrontasi and were eager to deal with internal issues rather than further expansion in the region. This link, together with gradually healing relations with Malaysia, helped the three countries, together with Thailand and the Philippines, to move toward a regional understanding among the anti-communist states of Southeast Asia. This resulted in the formation of the Association of Southeast Asian Nations (ASEAN) in 1970.

It was perhaps under Rajaratnam's guidance that the military alliance with Israel was conceived at about the same time. Israel, seen as a small state surrounded by hostile Muslim neighbours, seemed to share a common situation and world view with Singapore. The PAP looked to Israel for advice in building and training a tough military and a mobilized society. Internationally, this put Singapore in league with the group of pro-US, anti-communist countries without having to rely on direct military and security aid from the USA itself.

Internally, Singapore may be said to have ceased the practice of politics as they are usually understood in a democratic society. In fact, many would hesitate to continue call Singapore a democratic society, despite the holding of regular elections. Domestically, as well as internationally, the revolution was over. For all practical purposes, the left had been crushed even before Singapore entered Malaysia, and once outside it, the PAP took steps to ensure that no opposition party would ever be able to rise again. Legislation was enacted that made it virtually impossible for an independent group to amass the financial and public resources to field a credible opposition party. Given that Singapore is a relatively small place, and most available resources are easily accounted for, it was difficult to develop any sort of base among the population or to amass the finances necessary to run a political campaign without drawing attention from the government. To this was added the government's complete control of the media and its power to authorize or ban any kind of organization. The Emergency Regulations, the ISA and the PPSO have all remained in force with the excuse that the state is under continual threat.

This sense of threat, of an imminent emergency that would "destroy national stability," has been a major propaganda weapon of the government since its foundation. The possibility that Singapore's security and prosperity might be subverted by domestic foes or confiscated by external enemies (read Malaysia or Indonesia) has been a persistent subtext in most of these messages. At the same time, anything that threatened the power of the PAP government was usually interpreted as a threat to national security. The

"Rugged Society" (one of the PAP's campaign slogan from the late 1960s and early 1970s) was one that not only worked hard to insure economic survival and to make a place for Singapore in the global economy but one that was also disciplined, obedient and quiescent.

The key threat, domestically, continued to be the ethnic Chinese – the Chinese-educated, or what Lee would style "Chinese chauvinists." This group, the majority of Singapore's population, continued to present an unre-solvable dilemma. The PAP needed their votes to continue to win elections, but it was determined to prevent them from developing an autonomous political or social presence. This meant crushing not only the left, what remained of it in the Barisan Socialis, but every sort of organization that grew out of the Chinese-educated population. This included everything from secret societies, to the SCCCI,[37] to temple and cemetery organizations, to Chinese-language schools and newspapers.

Singapore under Lee & Co.

Modern Singapore owes much to Lee Kuan Yew's ideas. Two of these in particular, which have been highlighted by Michael Barr and others, are his belief in elitism and meritocracy (Barr 2000). Both of these have had a profound effect on the development of Singapore's political system since independence. Barr suggests that, among other things, Lee was influenced by the ideas of Arnold Toynbee on the importance of a dynamic elite class in the achievement of social and political progress. If Singapore was to develop, it needed a self-renewing elite group. Lee had little faith in the masses of the population, whom he considered as mere "digits." They needed to be led.

Lee also believed that it was necessary for the government to nurture an elite. He was doubtful that Singapore, with its small population, would be capable of producing people with the necessary talents and character without careful training and the systematic dedication of resources to accomplish the task. The members of this elite had to be selected on the basis of merit. To a great extent, this became one of the guiding principles of the educational system, which will be covered in greater detail in Chapter 5.

A number of other ideas together with the above came to form an ideo-logical constellation that have become the guiding principles of Singapore. During his education in Britain, Lee was certainly influenced by Fabian socialist ideas, and to some extent these provided a rationale for his anti-colonialism and his socialist policies. However, it is clear that Lee's practice of socialism has been highly selective. Populism and popular democracy have no place in Singapore. Aside from a large-scale, self-funded public housing program, a self-funded pension plan and free education, Singapore is not a full-scale welfare state. There is no unemployment insurance, or free medical care and no dole; nor is there a state-sponsored pension plan for those outside the formal workforce. Trade unions in Singapore have been amalgamated into the NTUC, are strictly controlled by the government and have no independent voice. The aspects of Fabianism that Singapore has adopted have been its paternalistic and managerial elements.

For the party and the political system, the elitist and managerial ideas have meant that the leadership of the party was not to be selected from among those who faithfully worked their way up in the rank and file of the party organization. Rather, the party turned toward a more corporate model of headhunting. It recruited top university graduates and those who had already distinguished themselves in academia, business, management, the military, or government administration. Ultimately, a rigorous system of tests, mostly psychological, interviews and other methods of determining loyalty and suitability were devised to screen these individuals before they were recruited into the party. Often the newcomers were immediately given positions as MPs or even cabinet ministers. Many were called, but in the end, few were chosen. Not all could live up to the rigorous standards set by Lee Kuan Yew. Those who did not pass the performance standards were summarily dismissed and left to slide back into obscurity. By the 1970s, service in the party leadership was the highest goal to which an individual Singaporean could aspire. Unless one left the country to seek opportunities abroad, there were few alternative possibilities.

The chosen individuals tended to have backgrounds in law, engineering, science, business management and other essentially formalist or quantitative disciplines. They were technocrats. The PAP thus came under the control of a technocratic elite representing not the people who elected them but a sort of "non-ideological" or positivist commitment to "universal" standards of rationality and professionalism. In other words, they represented no one but themselves and their own ever-changing interpretation of those standards of which they were the sole custodians. Herbert Marcuse's one-dimensional man had come of age (Marcuse 1964).

Another key element of Lee Kuan Yew's political philosophy was that of multiculturalism. This was not original to him: all the progressive groups in Singapore championed some version of this goal. Prior to Singapore's inclusion in Malaysia, and while it was part of Malaysia, Singapore's leaders supported this ideal, along with the belief that since Malays were the indigenous peoples they and their culture deserved a special status. This meant, in practice, certain privileges for Malays in Singapore (although not so many as in the Federation) and special status for the Malay language, which would be Singapore's national language. Beyond that, all races – Chinese, Malay, Indian, others – were to have equal status, and all four languages would be considered "official" languages (i.e. Mandarin, English, Tamil, Malay).

Politically, this program won few points with the leaders of UMNO, who wished for a much greater Malay preference, but all things considered, they could hardly hope for more in a place where Malays made up only 10 percent of the population. In the long run, however, and this is clear in

Singapore's social programs, it meant that there would be no ethnically based political parties and no ethnic residential strongholds in Singapore. As Lily Rahim has pointed out, the result of Singapore's public housing and resettlement programs meant the end of ethnic *kampongs*. Ironically, this has meant the *de facto* creation of Chinese majorities in every constituency (Rahim 1998). Attempts to create or demand ethnic constituencies dominated by either Malays or Indians would be treated as expressions of "chauvinism," as would any other ethnic or culturally based challenges to PAP social or political policies.

The charge of "chauvinism" became the polar opposite of Singapore's multiculturalism, and since the government controlled the political discourse, any expression of a political or social nature that came from an ethnic source could be tarred with the label "chauvinist." This became particularly effective after the events of May 1969 in Malaysia, when racial riots broke out in Kuala Lumpur. Many voluntary organizations in Singapore, most of which had some sort of ethnic basis, found themselves severely restricted in their areas of operation. Many were Chinese clan organizations, regional organizations, temple or mosque groups, etc. In essence, these were forbidden to engage in any kind of activity that might be considered "political." These moves went a long way toward closing down much of Singapore's hitherto vibrant civil society. Singapore had become, in most meanings of the word, a dictatorship. Perhaps it could be styled a benevolent one, but it was a dictatorship nonetheless. Chan Heng Chee has called it the "activist" state, but there may be no need to invent new words to describe the concentration of all power in the hands of a small clique, and perhaps in those of one man.

Chan has argued that a part of Singapore's colonial legacy was the British parliamentary system, which was subsequently jettisoned by Lee Kuan Yew. This is not exactly correct, since Singapore was never governed by a parliamentary system while it was under colonial rule. Perhaps the real legacy was the experience of 130 years of autocratic colonial rule by an unresponsive bureaucracy and an ambitious and exploitative economic elite. In modern Singapore, as in China or North Korea, political life has been made the sole property of the narrow elite of an exclusive party. The main political project of the period between 1959 and 1975, and thereafter, has been the elimination all forms of civil society. Most of all, the PAP worked systematically to erase all those impulses of political activism that might have allowed the expression of political demands from the people and independent intellectual critics who might challenge the agenda of elite dominance (Chai *et al.* 1991: 176). Elsewhere, Chan has sharpened this argument, noting that intellectuals were not permitted an independent voice in Singapore:

> In Singapore today, the views of independent intellectuals receive no favour and if his views are critical of governmental power, this function

is not recognised as legitimate. Such an intellectual is vilified on the grounds that his claim to the right of criticism is an alien tradition borne of Western liberal thought; that new states need more power not less, more stability not instability.

(Chan 1976: 11)

This trait was made explicit in the early 1970s when the independent newspaper *The Nation* adopted an editorial policy that was critical of government policy and was quickly shut down. About the same time, a group of independent planners and architects, the Singapore Planning and Urban Research group (SPUR), raised questions regarding the design policies of the HDB. Very shortly, a number of individuals in the group, particularly architect Tay Kheng Soon, found it difficult to obtain work in Singapore. In 1994, the world-famous Singapore author Catherine Lim dared to raise a small voice of criticism in the local press. The *Straits Times* published two op-ed pieces by the PEN winner. One commented on the "great affective divide" between the PAP government and the people, noting that people feared and respected the government but did not love it (Lim 1994a). A second article, published a couple of months later, commented on the increasing arrogance of the PAP government under the new prime minister, Goh Chok Tong (Lim 1994b). Although the articles were couched in rather restrained language, they were taken as unconscionable smears on the PAP and the personality of the prime minister. Both were met with stinging rebukes from both Goh and Lee himself, who had by then resigned the premiership and become "senior minister."

This thin-skinned attitude toward criticism or dissent of any kind had become characteristic of the PAP's stance since the early 1970s, when it crushed *The Nation* and arrested staff members of the Chinese-language opposition paper, *Nanyang Siang Pau*. In their turn, even international media such as the *Far Eastern Economic Review* and the *Asian Wall Street Journal* found their publications banned, their issues confiscated and their reporters declared *persona non grata*.

Another and perhaps more troubling attack, since it signaled that nothing was sacred, came in the mid-1980s. This was launched against the Catholic Church. As Singapore gained affluence on the crest of the Asian boom, there arose a need for domestic help. Local Malays and Chinese had priced themselves out of the market, and most had found other jobs in industry. Singapore's newly affluent bourgeoisie now found it "necessary" to bring in "guest" workers: in this case young women from the Philippines to work as domestic servants. These were considered ideal, since they were seen as docile and English-speaking, and because they were expected to return home after a few years.

Neither their own nor the Singapore government took any responsibility for the welfare of these people. They were brought in by private contractors, and there were numerous instances of fraud and mistreatment. There were also reports of both sexual and physical abuse by some of the families who hired them. Their complaints received less than adequate attention from the Singapore authorities, and in desperation they turned to the one organization that they felt could represent their concerns: the Catholic Church. Attempts at publicizing their complaints or at reform of these abuses by members of the clergy led to the expulsion of a number of priests and warnings to the hierarchy that the Church should reduce its involvement in social action to protect workers.

The government's defense of the stifling of dissent and criticism was to be Lee Kuan Yew's next idea: that of Asian values. In the case of Singapore, this meant traditional Chinese, or Confucian, values. These values favored the interests of the community over those of the individual and placed stress on hierarchy, respect, consensus, discipline, obedience, hard work and frugality. As interpreted by Lee and other Asian dictators, they meant docile acceptance of state authority and were developed as a critique of "decadent, Western, liberal permissivism." Western, secular values were alien to Asian people. Asian values proved a useful foil to fend off charges of human rights abuses and undemocratic practices from Western governments, intellectuals and the media. At the same time, the idea resonated favorably with other Asian states with even bleaker human rights records, such as the People's Republic of China, Indonesia and Burma.

As Michael Barr has pointed out, Lee has harbored a deep but contradictory admiration for Chinese culture and civilization. On the one hand, as an English-educated Baba Chinese, there is little about him that could be considered truly Chinese. English and Malay were his first languages, and even today his Mandarin remains substandard. His greatest political enemies were always the "Chinese chauvinists." In truth, multiculturalism was a defense against the masses of the Chinese-educated. On the other hand, he deeply admired people like Lim Chin Siong and many others who had been the shock troops of the anti-colonial and independence movement. He respected the dedication and commitment of the communists, who alone had stood up to the Japanese in the Malayan jungles and had later fought the British during the Emergency. It was the Chinese-educated, some of them communists, who had organized the labor unions in Singapore, fought the secret society thugs hired by management, stood against police batons and, when necessary, gone to jail. None of these were things that Lee himself would ever have done.

In Lee's mind, these people were strong and determined because they had what he called "cultural ballast." He saw people of his own class and background, English-educated Asians, as lacking deep cultural roots and were thus unable to commit themselves to some great task. Paradoxically, he did not include himself in this category; however, he spoke with scorn about individuals such as Jamit Singh, the Sikh leader of the harbor unions, who had shaved his beard and cut his hair. Despite Singh's considerable achievements, he was unreliable in Lee's eyes (Liew 2003). It was for this reason that Lee sent his own children to Chinese primary schools and to ensure that they grew up with the correct values.

It was in this spirit, in his pursuit of Asian values, that Lee began to tinker with social and educational policies that in many ways actually began to undercut the earlier multiracial policy. By the late 1970s, the government had begun to tilt markedly in favor of the Chinese and things Chinese. After nearly two decades of policies that disadvantaged Chinese education, the government launched its "Speak Mandarin" campaign. This was partly an attempt to further restrict the Chinese-educated by reducing the use of the dialects. The program also saw the promotion of bright students (those who were good at exams – usually Chinese) into special fast-track programs and the development of an Asian values curriculum in the schools. Many of these programs were dismal failures, but some have persisted, and they all reflect the government's aim of tailoring programs that appear to favor the Chinese. Michael Barr and Jevon Low have recently attempted to examine the long-term direction of multicultural programs (Barr and Low 2005). At the same time, as Lily Rahim has noted, there was a clear cutback in programs designed to favor Malays, so that by the beginning of the 1990s, virtually all of the Malay preferences that had previously existed in Singapore had been withdrawn.

Elections and Parliament

The third phase of Singapore's political development seems to have begun around 1985 or 1986, with the economic crisis of that year as the key event marking the transition. We might take the "Speak Mandarin" campaign, which began in the late 1970s, as the first indication of this shift, but the economic crisis gave it a certain focus and purpose that it may have lacked originally. The economic crisis was simply the final proof that things were going wrong in Singapore. The policies that seemed to have been appropriate for the 1960s and 1970s had begun to fray around the edges with the appearance of unforeseen developments that had come to trouble Lee and the PAP leadership.

While many of these issues will be dealt with in the next two chapters, it was clear that there was a growing cultural, social and spiritual malaise. A new generation was coming of age that had never known colonialism, discrimination, poverty, crime, substandard living conditions, poor education or unemployment. They were hard workers and high achievers, but they were selfish and despite a steady diet of government propaganda, had little sense of social responsibility. They wanted better housing, better cars, better TV sets and appliances, and greater personal prestige. They expected opportunity, advancement and material success as their birthright. The PAP leadership became aware of this "malaise" with the economic slowdown and began to rethink its strategy.

The question of opposition and dissent resurfaced. Throughout the 1960s and early 1970s, the PAP had destroyed every vestige of organized opposition in Singapore. Between 1965 and 1982, not a single opposition MP had been elected to the Singapore Parliament. The election of Joshua Jeyaretnam in that year was little more than a microscopic crack in the otherwise impregnable armor of the PAP, but to many in the party it seemed as though the sky had fallen. When another opposition member (from a different party) was elected in 1985, they were sure it had. The loss of the two seats was largely symbolic for the PAP and meant very little in the long run. However, these concerns were not entirely without reason, for despite its domination of Parliament, the PAP's share of the vote had been declining steadily since the early 1980s. Between 1963 and 1984, the party had averaged about 75 percent of the total vote. In 1984, there was a swing of 13 percent against the party, and by 1991 its share of the vote had fallen to 60.1 percent. There was an opposition in the populace, but it could not get organized (Rodan 1993: 83–4, 97).

Nevertheless, the losses did galvanize the PAP into action. On the one hand, it moved to provide alternative avenues of public involvement in government, while on the other, it took steps to strengthen and prolong the life of the one-party state. One of the results of this period was the creation of appointed, non-constituency (and non-PAP) MPs (NCMPs). These would be free from party discipline and could, theoretically at least, provide a disinterested opposition that would thus remind the party that it was subject to some scrutiny. In 1985, a Feedback Unit was created that would conduct feedback sessions in the various community centers and party branch offices to canvass the feelings and opinions of the citizenry on specific issues. However, as Garry Rodan points out, the majority of these feedback sessions were targeted at professionals and white collar workers. The working class and, to some degree, women were forgotten. This was somewhat off-target, since much of the opposition came from the working class. Other means of broadening governance included the creation of town councils, the introduction of Government Parliamentary Committees (GPCs) and the creation of the Institute of Policy Studies (IPS) (*ibid.*).

While these measures created only a token opposition and token dissent, they were all that the PAP would allow at the time. The PAP was, after all, trying to short-circuit the development of an opposition by providing non-confrontational methods of discussing the impact of government decisions and of obtaining citizen input in the development of policy. Although the government listened, there was nothing that said it had to take the advice of these citizens.

At the same time, Lee Kuan Yew began to plan for his own succession. This has turned out to be a carefully stage-managed process. It is of interest that as Lee aged, he placed less and less trust in the party apparatus, including his most trusted and dependable lieutenants. The movement toward the recruitment of outside talent to fill top posts in the government/party continued, while the men who had built the party with him and who had been at his side from the beginning were gradually retired or pushed out of the party. This applied to key figures such as Goh Keng Swee and S. Rajaratnam as well as many lesser ones. In fact, by the time he retired to the post of senior minister, a post with almost as much power as prime minister, there was no one in his age cohort, or the one immediately below it, to succeed.

Instead, in 1985, Lee reached down into the upper ranks of the party's middle generation, among men (no women, of course) only in their late 40s, to begin grooming his successor, Goh Chok Tong. Goh's career is instructive. He was born in 1941, attended Raffles College and graduated from the University of Singapore in 1964 with first class honours. He worked as an administrative officer in the Administrative Services of Singapore until 1969, but two years of that period was spent acquiring a master's degree in economics at Williams College in the USA. After 1969, he spent eight years working for Neptune Orient Lines, leaving its employ as managing director. He became MP for Marine Parade in 1976 and left Neptune Orient the following year to take up the position of senior minister of state for Finance. Between 1977 and 1990, he held the portfolios for Trade and Industry, Health, and Defence. In 1985, he was appointed first deputy prime minister. When Lee Kuan Yew became senior minister in 1990, Goh became prime minister at the age of 49 (Singapore government website: http://www.cabinet.gov.sg/pmgoh.htm, "The Cabinet," 2 August 2004).

At the same time as Goh became prime minister, Lee promoted his own son, Lee Hsien Loong (then the youngest brigadier-general in the Singapore armed forces – he was 32 when he attained the rank) to the post of deputy prime minister and minister for Trade and Industry. It now became clear that "the BG" (as he is known) was in line for the top job in Singapore. Lee was in the process of creating a dynasty. It appears that in Singapore, Asian values also include hereditary succession. On 11 August 2004, Lee Hsien Loong became prime minister. Despite charges of nepotism, one cannot deny Lee Junior's competence; on the other hand, one must ask if he would have attained that position had he not been the son of Lee Kuan Yew. Given the examples of dynasties appearing in places as diverse as North Korea, the Philippines, Indonesia, Pakistan and India, it may be that the tendency is a distinct part of Asian culture.

5 The managed, middle-class, multiracial society

One of the major changes that took place in Singapore with independence was the level of control that the government came to exercise over society. As a colony, Singapore's social life was relatively free. So long as people were not forming secret societies or attempting to overthrow the government, or form labor unions, the government took a *laissez-faire* attitude toward social activity. With the upsurge of political and social action that characterized the immediate postwar period, even most of those restrictions were lifted, for a time at least. The rise to political dominance of the PAP after 1959, and its subsequent movement to shut down civil society, brought a new kind of discipline and order to Singapore's society.

It was not merely through political dominance and the use of the ISA and the PPSO and other overt acts of coercion that this order was achieved. Rather, the party/state now took full responsibility for almost complete management and surveillance of society. Its power was reflected in every agency, from housing, to education, to economic development, to labor organization, to traffic control, to control of fertility, to cultural expression, to religion. In every aspect of life, government regulation became paramount. Aspects of everyday life such as dress, habits of cleanliness and hairstyles also became matters of state concern. As Singapore became a global city-state, even its vegetation was brought under control, as specific varieties of trees, grass, shrubs and flowers were selected for the carefully manicured parks and other public plantings. As one wag styled it, Singapore became "clean and green, beautiful downtown Southeast Asia."

For Lee Kuan Yew and the PAP, Singapore was a *tabula rasa*, a clean slate on which they had everything to make anew. Ironically, they shared this attitude with Thomas Stamford Raffles, who in 1819 also saw Singapore as a place where he could recreate society and found a system of "order and purity." For both, the past was no guide to the future. It was to be rejected. In fact, during the early years of Singapore's independence, the history of Singapore was virtually ignored in the schools. Nonetheless, history had a way of insinuating itself into the plans of the PAP just as it had with Raffles. Given the level of power exercised by the PAP, and the fact that within the party Lee's word became virtually unchallengeable, it often seemed that it was a one-man show.

It is thus important to understand Lee's ideas when examining the development of social policy in Singapore during the years after 1965. Lee's ideas about meritocracy, eugenics and elitism, his distrust of democracy, and his biases about things Chinese all came to be of significance in the playing out of events. Michael Barr has stressed the significance of these ideas in Lee's personal belief system (Barr 2000). Because of Lee's authority, particularly during the 1980s and 1990s, when everyone of his own generation had retired from political life and the party was led by younger men, there was no one who dared to contradict him. As a result, government policy sometimes seemed highly idiosyncratic.

Some would argue that this project in social reconstruction has been largely successful. Those who have followed the development of the city since the early 1960s would have to admit that the entire island has been physically and socially transformed. The city reached full employment and eradicated poverty. The housing shortage was solved, and Singapore has avoided racial and class conflict. The crime rate is one of the lowest in the world, and the government has a reputation for honesty and integrity that few others can match, even in the developed world.

Singapore's social order has been radically changed as well, but it has not always had the result that was intended. Singapore's transformation has been a struggle with history and tradition. In some cases, aspects of society that the government attempted to change have proved remarkably resilient. The question of whether such close management can successfully create a self-sustaining and creative culture may remain open.

It is useful to look at some of the various arenas in which the PAP government has been able to develop its control over society. Aside from claiming that there was a need for social stability to achieve economic development, some important areas in which the PAP found justification for its social engineering agenda have been multiracialism, national identity and meritocracy. The government has sought to use housing, education and family policies to achieve its ends. Like Mao Zedong in China, Lee Kuan Yew sought to create a cultural revolution. However, Lee's revolution was not a proletarian but a bourgeois revolution. Rather than mobilizing the masses, Lee and the PAP worked to immobilize them.

Government policy was a key factor in the long-term changes taking place in Singapore during these years. Once in power, the PAP set about the task of carefully managing social development in Singapore. Gradually, all alternative paths or options were systematically eliminated. John Clammer has outlined the government's ideology as it grasped power. The first tenet of the system was the assertion of the overarching hegemony of the state in all areas of life. This was justified by the need for political stability in order to bring about economic growth. The goal of economic growth also required central planning and control. It was assumed that the people could not be trusted to make their own decisions. This paternalism pervaded the social order and was reproduced in the bureaucracy, education, public enterprises and community centers. It has been sustained by the provision of material rewards and technocracy, with the primary goods being economic in nature. Clammer described it as "quasi-Marxist materialism" (Clammer 1985: 160).

It is easy enough to account for this detailed management of society by looking at the PAP's ideology, which claims complete authority for the state. The more significant question is why does it work? John Clammer points out that in Singapore there are "no seriously contending alternatives" (*ibid.*: 159–60). It is clear from the course of Singapore's political development that virtually every social or political group that might have constituted an independent voice in Singapore was either co-opted, intimidated or eliminated during the first decade or so of PAP rule. Another factor that facilitated its success was that the government seems to have had a clear plan that took it a good part of the distance. Moreover, it is quite sensible to assume that many in Singapore supported the direction chosen for them by the government. Certainly, material wealth and physical comfort are hard to reject when the possible alternative is made to seem so negative.

The multiracial society

One of the key areas of Singapore's development that lent itself to control was the issue of multiracialism or multiculturalism. The stated goal of most political leaders and movements in postwar Singapore was "multiculturalism." This was a term that could have many meanings, but in the most general sense, it meant an attempt at creating a society that did not allow the issue of race to divide people and that tried to erase the heritage of colonial communalism. In 1945, Singapore was still a plural society. Malays, Indians and the "five kinds of Chinese" lived alongside English-educated Straits Chinese, Eurasians, Indians, Armenians, Jews and the English themselves. They all mixed, but as Furnivall has said, they did not mingle. By 1965, this aspect of Singapore had not changed very much.

Multiracialism, or multiculturalism, was still an aspiration. It represented an intention to change what was there and to create a society that did not pit people against one another because of skin color, religion, ethnic origin or culture. It was an ideal aimed at changing an unacceptable reality for a more desirable future social construct. For a generation that had lived through World War II, this seemed a commendable and necessary aim.

Given the history of race relations in Malaya and Singapore during and after the war, multiracialism seemed a sensible way to avoid racial conflict. For those who believed in democracy, it was a way to create a more equitable society. Finally, if Singapore was to be a viable nation-state, a national identity to which all citizens could subscribe seemed important. Social peace, stability and unity all depended on the creation of a truly multiracial society. This ideal also opened the way for social management.

There were also selfish reasons. The race/culture issue could also unite some of the people against others. It can thus be argued that some aimed to prevent domination of the society by "chauvinists," either Malay or Chinese. Most intellectuals, many among the wealthier elite, and many leaders were English-educated and thus belonged to that "deracinated" minority that Lee Kuan Yew so detested. It was, in fact, his own class. They were the ones who had been closest to the British, and they were the obvious successors. Despite the tenuous hold that they already had on power, both demography and geography were against them. The Chinese-educated outnumbered them, and in a democratic society where the majority ruled, the English-educated stood to lose. In addition to numbers, the Chinese-educated had been mobilized by a communist party that promoted a heady mix of Marxism, Maoism and Chinese nationalism.

On the other hand, around them was a "sea of Malays." The Malay states of the peninsula had already been separated administratively from Singapore by the British for the express purpose of preventing a "Chinese takeover." By the early 1950s, Malaya had come under the control of a clique of Malay aristocrats and administrators who held power on the basis of a racist mandate and who promised to uphold Malay privileges. They had formed a partnership with the clique of wealthy Chinese businessmen who ran the MCA. Both were interested in limiting the power of the Chinese working class of Malaya. On the other hand, there was also Indonesia, whose fervent nationalism and anti-colonialism often masked deeply held anti-Chinese feelings.

As Singapore moved toward independence and began to chart its own future, the battle for a multicultural society was fought out on a number of fronts, including language, education, housing, political organization, the economy and the government service. It was an issue that attracted a great deal of rhetoric from all sectors of the political spectrum. One of the first attempts to realize this goal was the move to give all four languages (English, Malay, Chinese, Tamil) equal status in the Singapore Legislative Assembly under David Marshall in 1955. At the same time, questions regarding the policy toward Chinese and English education were raised, as was the issue of Malayanization of the government service and the elimination of racial preferences that had favored Europeans.

Between 1955 and 1965, when Singapore aspired to merge with Malaya, Singapore's leaders, particularly those in the PAP, sought to promote multiculturalism as an alternative to the pro-Malay policies in the federation. All four languages were accepted as "official," and Malay was taken as the national language. Once outside of Malaysia, Singapore dropped Malay as the national language, but language policy has remained a highly political one.

As an excuse for the paternalistic management of society, the multiracial agenda justified the government's structuring of education, housing and the new identity to which all Singaporeans were expected to subscribe. At the same time, any attempts by members of a specific cultural community to gain consideration for themselves have been treated as expressions of chau-

vinism by the government. The possibility of racial violence or outside intervention, should the government's brand of multiracialism fail, was presented
as a constant threat to Singapore's "survival" and thus became an unchallengeable article of faith.

Sociologist Chua Beng Huat has analysed the government's strategy and
argued that the state has set itself as the "neutral" party above contending
groups, and it alone looks after the national or collective interest. In order to
avoid any existing cultural group, the state has embarked on a program of
"Asianization," which steers the national culture away from undesirable
Western, liberal impulses and at the same time rejects local cultural
constructs that the state does not already control (Chua 1995).

To a certain extent, the urge to recreate Singapore on the part of the
English-educated classes may be seen in relation to the crisis of the Straits
Chinese or Baba community. As noted in Chapter 3, Chua Ai Lin has docu-
mented the emergence of the English-educated domiciled community during
the period between 1920 and 1945 (Chua 2001). Jürgen Rudolph has called
attention to the consequent decline of the Straits Chinese or Baba community after the war. During the war, the Japanese, who did not distinguish the
English-educated Chinese, forced them together with the Chinese-educated,
and their unique status was lost. With the rise of communism among the
Chinese-educated and their increasing self-confidence in the anti-Japanese
resistance, the Babas found themselves scorned for their inability to speak
Chinese and for their loyalty to the British and the empire.

During the war, *nyonya* women, who were the upholders of domestic
Baba culture, were forced to labor outside the home. The maintenance of
ceremonies and Baba culture became too expensive and time-consuming.
There was a decline in the use of the Malay language, and "the once flourishing literary activities in Baba Malay came to a grinding halt and *wayang
peranakan* and *dondang sayang* were in a crisis. Thus, the most important
'Malay' aspect of the previous 'Baba identity' was indeed on the decline." At
the same time, relations with Malays deteriorated, and the latter became
more nationalistic and anti-British (Rudolph 1998: 408–9).

In the postwar years, ironically, the British again favored the "Queen's
Chinese" and the members of the Singapore Chinese Peranakan Association
(SCPA) as the "natural leaders" of the Chinese community. City councilors,
executive and legislative councilors, and the heads of the leading political
parties were mostly Babas. They were all conservative and not really in
touch with the masses. The Babas were thus isolated and went into a state of
shock, trying to be inconspicuous and hide their identity. Rudolph has
further noted:

> The second, usually ignored, turning point was marked by self-rule and
> the takeover by the PAP. Although leading members of the PAP such as
> Lee Kuan Yew, Dr. Toh Chin Chye and Dr. Goh Keng Swee were
> publicly described as English-educated "Babas," the Babas as a "group"

were openly belittled as "deculturalized." As a result, the Baba's influence as a group further declined in every respect.

(*ibid.*: 410)

With the PAP victory, the SCPA and its affiliates or successors became politically impotent and so turned apolitical and just tried to preserve the heritage. Heavy stress was placed on the political correctness of "Chineseness," which led to radical changes in Baba culture in the 1960s and 1970s. The era saw increasing intermarriage with other Chinese and a decline in the demographic concentration of Babas. There was also an abandonment of family ceremonies, and many Babas embraced Christianity, especially Catholicism. Women stopped wearing the *sarong kebaya*, and there was a simplification of cuisine (*ibid.*: 411).

If the rise in the importance of "Chineseness" helped to undermine the Baba community, that stress upon Chinese identity also came under attack from the government. The so-called Chinese "chauvinists" who promoted Chinese education and culture, who expressed admiration for the People's Republic of China and who defended the use of Chinese were criticized by the PAP and accused of attempting to intimidate the other races of Singapore.

The Chinese-educated were associated with the masses. They were generally more left-wing, and they made up the ranks of the Chinese student unions and labor unions. They were the bulk of the working class, but they also had important sympathizers among the wealthiest individuals in the city, including rubber barons such as Tan Lark Sye and Lee Kong Chian. They had a powerful voice in the Chinese press and a prestigious intellectual center in Nanyang University, the only Chinese-medium university outside China. As a social group, they represented an active cultural movement in the immediate postwar years, publishing books, short stories, poems and their own magazines as well exercising a powerful political and social force (Han 1964). They represented a major threat to PAP dominance after 1963 and became the target of severe restrictions in the ensuing years.

The Malays of Singapore represented yet another cultural threat to the English-educated leaders of the PAP. Their links to Malays in the federation made them suspect as citizens. Even today, Malays are rarely taken into the Singapore military, and when they are, they rarely become officers; nor do they occupy any strategically important role in national defense. However, they had to be treated with a certain care. If they were too badly mistreated and discriminated against, some in the federation might spring to their defense. On the other hand, too enthusiastic support would alienate many Chinese. Even though the Malays were the most disadvantaged economically, there were also many Chinese who were no better off. Expressions of discontent by those at the bottom of Singapore's socio-economic pyramid have been treated by the government as the "politics of envy," and thus all expressions of protest have been delegitimized.

While these efforts have brought social stability, there has been a clear lack of commitment to the hybrid identity promoted by the government. Given the failure, in recent years, of multiethnic states such as Yugoslavia and the Soviet Union, the leaders of Singapore are conscious that their goal of creating a successful cultural revolution is as yet unachieved.

The management of living spaces

Housing was one of the key areas where the process of managed social change was most clearly visible. The handling of the housing problem has been seen as one of Singapore's great success stories. Within less than two decades, over a million people have been moved out of substandard housing and into new, clean and convenient high-rise flats, many of which they now own. Living standards and quality of life have been markedly improved.

Figure 5.1 A young Chinese family at dinner in Singapore, 1948.

During the late 1940s and through the 1950s, the housing shortage was seen as a key problem area in Singapore. It was considered to be in a state of crisis. With a population of just over a million and most of them below the age of 15, Singapore faced a major challenge to its basic infrastructure. While the colonial government had begun to address the housing problem, it was not until independence that a solution seemed possible. Rehousing the population also provided an opportunity for the government to begin managing the people in ways never before imagined.

The housing issue was the focus of a number of important sociological studies done in the colonial period. One very extensive study was done in 1918 and another in 1947 and a third in 1953–54 (Singapore 1918; Department of Social Welfare 1947, 1958). Another study was done by Barrington Kaye, a social research fellow at the University of Malaya in 1954–55, which has been published as *Upper Nankin Street Singapore: A Sociological Study of Chinese Households Living in a Densely Populated Area* (Kaye 1960). All these studies show that Singapore had faced a severe housing shortage, at least in the Chinatown area, for at least half a century. Brenda Yeoh has cited the 1918 study, pointing out that, in the years 1906–17, "Block densities varied between 635 and 1,304 persons per acre while house densities ranged from 18.7 to 44.5 persons per house" (Yeoh 1996:138) Kaye found similar densities when he surveyed Upper Nankin Street in 1954. At that time, 1,814 people lived in the one-block street, and overall population densities in Singapore's Chinatown were close to 450,000 persons per square mile in some districts (Kaye 1960: 2).

While the urban areas of Singapore were crowded, at least they had the benefits of running water, electricity, sewerage, garbage collection and public transportation, however inadequate. Another large portion of the Asian population lived scattered around the island in the *kampongs*. Many of these had only limited supplies of running water and electricity, no sanitation facilities, poor transportation links and few of the other amenities of urban life. There were few shops, not many schools and little in the way of medical facilities, and it was difficult for these people to commute to their places of employment. They were also seen as breeding grounds for crime, and secret society or Communist Party organization. Beyond this, Singapore's population growth rate in 1957 was 5.4 percent, and even though this declined quite significantly in subsequent years, the overall population increased from 1.4 million in 1957 to nearly 2.3 million in 1976 (Varma 1969: 135).

From 1960 onwards, the government undertook a vigorous program of public housing construction. By 1977, the Housing Development Board (HDB) had built 235,000 high-rise flats and had accommodated 51 percent of the population; by 1989, an additional 600,000 flats had been built and virtually the entire population had been housed (Tai and Chen 1977: 4). At first, housing was low-cost and consisted of three- or four-room flats. Later they were constructed with five rooms. The government then started the

Housing and Union Development Company (HUDC) and began to construct middle-income housing, while private developers began to build luxury flats for the more affluent.

In 1989, S. Dhanabalan, the minister for National Development, spoke of the accomplishments of the housing program and outlined the government's

Figure 5.2 Disappearing Chinatown. New shopping centres and shophouses ready to be torn down, *circa* 1990.

policy on achieving multiracial communities through housing. He pointed with pride to the achievement of building "whole new communities, based on social and racial integration." The creation of HDB estates had enabled the government to mix the population, breaking up the old racial enclaves in the *kampongs* and urban neighbourhoods that had characterized Singapore before independence (Dhanabalan 1989). Now Malays and Indians lived together with Chinese in multistory apartment blocks. So far as appearances were concerned, the plural society was gone.

This project in social engineering was not an unqualified success. There were still lingering pockets of dissatisfaction. As early as 1977, sociologists were starting to calculate the pluses and minuses of the HDB project:

> In general, HDB residents feel that they are provided with good recreational facilities, good commercial and community services, adequate play facilities for children, convenient public transportation and other infrastructure facilities, but they are usually annoyed by noise pollution, poor social environment and crowding. There are also lack of mutual assistance from neighbours, weak public security in the neighbourhood, lack of a strong sense of belonging to the community, little neighbourliness and weak primary group contacts. Although kampong and rural people face problems of poor transportation facilities, inadequate drainage facilities, unhealthy environment and inadequate public utility facilities, they enjoy, however, close community ties, good neighbourhood relationship, close attachment to the community, strong familial ties and primary group contacts.
>
> (Wang 1995)

During the next decade, the government failed to deal with this negative aspect of HDB housing. By 1989, Dhanabalan warned of new and disturbing trends: "which, if left unchecked would undermine our efforts to foster social and racial integration." He observed that people were moving back into racial enclaves in search of that sense of community that continued to be lacking in the world the PAP had made. Malays were moving to Bedok and Tampines, while Chinese were attempting to find flats in Ang Mo Kio and Hougang.

With people now purchasing their own flats and the appearance of a growing resale market for flats, this tendency to regroup along racial lines was gathering momentum. There were now neighbourhoods in Bedok/Tampines that were more than 30 percent Malay, and areas of Hougang New Town where Chinese households constituted 90 percent of the population. In a speech to community leaders, Dhanabalan told them: "We cannot allow this to go on. We must introduce open and clear policies that will prevent such concentrations from developing." He went on to outline practical steps that leaders could take to implement the policy and laid out the thrust of the government's general policy:

A balanced racial and social mix in practically every constituency today has helped us to avoid social tensions. It leads to harmonious living and better understanding among the races. This policy is necessary for the long-term stability of our nation.

(Dhanabalan 1989: 6)

However, people had seen the future, and they did not really like it. There has been a quiet but inexorable resistance to government efforts to engineer its own version of community.

The government seems to have been less concerned about the appearance of *de facto* segregation by socio-economic level. Luxury and middle-class housing areas have not been located in the same areas as the HDB flats. Rather, they are in preferred areas, such as closer to the sea, possessing a view and closer to better facilities. If segregation by race had ended, segregation by class and income had become more pronounced.

Singapore's new middle class

While the debate over multiculturalism progressed, there were also other fundamental changes at work in society and the political and economic orders that were inexorably altering the very ground upon which the discourse was based. Government policy and economic change had significantly changed society. By the mid-1980s, Singapore had been transformed from an Asian port city of coolies and *taukehs* to a global metropolis inhabited by an affluent middle class and a fully industrialized and reasonably well-paid working class. This development brought new and unforeseen changes.

Economic development, industrialization and the placing of 86 percent of the population in some form of subsidized housing by the end of the 1980s had created a society that saw itself as middle-class, and one that moreover considered itself upwardly mobile. Singaporeans eagerly embraced the material prosperity that the PAP promised. Parents hoped to provide their children with better education as this was seen as the path to greater success. People also had money to spend on consumer appliances, hobbies, sports and vacations. Even though most could not afford to own automobiles, many were able to purchase them, and Singapore became laced with broad freeways, parking lots and even some bedroom suburbs (Federal Research Division 1989). To check this trend, the government made car ownership in Singapore one of the most heavily taxed and restricted activities of any country in the world, but people continued to find ways to acquire this precious item of status and convenience.

Part of the new prosperity was brought about by the entry of more and more women into the workforce. In 1970, only 24.6 percent of women worked outside the home, but by 1988 this number had risen to 48 percent. At the same time, 79 percent of Singapore's men were employed. For all Singaporeans, the employment situation had seen a dramatic improvement from the 1960s, when the country faced a 10 percent unemployment rate. However, the resulting prosperity and the trend toward nuclear families left a gap on the home front.

There was a need for a group of workers to undertake the domestic tasks left by Singaporeans entering the job market. In 1978, the government issued the first work permits for a limited number of foreign maids to be recruited from Thailand, Sri Lanka and the Philippines. It took ten years for the number to rise to 20,000, but the number reached 40,000 by the end of 1988. By 1999, there were 100,000 foreign maids in Singapore, three-quarters of whom were from the Philippines, or one maid for every eight households (Yeoh *et al.* 1999). These women are not protected by the Employment Act because the government treats them as working under private contracts between maid and employer and thus leaves wages and conditions to the "free market," a situation that disadvantages most maids.

With the industrialization of Singapore's workforce, many other foreign workers came in to fill sectors of the economy no longer favored by locals. By 1997, there were 560,000 foreigners in Singapore, making up nearly 30 percent of the workforce of 1.8 million. Among the men, one of the largest groups was Thais working in the construction industry. Despite the fact that many of these workers are protected by government legislation, their temporary status and general ignorance of local conditions "creates a pool of low cost, compliant labor" (*ibid.*).

The distinction in the domestic population now recognized by the government is one made by Prime Minister Goh Chok Tong in 1999, between "cosmopolitans" and "heartlanders." The former are the English-speaking and university-educated, upwardly mobile professionals, while the latter are parochial dialect speakers living in HDB flats (Low 2001).

This growing gap between the elite of the population, who are comfortable in the globalized world, and "Ah Beng" and "Ah Lian," and "Mat" and "Minah" (pejorative terms for the Chinese and Malay everyman and woman of Singapore) is a troubling one for the government (Chua 2003: 92). Much of the dissatisfaction shown in elections during the 1980s and 1990s actually came from the latter groups. Many of these feel left behind in the new wave of managed elitism that is driving Singapore into the knowledge-based economy. Even more worrying is the general lack of loyalty from the former group. A significant number of these, once having amassed a sufficient nest-egg, grow bored with "living in the sixth form" and cash in their luxury flats or terrace houses and move to Australia or Canada. By the 1990s, each year 4,000 to 5,000 families were leaving Singapore.

The management of education

The educational project of the PAP has made long , slow and sometimes faltering progress. The main issue in 1959 was the deep division between the English-educated and the Chinese-educated and the ambiguous political stances of the two groups. On the one hand, the English-educated included people (like Lee Kuan Yew) who were of Chinese ancestry and who felt themselves at something of a disadvantage in a society where the Chinese-educated outnumbered them by such an enormous margin. Even less secure were those Indians, Eurasians and others of the English-educated who saw themselves as an endangered minority among the Chinese. Nonetheless, these were the people with the skills and ideas who dominated the state, both as bureaucrats and as politicians. They made up the right wing of the PAP. They included Goh Keng Swee, Toh Chin Chye and others like Rajaratnam. Even though they were "his" people, as a group Lee Kuan Yew saw them as "rootless" and "without foundation." His criticisms of individuals like Jamit Singh, the dockyard labor leader, exemplify this attitude.

> You know, every time I think of people whom I have met and known as friends in school or in college, I think of those who become decultur-alised too quickly. I had a friend who was a Sikh. He threw his past away: he shaved his beard: he threw away his turban: he had a haircut. No harm at all. But, something happened to him and in next to no time, he was doing foolish things. He lost his anchorage. You know, it gets very difficult for a ship without an anchor in a harbour when it gets stormy.
>
> (Liew 2003)

On the other hand, there were the Chinese-educated. They made up the majority among all groups in Singapore. Despite dialect differences, they all had Mandarin in common. They were thus all oriented more toward China than to the West. They were led by different union and student firebrands like Lim Chin Siong and Fong Swee Suan, who spoke to their hearts. The power of such individuals was the major threat to Lee and the English-

Table 5.1 Numbers of Chinese- and English-medium schools and students in Singapore, 1947–55.

Year	Chinese		English	
	Schools	*Students*	*Schools*	*Students*
1947	154	53,478	70	28,840
1948	184	58,096	85	33,214
1949	271	68,434	102	37,655
1950	287	76,200	120	49,676
1951	288	75,974	139	54,812
1952	279	74,104	150	63,271
1953	273	79,272	276	71,297
1954	277	81,605	204	84,418
1955	277	94,244	239	96,658

Source: Compiled from annual reports of the Department of Education (Yong 1992: 93).

educated leaders around him. In addition, there were the *taukehs* represented by the SCCCI, which in 1959 controlled about 30 percent of
Singapore's economy. They dominated the Chinese economy of Singapore,
and it was this group that supported the Chinese-medium school system.

In the years immediately following the war, the Chinese-medium schools
were the most numerous in Singapore and taught the largest number of
students. By 1950, however, it was clear that the number of English-medium
schools was increasing at a faster rate, and by 1954 there were more students
enrolled in English-medium schools than in Chinese (see Table 5.1). The
persistent decline in Chinese education was a disturbing trend for those in
the Chinese-educated community, and the issue of preserving Chinese education was one of the major political questions of the 1950s and early 1960s.

The policies of the PAP after 1959 did little to allay the fears of the
Chinese-educated. Seeing them as both political and cultural threats, govern-
mental policy worked to systematically undercut Chinese education as it then
existed. Despite a strong emotional attachment to the Mandarin-language
schools, most Singaporeans understood that graduates of English-medium
schools simply possessed greater opportunities for jobs and further education. When Singapore left Malaysia in 1965, children were given the option of
attending school in the language of their choice: English, Mandarin, Malay
or Tamil. As it turned out, there was a strong tendency to choose English,
and enrollments in Chinese-medium schools began to drop quite sharply.

By 1959, there were already more Singaporeans enrolling their children in
English-medium schools than in Chinese. Within less than a decade, enrollments had dropped from just under half to only one-third, and by the end of
the second decade of PAP rule, annual enrollment in Chinese primary
schools had dropped to just over 11 percent of the total, while enrollment in
English-medium schools was at nearly 80 percent (see Table 5.2).

Table 5.2 Primary school registrations in Singapore, 1959–78.

Year	English stream	Chinese stream	Chinese as percentage of total *
1959	28,113	27,223	45.9
1962	31,580	22,669	38.4
1965	36,269	17,735	30.0
1968	34,090	18,927	33.6
1971	37,505	15,731	29.0
1974	36,834	10,263	21.7
1975	35,086	9,112	20.5
1976	35,035	7,478	17.5
1977	40,622	6,590	13.9
1978	41,995	5,289	11.2

Source: Goh (1978: 1–1).

Note: * Total includes Malay and Tamil streams.

There were powerful groups in Singapore's society that needed to be neutralized if the government's control of education was to succeed. On the one hand, there were the students themselves. Since the 1950s, Chinese students had organized student unions that were said to be controlled or at least influenced by the MCP (Singapore Legislative Assembly 1956). During the 1950s and early 1960s, they were an important political force, as they supported or opposed various political contenders. They were powerful auxiliaries for the labor unions, particularly during strikes such as the Hock Lee bus strike in 1955. Prior to 1959, they had been strong supporters of the PAP. Once in power, the party moved to reduce their influence and used the Emergency Powers of the ISA, the power of deportation, and the repatriation (of Malaysians) to break the power of the Singapore Chinese Middle School Student Union (SCMSSU) and the unions of high school and university students. At the same time, wider social and economic forces worked to reduce the numbers and influence of the Chinese schools; these trends were strengthened by government policies.

The other group that stood in the government's path was the SCCC. The Chinese Chamber of Commerce represented the major funding and controlling body for Chinese education. Chinese schools had been founded, supported and governed by the Chinese merchants of Singapore. The SCCC saw the schools as its pet cultural project. and its members felt that as representatives of the Chinese business community, a large part of their prestige in the community was based on their patronage of the schools and on their support for Chinese cultural and charitable projects in general.

Despite the contradictions of their class and economic aspirations, the students and the *taukehs* were often allied against the colonial government in their defense of Chinese education. There were, in fact, a number of truly left-leaning businessmen, such as Tan Kah Kee, Lee Kong Chian and the founder of Nanyang University, Tan Lark Sye. Together the chamber and the students were a formidable political and social force linking youth and organization with wealth and respectability. It was against groups such as these that the charge of "chauvinism" was most often leveled.

As Visscher has shown, the PAP had courted the SCCC during the vote for its Malaysia plan and against the Barisan and others. They proved instrumental in getting out the Chinese-educated vote for the PAP plan. Once in Malaysia, however, Chinese businessmen were among those affected most negatively by Malaysian economic policies. In the years following separation from Malaysia, the PAP government was increasingly critical of the SCCC and its successor, the SCCCI (the Singapore Chinese Chamber of Commerce and Industry). In addition to its charges of chauvinism, the government saw no place for the small and medium-sized Chinese family businessmen, who made up the vast majority of SCCCI members, in their economic plans (Chapter 6); nor was it happy to allow the *taukehs* to exercise influence over Singapore's social and political development. The government first worked to undercut the power of school committees and later muscled the SCCCI, as a group, out of its longstanding position as upholder of Chinese culture (Visscher 2002).

From 1968, the government attempted to maintain a bilingual program in which students in each of the four streams would also study one of the other three languages as a foreign language. By 1978, it was recognized that this policy was not working. The Ministry of Education discovered that over 60 percent of students who sat the primary school-leaving exams and O-level exams failed in one or both languages. In particular, facility in English was found to be lacking, even in the English-medium schools, to say nothing of the Chinese schools. To make matters even more critical, in 1978, the government decided to shift Nanyang University to an English-medium curriculum. This meant that there was no tertiary alternative in Singapore for students graduating from Chinese-medium secondary schools.

For many, this was not a significant issue, since it was also discovered that fairly large numbers of students did not even finish primary school. In a study done by the government, only 71 percent of a Primary I cohort actually reached secondary school. This compared unfavourably with 92 percent in Taiwan and 100 percent in Japan. Only 9 percent of the cohort in Singapore reached university, compared with 20 percent in Taiwan and 38 percent in Japan (Goh 1978: 1–3). These rather depressing findings led to one of the first major reforms of the educational system: the introduction of a streaming system that would be structured around a battery of examinations. (*ibid.*: 4–6).

The language policy was adjusted so that students would be required to choose their "mother tongue" as a second language if they were in an English-medium school. Otherwise, they were required to enroll in a school taught in their "mother tongue" and to study English as a second language. While Malay was the mother tongue of most Malays, Tamil was not the mother tongue of all Indians, and Mandarin was not the true mother tongue of anyone in Singapore. These changes have remained features of Singapore's educational system to the present.

Lee Kuan Yew's belief that Singapore should be a meritocracy saw greater stress on testing regimes. Those Singaporeans who hoped to advance their children's career prospects had to embrace these opportunities, regardless of the conditions imposed by the government. The limited number of places in tertiary institutes meant that competition for places in the National University of Singapore (there was only one) was extremely fierce. Even by the beginning of the twenty-first century, when there were more universities,[39] successful entrance was still open only to those who had run the gauntlet of IQ, achievement and suitability tests that screened and streamed the students throughout their academic careers. By 2000, it was necessary for a toddler to enter the right preschool, so that they could be prepared for kindergarten, gain entrance into the right primary school and thereby qualify for the best secondary school.

Ironically, or so it has seemed to outsiders, the sorry state of Chinese education at the end of the 1970s was the occasion for the government to introduce the "Speak Mandarin" program. This was part of the "Asianization" project of the PAP and was partly aimed at counteracting the "liberal ideas" that were imbibed with Western culture. The project was also intended to help to restore some "cultural ballast" to those being educated in English. The fact that not all Asians in Singapore were Chinese was at times lost on the government. There was also an opportunistic element in the new stress on Chinese. That was in the reforms then beginning in the PRC with the rise of Deng Xiaoping and China's opening to the West.

These government programs have not always been fully successful. Attempts by the government to suppress the use of "dialects" (e.g. Hokkien, Teochew, Cantonese, Hainanese, Hakka) during the 1980s have been without much success. An attempt in the early 1980s to force people to stop transliterating their names according to their dialect, which is the common practice in Singapore, failed miserably. When the Department of Education required parents to transliterate their children's names according to the Mandarin pronunciation in *hanyu pinyin*, the parents simply refused.

The "Speak Mandarin" campaign and other cultural policies that followed it suggest that a definite bias has developed in the Singapore government's definition of multiracialism. The weight of numbers and the inherent prejudices of the rulers are beginning to show through. Michael Barr has suggested that this has been a fundamental leaning in Lee Kuan Yew's personality from the beginning (Barr 2000). In a more recent study of kindergarten and primary education, Barr and Low have noted a number of policies at this level of the educational system that put Malays at a disadvantage (Barr and Low 2005). A more general critique of the manner in which the system has impacted on Malays has been presented by Lily Rahim (Rahim 1998).

It is difficult to tell at this point, but there seem to be signs that Singapore is once again responding to the call of China. The opening up of China in the past few decades has been an important economic boost for Singapore, as well as the other countries of Southeast Asia. Singapore's rulers have carefully sought to realign their country to take best advantage of China's growing wealth and influence by urging businessmen to seek opportunities in China (see Chapter 6) and by encouraging the migration of selected individuals from the "homeland."

At the same time, the popularity of East Asian popular culture in Singapore shows that it is not only the government that is interested in Asian culture. One may question whether Japanese *manga* recycled through Taiwan and Hong Kong, Cantopop and bronze-colored hair are exactly what Lee Kuan Yew had in mind. Nonetheless, their popularity seems to have seen a rising level of Chinese literacy among Singapore's young people.[40]

On the other hand, some of Singapore's television producers and dramatists are beginning to speak in their own argot, again somewhat to the dismay of the keepers of public propriety. The growing stature of "Singlish," the local patois of English mixed with Malay and Hokkien terms and often presented in indigenous grammatical patterns, is another source of concern to the government, which is as opposed to Singlish as it is to the other Chinese languages commonly spoken in Singapore (Chua 2003: 92–4). Despite this critical attitude, a number of television sitcoms (e.g. "Phua Chu Kang") that rely on a Singlish discourse have proved so popular that the government has been reluctant to forbid them.

The managed society

One of the areas that seemed most pressing in the early days of Singapore's independence, and one that offered considerable latitude for social control, was in the area of population. Singapore's high unemployment, overcrowded housing and limited resources all seemed to point to an impending crisis in the early 1960s. Between 1947 and 1957, the rate of population increase was 4.4 percent, 3.4 percent of which was the result of natural increase. This marked a radical change in the context of Singapore's earlier demographic history. From a city of migrants, Singapore had become a country to which migration virtually stopped. For the next two decades, the population continued to increase, albeit at a slower rate, and migration was reduced even further. In 1947, 56 percent of the population had been born in Singapore, but by 1980, over 85 percent of its citizens were locally born (Federal Research Division 1989: 71–2).

Singapore had become a city of families. While the government was adept at providing jobs, housing, education and health care for its population, it also realized that rapid population growth now constituted a threat to those living standards. As a result, from 1965, it embarked on a vigorous policy of population control. A Family Planning and Population Board was established, and abortion and voluntary sterilization were legalized.[41] To further check population growth in the 1970s, a set of disincentives was put in place. These included raising the costs of bearing a third or fourth child. There was no maternity leave for civil servants who had a third child: hospitals charged higher fees for third and fourth children; there were no income tax deductions for additional children; and there was no consideration for larger public housing accommodation. For those who followed the government's injunctions to "stop at two," it was easier to gain access to better primary schools, and there were further incentives for those accepted voluntary sterilization (*ibid.*: 73–4).

The history of the population control project serves as an interesting example of the Singapore government's impulse to manage society. Beginning in the 1960s with the aim of averting the strain on limited resources that would result from excess population, the PAP was successful in putting together a multifaceted program. In addition to the system of incentives and disincentives, there was an intensive advertising and propaganda campaign. Such campaigns are typical of the Singapore style, and almost every major government initiative is accompanied by billboards, radio and TV ads and programs, speeches by public officials, posters, and the mobilization of civil servants, party officials and the various community centers.

The population control program succeeded quite rapidly. By 1975, the growth rate had fallen to 1.006 percent, which is seen as the replacement rate, while the overall population had risen to about 2.4 million. The rate of increase then proceeded to decline even further and went into negative territory. At the same time, Singapore's demographic transition was accompanied by increases in income, women's participation in the workforce, and better nutrition and health. Women married later, and families were smaller. These were typical phenomena of the transition to a developed industrial society.

The decline in birth rates was not evenly spread across the population. Poorer and less-educated women continued to marry earlier and to have larger families. This development was seen as a threat to the long-term welfare of society. Lee Kuan Yew firmly believed in the need for the existing population to produce an elite to administer the country in the future. He claimed that Singapore had developed so rapidly because it had possessed "an extra thick layer of high-caliber and trained talent." However, the problem for the future was that with the declining birth rate it might not be possible to produce enough high-caliber minds to govern the country. Michael Barr has quoted a telling speech in which Lee set forth his rationale for his eugenics program.

> We must be grateful that the talent profile, or IQ spread, of our population enables us to produce, from a yearly birth rate, in the 1950s and 1960s, of 60,000 to 50,000, or about 50–60 first class minds, an average rate of 1 in 1,000. Alas, not all of these bright minds have strong characters, sound temperament, and the high motivation to match their high intelligence. I have found, from studying PSC [Primary School Certificate] scholarship awards for the last 15 years, and reading confidential reports on their work in the public service and the SAF [Singapore Armed Forces], that the scholars who also have the right character and personality, effectively works out to 1 in 3,000 persons. In the 1970s, our annual births went down to 40,000. The number of talented and balanced Singaporeans will be between 12–14 persons per annum at one per 3,000.
>
> (Barr 2000: 122)

According to Barr, Lee's concerns were sparked by the 1980 census, which showed that better-educated women were having fewer children or (worse) not marrying at all. On the other hand, poorly educated women were having more children:

> If we continue to reproduce ourselves in this lop-sided way, we will be unable to maintain our present standards. Levels of competence will

decline. Our economy will falter; administration will suffer; and society will decline. For how can we avoid lowering performance when for every two graduates (with some exaggeration to make the point) in twenty-five years' time there will be one graduate, and for every two uneducated workers, there will be three?

(*ibid.*: 123)

These remarks sparked the "Great Marriage Debate" and led to the formation of a unique Singapore institution – the Social Development Unit. This was a special agency set up to lift the birth rate of university graduates. It organized "seminars," which were weekend retreat-style gatherings of marriageable graduates. There were equal numbers of men and women, and they were encouraged to meet and mix. There were also dancing classes, and instruction in table manners and basic social skills. These events were overseen by facilitators, who worked actively as matchmakers. The aim was to promote an increased number of marriages between university graduates. Barr observed:

Lee's views on the genetic nature of talent have led him to approach his self-appointed task of elite-building from an extremely blinkered and idiosyncratic perspective. Once it is accepted that talent is inherited from one's parents, and that no amount of education or nurture will lift the proletariat into the ranks of the elite, then it makes no sense to expect the sons and daughter of the "broad base" to do more than master the technical skills needed to be productive, work hard and learn not to "spit all over the place."

(*ibid.*)

The problem for Singapore may be that it will continue to be a large classroom to improve the behaviour of the Asian lower classes. The demographic changes of the past twenty-five years have seen a new migration into Singapore. The arrival of tens of thousands of Filipina, Indonesian and South Asian domestic servants is only one aspect of the current situation. Singaporeans now prefer to let foreign contract laborers do the low-skilled jobs, particularly construction work. These jobs are now filled by Thais, Indonesians and Indians. Singaporeans can occupy themselves with steady jobs in factories and offices with regular hours and the usual benefits and protections.

The government has, with the exception of the maids, generally favored this development, since it is possible simply to send these laborers home when there is no work for them. Until recently, it seemed like a perfect solution. The dirty jobs got done, and when they were finished the idle workers were not a burden on the public purse. Because they were on contracts with private companies, usually based in their home countries, no Singapore-based companies need take responsibility for them. They slept on the building sites, provided their own food and moved with the work. Because of the language and cultural barriers, they have been slow to take advantage of the few rights they do have. Thus they have often been exploited.

Few Singaporeans have worried about the welfare of these individuals, seeing them as birds of passage. However, they are having an impact on the social scene, and it remains to be seen whether they will continue to be a disposable workforce. Already, certain sections of town are becoming "little Bangkoks" or "little Manilas," with shops that rent Thai or Filipino videos, sell food, book travel, send money, sell phone cards and provide a whole range of services for these sojourners. Areas such as these have become major gathering places for these individuals on their days off. On any Sunday, one can find crowds of maids and laborers in the shopping malls, parks, public spaces around MRT stations, bus stations, churches and other places where they gather. Many Singaporeans find these gatherings objectionable and complain about the possibility of violence, litter, congestion and inconvenience.

Government control of housing and other basic facilities has prevented the establishment of permanent communities of these foreigners in Singapore itself, but one wonders whether these policies can be successful over the long run. It seems that the government has already understood the fact that migration from surrounding areas will persist into the foreseeable future, thus new immigration policies have been put into place. Singapore has been encouraging the immigration of Chinese since the 1980s under a variety of circumstances. At first, it was only migrants from Hong Kong and Taiwan who were relatively affluent or who possessed high-level educational qualifications who were welcomed. More recently, a wider variety of migrants have been coming from the PRC under very attractive conditions. These include a number of "silent" movements, such as Chinese students coming to study in Singapore's universities and high schools. Not only do they provide extra income, but the mothers of school students are also allowed to accompany them and are permitted to seek jobs and are eligible for HDB housing.

Conclusion

Singapore's society has been radically reshaped over the past half-century. The city once possessed a chaotic social order characterized by sharp distinctions between ethnic groups, dominated by a colonial power, and marked by extremes of poverty and wealth. This has been transformed into a well-ordered, affluent, middle-class metropolis. The dirt, crime and slums have been replaced by carefully landscaped parks and green areas, safe streets, and well-kept high-rise blocks and suburbs.

The social engineering of ethnicity has seemingly ended the tendency of racial strife that seemed immanent in the 1960s. People speaking a variety of languages and practising the entire range of religions and cultures live together in harmony. On the other hand, there are ripples of disquiet.

Despite the best planning, there is the tendency for people to resist the "mixing" that has taken place in HDB housing, and to regroup with their families and co-religionists and ethnic brothers and sisters. One is reminded of the failures of other forced deculturalization projects in places like the former USSR and Yugoslavia. Racial and ethnic groups do change over time, but it is not clear that such "management of ethnicity," as Raj Vasil has termed it, can have a permanent impact. Given the government's tacit preference for new Chinese migrants and the pro-Chinese slant in education and other social policies, not all citizens see the state as totally objective.

The government's meritocracy policy has created a diligent and flexible workforce. The educational system is producing intelligent and highly qualified employees, and the state has been able to ensure a supply of skilled managers for its own enterprises. The dynamism of Singapore is unmistakable evidence of its competitive spirit and will to succeed. On the other hand, the same policies have produced a society that is materialistic and unpleasantly aggressive, or *kiasu*. One may also wonder whether these qualities were already there and only needed some room to grow. It is growth that may be the problem.

While it is clear that the government has been able to pilot Singapore's society through the first and perhaps the second transitions through industrialization and into the knowledge economy, one may wonder about the next move. Singapore has been going through a period of sustained growth for the past four decades. What will happen when that growth slows? Population growth has slowed, and with it, the growth of what Lee Kuan

Figure 5.3 One of Singapore's many housing estates: Holland Road, 1990.

Yew has seen as the most important element of society. Will his dire predictions of genetic degradation be proved valid? Even more disturbing is that a number of the talented and successful have chosen, at the most productive period of their lives, to pick up and leave Singapore.

One unfavourable side-effect of the government's careful management of society has been the stifling of initiative. In the economic sphere, government has come to see the need to foster entrepreneurship, which, it seems, must come from small and medium-sized enterprises, such as the traditional Chinese businesses. At the same time, however, intellectual and artistic creativity have been stifled by censorship, lawsuits, hectoring, arrests and a careful policing of "out-of-bounds markers" (or "OB markers," as they are popularly known). Naturally, vehement and telling criticism of the government is one of the no-go zones of public discourse in Singapore.

Chua Beng Huat has pointed to yet another problematic area of Singapore's social development. He has called attention to the growing gap between the rich and poor. The Asian economic miracle and very generous salary scales for top-level government and corporate administrators has created a class of very affluent citizens. They live in private housing, drive their own cars and send their children to the top schools and often to universities in the USA, the UK and Australia. They employ Filipina or Indonesian maids and live in a permanently air-conditioned world. They are the cosmopolitans. Those who call attention to the differences between these affluent few and the "heartlanders," the many who live in public housing and rely on public transportation, are accused of encouraging the "politics of envy" (Chua and Tan 1999).

For the time being, according to Chua, many in the working class aspire to this middle-class standard. They have seen their own family members and acquaintances benefit from the social mobility of Singapore's era of prosperity, and they still feel that such dreams are not out of their reach. Singapore has no entrenched working-class culture, but this too could develop. The question for the future is whether it will be possible to maintain a similar level of prosperity to meet these ever-rising expectations.

Finally, there is the question of immigration. The twentieth century has seen Singapore experience a wave of large-scale immigration, followed by a decline to the point of virtual standstill in the years between 1930 and 1980. Since then, immigration has once again picked up; as Singapore's working class has moved up into the middle class, it has created a vacuum at the bottom, bringing in yet another wave of hungry members of the Asian proletariat as well as a smaller group of highly skilled cosmopolitan specialists, few of whom have any commitment to the "nation" of Singapore. Will it be possible to continue to treat these guest workers as a permanently disposable underclass, or will they too be able to demand a secure piece of Singapore's prosperity?

6 Singapore's economic transformation

The major shift in Singapore's economy during the first decades of independence was the creation and growth of a manufacturing industrial sector. Economically, this meant a de-emphasis and a shift away from trading. The turbulent postwar years of global boom and recession and local labor activism and unemployment had left a difficult situation for the government of independent Singapore. Between 1965 and 1975, the PAP formed an alliance with international corporate capitalism to create a booming manufacturing industry that gave Singaporeans full employment and domestic prosperity.

The government could exercise almost complete control over most features of the domestic economy, although the security of links to the global economy naturally remained beyond its grasp. Singapore was thus subject to the vagaries of the world market and the fluctuations of international business cycles. And these ups and downs became not only bumps on the road to Singapore's development but also opportunities for reflection and readjustment by Singapore's economic planners. Their continued success has given Singapore's leadership not only greater credibility in providing material wealth but also more extensive control over the economy.

Singapore's first spurt of growth came to an end with the recession of 1985. After a re-examination of Singapore's changed economic situation, it was decided to take the next step up the economic ladder and to move out of manufacturing industries that depended on cheap labor. At this point, it was discovered that there was a place in the grand plan for small and medium-sized enterprises (SMEs) such as the Chinese family firms. Also, the orientation of Singapore's economy began to shift toward the new opportunities presented by the PRC. Singapore also began to seek ways in which to upgrade the skill level of its workforce.

These reforms were followed by another decade of renewed growth, which saw considerable investment in the economic developments taking place in Malaysia, Indonesia and Thailand. This wave of expansion suffered an abrupt jolt with the currency crisis that hit the developing economies of Southeast Asia in 1997. The simultaneous collapse of the Indonesian rupiah, Thai baht, Philippines peso and Malaysian ringgit was a severe blow to Singapore, whose banks had large holdings in those currencies. After some retrenchment and further belt tightening, Singapore was able to struggle back toward former levels of prosperity, but then it was hit by the same blows as the rest of the world when Muslim terrorists struck on 11 September 2001. This was followed by the severe acute respiratory syndrome (SARS) crisis in 2003, which almost brought Singapore's tourist industry to a halt.

Today, Singapore is once again at a major economic transition point. One global crisis seems to follow another in rapid succession. At the same time, the alliance with international capital and the neoliberal agenda of the World Trade Organization are placing additional demands on the structure of Singapore's political economy. Domestically, the government's hold on power has been typically justified by its ability to provide continuing economic growth and prosperity while controlling and exploiting the talents of its creative elite. Some observers suggest that the distance between these two objectives is beginning to widen. It is worth looking at the course of Singapore's recent rise to the status of a developed country to understand the dimensions of the current dilemma.

The last days of the colonial economy

In the 1940s and early 1950s following the war, it did not appear that the future of Singapore's economy was particularly bright. Despite some international preparations for a postwar slump and reconstruction, such as the Marshall Plan in Europe, there was little help for Asian economies. Most of the imperial powers had suffered severe damage to their own metropolitan regions, and they had little money to spare for the reconstruction of their colonies. In fact, in some cases, the colonies were expected to help to pay for rebuilding the metropole. Even if they were not overtly exploited, they were expected to pay their own way while still serving the empire.

With the war over, there was little demand for rubber and tin, the mainstays of Singapore's economy. Moreover, much of its infrastructure had been damaged or had fallen into disrepair, particularly the harbor facilities (L.S. Chia 1989). The economy and the process of rebuilding lagged throughout the late 1940s, but with the outbreak of the Korean War in 1950, all this changed. There was immediate demand for the products of Malaya. In fact, the Korean War boom lifted all the Asian and Pacific economies. From Japan to Australia, heavy procurement expenditures by the USA got the wheels moving again.

The collapse that followed the Korean War taught some in Singapore that necessary as it may be, the *entrepôt* trade on its own would not be sufficient to maintain a reasonable life for the greater portion of the city's inhabitants. Moreover, an economy tied to the market for primary products like rubber and tin, together with the fact that the sources of both were also beyond its control, left Singapore constantly vulnerable. Between 1950 and 1960, rubber constituted two-thirds of Singapore's exports. Half of this came from Malaya and the other half from Indonesia. In 1960, Singapore was the world's largest rubber exporter, with sales constituting 37 percent of global output (Visscher 2002: 130).

Throughout the 1950s, rubber was both Singapore's strength and its weakness. It struggled with uncertain suppliers, volatile markets, limited reserves of domestic capital, a rapidly growing population and high unemployment. Whatever industry Singapore had was related to the processing of primary products from Indonesia and Malaya, or else to the port itself. Relations with both countries were uncertain during these years. In Indonesia, President Sukarno attempted to force all trade through Jakarta, blocking the previous trading relations that had existed between Sumatra and Kalimantan with Singapore. This Indonesian policy was largely unsuccessful, and its failure further soured relations between the two countries. Indonesian traders knew they could get higher prices for their products and pay lower prices for their purchases in Singapore, so despite the laws, there they came. Singapore's authorities welcomed these "barter traders" and turned a deaf ear to protests from the Indonesian government. The fact that much of the trade was in the hands of Indonesian Chinese did even less to endear them to the Indonesian government.

Trade with neighboring Malaya was less troubled, particularly since rail lines ran from Malaya to Singapore and both areas remained under British control, but the future of this trade was uncertain. Would Malaya continue to rely on Singapore as its *entrepôt* once it attained independence in 1957? For the short term, the trade was safe, but in the long run, there was every indication that Malaya would develop its own ports, particularly Penang and Klang, in competition with Singapore. This probability was one of the major reasons that many in Singapore supported a merger with Malaya.

Throughout these years, the mainstay of Singapore's economy continued to be the hundreds of traditional Chinese family businesses. Most of these were engaged in commerce, with the others providing services to the domestic market. These firms dominated the SCCCI and employed the largest number of workers. They also dominated Singapore's Chinese society as the patrons of Chinese schools, social organizations, cemeteries and temples. The chamber stood at the top of a vast pyramid of *huiguan*, Chinese trade, regional and linguistic associations that represented the core of the social and cultural life of Singapore's Chinese community.

Economically and socially, they faced rivals on the Left, both in the Communist Party and in the labor unions, and other agencies that called for social and economic reform. The high unemployment rate and the low wages and uncertain conditions of employment fostered continued labor unrest during the 1950s. There were a large number of strikes. Businesses were forced to deal with the unions, and wages began to rise significantly. Moreover, the labor movement developed considerable political clout. After

1955, Singapore's political parties sought the support of the Chinese masses and thus courted the labor movement. Left-wing parties such as the Labor Front and the PAP gained the support of the majority of Singaporeans and dominated the political scene. There was, it seemed, little reason for investors to risk their money in Singapore, and even domestic capitalists were reluctant to do so. As a result of their caution, domestic capital lost the initiative when it came to determining Singapore's economic future during the 1960s and 1970s. This loss of economic power was only partially responsible for the decline of the traditional Chinese elite. The SCCCI and its entire culture came under direct attack from the PAP, which saw it as a competitor for the hearts and minds of the Chinese masses. It was also the most powerful and durable structure in Singapore's civil society and thus constituted a threat to PAP dominance. As Visscher has pointed out:

> The erosion of the multi-purpose Chinese elite and of its underling social structure in the *huiguans* is not simply a victory of rational, formalized "modernity" over some organic "tradition." Status, money and power were important in both systems but the basis for status, the role of wealth and the use of power were different. Whereas in Chinese society personal wealth, or elite affluence, was an important provider of status and a means to accumulate power, the PAP's legitimacy was based on generating societal wealth and on its nation-wide distribution, or, in other words, on constituency affluence. To achieve this, however, the PAP was much more than an economic policy manager. It also included and appropriated the cultural and social realm, becoming a multi-purpose elite of sorts itself. The crucial difference was that the PAP claimed to be doing all this in the name of rationality, efficiency and, most importantly, in name of an abstract state.
>
> (Visscher 2002: 244)

The industrialization of Singapore

As a global *entrepôt*, Singapore had always been a marketplace, and trade was its life blood. In 1965, commerce made up nearly 30 percent of its entire GDP, while manufacturing accounted for only about 15 percent. By 1973, only eight years after independence, the contribution of commerce to the GDP had fallen to just over 26 percent, while manufacturing had risen to nearly 24 percent (*ibid.*: 237).

Ironically, preserving the commercial sector had been the entire economic rationale for merger with Malaysia in the years prior to 1963. Singapore's trading interests and its financial interests both looked on the Malayan peninsula as their hinterland. They imported and exported for Malaya. They invested in Malaya. They could see only disaster if they were shut out of Malaya. Although few of Singapore's Chinese traders relished the idea of being ruled by Malays, merger appeared to be an economic necessity.

Figure 6.1 Young women in a Singapore electronics factory, 1968.

The rise of nationalism in both the federation and Indonesia seemed to threaten Singapore's future as an *entrepôt*. Singapore's trading companies and banks were both deeply involved in servicing the primary production industries of both countries. Hundreds of Singapore's small family-run trading companies were likewise involved. Economic nationalism meant the restriction of trade to national ports, even when it was less convenient. While expulsion from Malaysia was welcomed by Singapore's ethnic Chinese for cultural and administrative reasons, the economic future appeared bleak.

The PAP government, with its emphasis on the creation of a manufacturing base, sought to create an alternative income stream while providing jobs for the large number of unemployed in Singapore. In doing this, the government virtually turned its back on most of those small traders, treating them as old-fashioned and lacking any potential for growth. The development of a manufacturing industry fundamentally altered the political economy of Singapore. In many respects, the PAP's economic program paralleled its political and social policies, which were characterized by a rejection of the interests of ethnic Chinese capitalists. On the other hand, the manufacturing jobs were intended primarily for working-class Chinese. It was an economic strategy that won over the PAP's most volatile constituency while undercutting the financial base of its strongest rival group.

Garry Rodan points out that Singapore's industrialization took a unique course because of the alliance during the 1950s and early 1960s between the PAP and the Chinese-educated left wing, which dominated the labor and student movements. While the relationship was tempestuous, it was crucial in shaping Singapore's economic and political direction. "In particular, it kept the government insulated from pressures by established business interests in the formation of a manufacturing strategy. There was no political necessity for a domestic, rather than an international, industrial bourgeoisie to prevail in any program to attract private investment." The state thus played a key role in Singapore's industrialization, not only through direct investment of its own but also by nurturing private investment from foreign sources (Rodan 2001: 143).

It may seem odd that the government would favor industrial interests over commercial ones. For a "nationalist" government, it was also surprising that they would seek foreign (and in particular Japanese) capital, rather than domestic capital, to build the industrial sector. Beyond this, the government created subsidies and other advantages for foreign investors that local investors did not enjoy, even when they did invest. To some degree, this policy replicated key elements of the colonial political economy. Once again, the government was in a virtual partnership with foreign corporate interests, and the local Asian traders and smaller business interests, which were neglected by the British, were now systematically disadvantaged by the government of independent Singapore.

However, there was a major contrast with the earlier period. The colonial government did not directly involve itself in the economy (save to protect

British interests); by comparison, the independent state now became deeply involved in the economy while continuing to actively promote policies that were beneficial to certain foreign interests. The PAP set up government-linked or government-led corporations (GLCs) and statutory boards, which often competed with local private interests. Instead of a free-trade economy, the Singapore economy came to be as closely controlled by the party/state as were the political and social sectors.

In developing its strategy, the PAP sought advice from the United Nations. The UN Industrial Survey Mission was led by Dutch economist Albert Winsemius. His report called for a program of import-substitution industrialization (ISI) led by state moves to attract private capital. It recommended control over labor and the holding down of wages, the provision of industrial estates, technical training, tax incentives and free remittance of profits.

In 1960, when these plans were being formulated, Singapore's *per capita* GDP was $1,330, which gave the country a middle-income status, according to Chia Siow Yue. Value-added manufacturing contributed only $235.6 million, or 11.9 percent of GDP, and manufacturing was still limited to processing locally produced primary products such as rubber and tin. It also included engineering services related to the British military base and a limited range of local consumer goods (Gunesekera 1989: 250).

Between 1960 and 1965, the PAP government following Winsemius' advice, concentrated on a locally driven import-substitution policy and offered protection to local industries. After 1965 and separation from Malaysia, the policy underwent a radical shift. Chia has divided the history of Singapore's industrial growth between 1959 and 1986 into four distinct periods. Between 1959 and 1965, growth was modest due to political uncertainties and industrial unrest, but there was considerable progress in laying the infrastructural foundation that contributed to later growth.

The second period, from 1965 to 1973, was the most spectacular. This period saw a major shift from ISI to export-oriented industry (EOI). The average annual growth rate in value-added manufacturing was 18.1 percent and was dependent upon a heavy inflow of FDI (foreign direct investment). These industries provided a large number of low-skilled, low-wage manufacturing jobs and did much to solve Singapore's chronic unemployment problems. Since the NTUC was now virtually an agency of the government, the state could guarantee labor peace and at the same time negotiate a reasonably attractive wage and benefit package for the workers.

The third period saw the annual growth rate decrease to only 8.6 percent due to the 1973 oil crisis and the global recession that followed; however, by the late 1970s, Singapore was back to double-digit growth figures. By the early 1980s, Singapore's early lead in the development of manufacturing was lessening, and there was increased competition from other lower-wage countries. The achievement of full employment in Singapore in 1972 had gradually tightened the labor market, and there was a rise in wages, which contributed to the overall cost of doing business (S.Y. Chia 1989: 253–4).

This period marked the beginning of Singapore's "Second Industrial Revolution." Productivity increased as more capital-intensive industries were lured to Singapore, and technical training programs were introduced to raise the skill level of the workforce.

Government involvement was crucial here in that it implemented a "corrective wage policy," which progressively raised wages and forced low-skilled, labor-intensive industries to either upgrade or find cheaper labor elsewhere. The government itself took a major role in investment in both the social and physical infrastructure, as well as in the industrial companies themselves. Rodan reports that by 1983 the government had invested in fifty-eight companies, which were used to promote higher value-added production. Industries such as electronics, machinery, chemicals and aerospace were all upgraded. FDI also doubled between 1979 and 1984 (Rodan 2001: 148).

Between 1960 and 1985, direct exports by manufacturing firms grew from $164.3 million to over $24 billion at an overall annual rate of 22.1 percent. The major new products in the mix of Singapore's manufactures were initially petroleum products. In the 1970s, these accounted for 38.1 percent of its industrial exports. By 1985, however, electronic products and components had become the top export earners, making up 34.5 percent of all manufacturing exports (S.Y. Chia 1989: 257).

The key factor after 1965 was the growth in importance of FDI in Singapore's manufacturing industry. In 1962, over 45 percent of Singapore's gross output of manufactures came from firms that were wholly locally owned and that accounted for over 66 percent of the workforce. Foreign-owned companies produced only 31.4 percent of gross output and employed only 14.1 percent of the workforce. By 1985, these proportions had almost reversed. Wholly foreign-owned companies produced 54.5 percent of the output and employed 41 percent of the workforce, while wholly locally owned firms produced 20.3 percent of the output and employed only 33.5 percent of the workforce (*ibid.*: 260).

This trend sharply curtailed the power and status of Singapore's domestic capitalists. The SCCCI was no longer the dominant economic body in Singapore. The state could take credit for providing a high level of material prosperity for the bulk of Singapore's population and for making Singapore Southeast Asia's first newly industrialized country (NIC).

The oil boom

A major boost for Singapore's economic development during the 1970s was the oil industry. Singapore was well positioned to take advantage of the global and Southeast Asian oil boom. Singapore's oil industry had actually begun in the colonial era, when bulk storage tanks for kerosene were built on Pulau Bukom in 1892. From that time until the 1960s, Singapore served as the storage, transshipment, distribution center for oil in the Far East and was thus a major regional center for the petroleum industry. In 1961, Shell established a small refining unit in Singapore with a capacity of 20,000 barrels per day, and during the 1970s other major companies followed suit (Doshi 1989: 82).

Singapore's location about halfway between the major producing areas of the Middle East and the major consuming areas in East Asia was a vital asset. Timing was also an important factor in the rise of the industry in Singapore. During the 1970s, just as the British were rolling up their bases in Singapore, the city benefited from the discovery of significant quantities of oil in the South China Sea. Oil had been an important export of Southeast Asia since the 1930s, with important fields in Brunei and the east coast of Kalimantan, but in the late 1960s and early 1970s major deposits were discovered in the Gulf of Siam, and under the Spratley and Paracel Islands in the South China Sea. Major new deposits were also discovered in Indonesia. By the end of the 1970s, Thailand, Malaysia, Vietnam and the Philippines had also become important oil producers.

Another important factor, according to one commentator, was the American war in Vietnam, which created a demand for high-quality petroleum products from a nearby source. At the same time, economic development taking place throughout Southeast Asia provided another growing market for petroleum products from Singapore.

While all of these countries benefited both financially and industrially from the oil, Singapore was the major beneficiary. It already had a head start with the beginnings of a refining and storage industry already in place. As the major transportation hub of the region, Singapore was able to expand these capabilities more readily than others. Mobil established itself in Singapore in the mid-1960s to support its Indonesian wells; Esso built a refinery in 1970; and Shell expanded its facilities in the mid-1970s; other companies such as BP and Mobil likewise established refining facilities of various kinds in Singapore. Caltex, C. Itoh and BP formed joint ventures with the Singapore Refining Company (another GLC) in distillation plants and refineries.

Oil companies and exploration companies also made Singapore their headquarters as they searched for oil in the surrounding waters. By 1980, Singapore was the center of Southeast Asia's booming oil industry. In 1989, Singapore had a refining capacity of just less than one million barrels per day. Despite the growth of the industry in nearby countries, Singapore continued to have an advantage in that these countries lacked the refining capacities appropriate to their needs and continued to rely on Singapore for the procurement of high-quality petroleum products. Singapore also became the region's "swing" refiner, balancing disparities between supply and demand for petroleum products by competitively filling the specific product deficits of a large number of countries (Doshi 1989: 80–90).

Between 1977 and 1982, Singapore's oil exports regularly made up nearly 40 percent of gross manufacturing exports and averaged nearly 6 percent of

GDP (*ibid.*: 85). After 1982, as other forms of manufacturing, particularly electronics, increased, oil declined as a part of total manufacturing exports to about 15–16 percent, a figure that it maintained throughout the 1990s. Given the combination of its refining, storage and shipment capacity, Singapore has become a key player in the global oil trading market. As part of Singapore's current drive to become a major financial center, it has also opened an oil futures market.

While Singapore's oil industry has been growing, there has also been a fundamental shift of economic interests within Malaysia and Indonesia. The rubber and tin industries upon which both Singapore and Malaysia depended during the 1960s have declined sharply. Rubber has almost disappeared altogether as a cultivar in Malaysia, while the importance of tin has dropped off in comparison with other products. In fact, much of the region's former dependence upon primary production and processing has disappeared. Manufacturing and the move, not only by Singapore but also by its neighbours, into the knowledge economy has changed the face of Southeast Asia, giving it a level of prosperity unimagined in the 1960s.

The port of Singapore

Concurrent with the process of industrialization and the development of the oil industry in Singapore was the growth of the port itself. The major development during the 1960s and 1970s was the transformation of the port from an *entrepôt* and transshipment center to one focused on servicing local industry. The development of major deep-sea harbors in neighboring countries has also enhanced this trend, with each country now sending goods directly from its own ports.

Starting in the early 1960s, as the PAP began its push to industrialize, the administrative authorities for the port were reorganized. The old Singapore Harbour Board, the Marine Department and the Marine Public Works Department were merged to form the Port of Singapore Authority (PSA). This was a GLC charged with the responsibility for maintaining the port, improving its services, providing pilotage, controlling navigation, and maintaining lighthouses and navigational aids. Starting in the early 1960s, moves were made to expand the area of the port, reclaim land and deepen the harbor and its approaches. The port was expanded to include five major wharves, including one on the northern side of the island at Sembawang, which mainly handles timber.

The changes in the port were mirrored by the shift in labor relations that took place with the rise of the PAP. The once-powerful group of unions that represented the harbor workers were suspended and merged with the SHBSA, and later in the 1960s, that union was itself reorganized and re-registered within the NTUC as the Singapore Port Workers Union. Increasing the efficiency of the port and reducing the number of workers on a stevedore gang was simplified with government control of the unions. The introduction of forklifts, pallets and other labor-saving technologies in the 1950s and 1960s also increased the capacity of the port.

In the early 1970s, moves were made to upgrade the port to handle containerized shipping, and in 1972, it handled its first cellular container vessel at Tanjong Pagar. By the late 1980s, there were nine container freight storage areas for different parts of the port. A computerized system for tracking each container from the ship to the wharf and beyond that until it left the island was also introduced in 1987. By the 1990s, Singapore was one of the four major ports in Asia, after Hong Kong, Kobe and Kaohsiung, and was handling over two million containers annually.

In order to service the growing industrial base and the growing petroleum industry, additional port facilities were constructed along Singapore's south-eastern shore. Singapore now has five major oil terminals, each operated by the oil company that controls the local refinery (i.e. Shell, Mobil, Esso, Caltex and BP). At Jurong, on the eastern side of the island, a major port was constructed to service the industrial center there (S.Y. Chia 1989).

Beautiful downtown Southeast Asia

Another key element in Singapore's growth over the past forty years has been the development of its infrastructure as a transportation and communications hub. Singapore was in the business of running a shipping port from its very inception, and it has kept pace with global developments in this area. While under colonial rule, the port had been the key reason for British possession of Singapore, and it remained so through the postwar years, continuing to ship tin and rubber to the industries of the West while importing Western manufactures for transshipment to Malaya, Indonesia and other parts of Southeast Asia.

Although shipping may have been occasionally deterred during the labor disputes of the 1950s, the Singapore Harbour Board and, later, the PSA generally continued to keep cargo moving through the port. Singapore remained one of the busiest harbors in Asia. In addition to handling cargo, Singapore was a major hub for passenger transportation within and through Southeast Asia. Travelers, tourists, businessmen, government officials, soldiers, migrants and pilgrims had always moved through the port, and they continued to do so in the postwar years and the early period of independence.

With the expansion of air travel in the 1950s and 1960s, Singapore began to expand its tourist infrastructure, building hotels and shopping areas and making its varied range of ethnic foods available to those passing through. Since the 1950s, Singapore had been a favored shopping stop for international tourists. It was, like Hong Kong, a free port, where one could purchase duty-free goods. In addition to high-quality but low-cost Japanese cameras, watches and electronic equipment, one could buy rapidly made suits, shirts, dresses and other hand-sewn clothing from the many Indian and Chinese tailors there.

During the 1970s, the Singapore government made a major effort to expand Singapore's tourist industry. As part of the urban renewal effort, key areas such as the Bras Basah/Orchard Road corridor were targeted for development as tourist areas. International hotels were encouraged to build in this area, and a number of shopping centers were created. Singapore was able to capitalize on the regional boom in the tourist industry in Southeast Asia, even though it really had little to offer in the way of exotic peoples, historic ruins, or natural wonders. As an efficient transportation hub, it was in a position to bring tourists in for a night or two before sending them on to Thailand, Indonesia, Malaysia, or elsewhere. During the 1970s, plans were laid for a large, state-of-the-art airport at Changi which would be linked to the urban center of Singapore by a network of superhighways. The investment in physical infrastructure paid off. People came for a brief stopover and a quick shopping trip and quickly moved on to their next destination.

This program initially focused on Europeans and Americans, who were just beginning to discover Southeast Asia as a tourist destination. Affluent, ignorant and impatient, Europeans appreciated Singapore's efficiency, its use of English, the relative ease of movement around the island and the lack of harassment from beggars, street peddlers and unscrupulous taxi drivers. It was "just like home," only different. It was "beautiful downtown Southeast Asia."

By the 1980s, the Singapore shopping stop had also become popular with the increasingly affluent classes of neighboring countries. With easy air links to Jakarta, Bangkok, Kuala Lumpur and Manila, flights to and from those countries soon filled up with well-heeled Southeast Asian neighbors of Singapore coming to spend a week or two at one of the five-star hotels on Orchard Road and to spend their days cruising the shopping malls and upmarket boutiques that were finding a ready demand for their products in Southeast Asia. The differential tariffs and poor infrastructure that kept such products from reaching their home countries at reasonable prices made Singapore an attractive destination for the wives, concubines and children of Southeast Asia's crony capitalists.

The shopping bug has not spared the residents of Singapore itself, who have proved to be among the most dedicated pursuers of fads and fashions. Singapore sociologist Chua Beng Huat has borrowed a phrase from former Prime Minister Goh Chok Tong, who noted that for Singaporeans, "life is not complete without shopping" (Chua 2003). Chua also notes that most Singaporeans find that private flats and automobiles are beyond their pocketbooks, thus they find ways to express their individuality through less expensive forms of consumption. The shopping mall has become a major arena for display and social interaction for many Singaporeans.

Along with the growth of Singapore's tourist industry came an energetic program of urban redevelopment, slum clearance and highway construction. Most of the two- and three-story Chinese shophouses were cleared from the urban areas of Singapore, and "Chinatown" and its people were moved to the HDB flats in the various "new towns" around the island. The areas they vacated were acquired by the government or affiliated developers, and by the 1980s, the skyline of Singapore had taken on a new look. Scores of multi-story glass and steel towers sprang up along the seafront, making Singapore one of the more spectacular ports of Asia.

The building boom in Singapore has a history of its own that in many ways parallels that of the city-state itself. Singapore architect Tay Kheng Soon has periodized the development of architectural styles in Singapore (Tay 1989: 865–6). Tay writes of the architectural styles of the period 1965–70, the first years of independence characterized by the industrialization of the economy

This period saw the introduction of assembly-line industries that began to restructure Singapore's predominantly *entrepôt* economy into a modern industrialized economy. Consistent with this process, the architecture of the period was characterized by unimaginative and utilitarian designs. Public housing of this period was typically uniform in design and regimented in layout. Other structures, including schools, community centers and commercial buildings, also displayed the same utilitarian and functionalist character. Innovation was not in architectural expression but rather in the organizational techniques and social engineering involved. Great innovations were achieved in the delivery system of housing but not in its design. It was characterized, he said, by "industrial forms and industrial mythic images; large blocks, and mechanical order" known colloquially in Europe as "brutalism" (*ibid.*: 865).

A second period was what he called the global city era, 1970–80. It was characterized by the "international corporate style of architecture". Again, most of the architects were locally trained and expressed a contemporary aesthetic that symbolized progress and modernity. Consistent with Lee Kuan Yew's desire to establish Singapore as a financial center, it exemplified "corporatist desires" as seen in the buildings constructed by government statutory bodies in the old urban areas along Shenton Way and its nearby streets.

A gigantism in the expression of buildings on Shenton Way can be seen in the stacking of building volumes. These volumes were disposed either horizontally or vertically as gigantic elements in the architectural composition. Thus buildings of around this period, such as the Telephone Exchange in Devonshire Road, the Public Utilities Board headquarters in Somerset Road, the People's Park complex, the Central Provident Fund Building and the Development Bank of Singapore, all displayed similar volumetric gigantism. The desire to project power cannot be mistaken: these buildings exuded a macho masculinity (*ibid.*: 866).

In the years since the mid-1980s, there has been a deepening of the corporatization trend, which has also reflected the growth of high-tech industry in Singapore. It has been characterized by two divergent trends. On the one hand, the continuation of corporate styles has persisted, often by foreign

companies as well as statutory bodies, with the employment of foreign architects with international reputations such as I.M. Pei and Kenzo Tange.
These constructions reflected an eagerness to acquire "all the excellence that
money could buy" and expressed Singapore's growing prosperity. This trend
can be seen in structures such as Raffles City, Marina Square, Marina City
and the Overseas Union Bank Headquarters.

At the same time, among local architects there has been the influence of
postmodernist trends together with the rediscovery of vernacular and
indigenous architectural forms. This has resulted in attempts to preserve
some key elements of Singapore's architectural heritage, if only in some
"boutique" format. Thus we have the attempts to create tourist nightspots in
the refurbished shophouses and godowns along Boat Quay and parts of
Chinatown. However, it remains to be seen whether these approaches will
solve what Tay sees as the problem of integration in the new city:

> It is always more convenient to separate than to integrate, but the
> resulting urban fabric reduces the connective quality of any city. In the
> absence of any corrective vision, the vitality and ambience for human
> interaction is inexorably reduced.
>
> (*ibid.*: 868)

Finally, an important factor in the whole urban development strategy has
been the means by which the government has managed to gain control over
much of the land area. At independence, the Singapore government owned
only about 10 percent of the property in the central district of the town. As
the government began to demolish shophouses and smaller buildings in the
1970s, property taxes were progressively increased in the inner city area. The
government also required minimum values and maximum quality for new
construction. New zoning regulations were also put in place restricting the
uses to which property in these areas could be put.

These regulations did little to discourage large land owners, who were
able to upgrade their holdings and who could afford to sponsor ambitious
new construction. However, smaller property holders were forced to sell out,
and usually to the government at very moderate prices. The government
eliminated the free market in urban property "to discourage speculation,"
defending itself with the assertion that it was government policies and activities that caused values to appreciate, therefore the government should reap
the benefit of the rise in real estate prices. It is noteworthy that much of the
new construction that took place in the Shenton Way area during the 1970s
was to house GLCs and statutory boards.

Singapore Inc.

With the partial exception of Hong Kong, none of Asia's NICs, of which
Singapore was one, did so without considerable government involvement.

In Japan, and later in Taiwan and South Korea, governments took an active role in encouraging manufacturers to open up shop; the same was true for Singapore. In addition to building infrastructure, restraining labor, providing tax breaks and insuring that profits could be repatriated, Singapore's government also created a unique place for itself in the economy by organizing statutory boards and the GLCs, which gave the government both control of and a direct role in major sectors of the economy.[42]

Two of the earliest statutory boards, and still among the most important, were the Central Provident Fund (CPF) and the Housing Development Board (HDB). The two, in fact, worked quite closely together. The CPF, Singapore's pension fund, has served as a major vehicle for enforced savings. While pioneer industries received many advantages, one obligation they had was to contribute a significant proportion of their employees' wages, together with a significant employer contribution, into the fund. An amount equal to 25 percent of the total wage packet of Singapore's workers has gone into the fund annually.

The fund, controlled by the government, became the major source of credit for the HDB's ambitious public housing program. The construction of Singapore's high-rise flats and new towns was almost entirely financed through the CPF, as were other infrastructure projects such as roads, water, sewerage, electricity and the island's rapid transit system, the MRT. By the late 1980s, as individuals began to purchase their own flats, they were permitted to draw on their own CPF accounts as a source of personal credit. Given the government's record for sound financial management and honesty, this has worked out quite well in Singapore, although there is some lack of transparency in the overall system. The government remains the banker for most of the population.

The pattern of statutory boards to undertake and manage large public enterprises and projects and the underlying strata of GLCs has become a key feature of Singapore's total political economy, as pointed out by Gary Rodan and other students of Singapore. In 2000, Singapore had approximately seventy statutory boards and more than a thousand state-owned or state-led companies in manufacturing and commercial enterprises (Rodan 2001: 151). The major players here were Temasek Holdings, Singapore Technology, and Health Corporation Holdings, in which the state was the sole if not the major shareholder. The total assets of these enterprises amounted to S$10.6 billion (*ibid.*: 167). It is also important to understand that control of these major holding companies is in the hands of key members of Lee Kuan Yew's family.

The GLCs and statutory boards are also important political tools within the state. They provide the government with a ready means of rewarding its bureaucratic allies with jobs as directors or managers of these enterprises. They also act as a recruiting ground for talent. It may be recalled that Goh Chok Tong himself began his career in Neptune Orient Line, the government-linked shipping company. Rodan has demonstrated that among the top 2,000 or 3,000 leaders in government, one finds the same names as in the upper ranks of the GLCs and statutory boards. In other countries, this might be considered a form of corruption or at least a conflict of interest, but in Singapore this system is at the root of the political economy.

New directions in the 1980s

The role of the GLCs and statutory boards became even stronger following the economic downturn of 1985–86. Singapore's leaders decided that they had reached the limits of manufacturing expansion and that it was time for Singapore to take the next step. Just as in the early 1980s, preparations for the transition of power to the next generation had taken place with ostensible bows toward consultation. The response to economic change seemed to suggest a retreat from tight central control, but it actually led to greater government involvement in and control of the economy.

The *Strategic Economic Plan* of 1991 set the new direction for the 1990s, calling for increased activism and expansion by SMEs (of which there were about 80,000) and for heavy investment in social and physical infrastructure. Sikko Visscher suggests that there were two reasons behind this move. On the one hand, it appeared that the partnership with foreign manufacturers had gone as far as it could. Singapore's labor costs had risen with economic development, and foreign manufacturers were opening new plants in Indonesia, Thailand and other countries where labor costs were lower. Singapore now found itself in the same situation as other developed countries at this stage in their economic development. There was a clear need for innovation, which could only come from within. The plan thus called for specific aid to entrepreneurs and for greater consultation by government with the private sector.

The second reason for the renewed interest in the SMEs was because the vast number of Singapore's smaller enterprises were run by ethnic Chinese. In the mid-1980s, the PRC was in the midst of its first wave of economic and political reform under Deng Xiaoping. The PAP began to see that it was time to de-emphasize links with the West and to re-establish economic ties with the PRC, thus restoring relations with one of Singapore's "traditional" trading partners. It also perceived that one of the most expeditious agencies for developing ties with China was the SCCCI. The chamber, because it was made up mostly of small Chinese businesses, bursting with entrepreneurship, had been pushing for links to China to be restored since the 1950s (Visscher 2002). Given its anti-communist stance and the generally hostile attitude within the government toward the Chinese-educated, those requests to open trade with China had previously met with rebuffs. In the late 1980s, that changed.

The PAP now came to look on the SCCCI, and the ethnic Chinese businessmen that it represented, as Singapore's bridge to China. Not only could they be the vanguard of Singapore's economic relationship with China, opening new markets, developing trade relations and finding investment opportunities, but they could also provide a service that could be marketed to others. Singapore would become a gateway to China for Europeans and Americans, who lacked the cultural *entrée* that Singapore's ethnic Chinese could offer. The SCCCI would serve as a broker between China and the world, and the Singapore government would manage the relationship (*ibid.*: 378). While these moves were less successful than had been anticipated, economic relations with the new China blossomed, and the "Speak Mandarin" campaign took on a new fervor as Singapore rediscovered its Asian values.

Business connections in China as well as in other parts of Asia now became increasingly important to the Singapore government. The third prong of the new economic plan involved overseas investment in the region. In addition to Singapore's ethnic Chinese investing in China, Singapore's large-scale capital enterprises, the GLCs, sought investment opportunities on a broader local or regional scale. Cash-rich with the savings of millions of Singaporeans, the directors of Singapore Inc. now saw that it was time for them to expand their horizons. Many of the new ventures were thus not carried out by SMEs on their own but in partnerships with GLCs. Government control of and involvement in the activities of the Chinese SMEs now actually increased.

These ventures have not been an unbroken series of successes. Some, particularly a major joint venture in Suzhou, turned into a fiasco resulting in a $151 million loss and a decision to turn over management control to China. Others may have been more successful. One major project has been the "Growth Triangle," which has brought Singapore investment and know-how into Johor and Indonesia's nearby Riau–Lingga archipelago. Here, Singapore's SMEs in partnership with the GLCs have led the way, embarking on extensive if not grandiose projects in the islands to the south, particularly in Batam and Bintan. To the historian, it seems ironic that the same geographical and socio-economic combinations that gave birth to Singapore's nineteenth-century economy should be revived at the end of the twentieth century.

Economic crisis and liberalization

Given Singapore's heavy investment in the regional economy, the Asian economic collapse of 1997 was a major blow that sharply curtailed the growth of the city-state's economy. Nevertheless, by 2001 the economy was on the mend, and Singapore's economic managers had sought to learn what they could from the debacle. Their conclusion was that with globalization, Singapore needed to expand and to become a global player. Prime Minister Goh Chok Tong declared: "We should now go global by forming strategic alliances or mergers with other major players. Indeed, we have no choice –

where the industries are consolidating worldwide, we either become major players, or we are nothing" (Rodan 2001: 157) The first moves toward implementing this policy were the appointment of international managers to executive positions in major state-owned companies. The government also moved to liberalize the financial and telecommunications sectors in response to WTO pressure. Another part of the new economic plan called for a shift away from the manufacturing emphasis and to develop a niche for Singapore as a regional provider of high value-added services such as accounting, law, training and management services.

This new impulse by Singapore Inc. has also included investment in the developed countries. SingTel has purchased a major share in Australia's number two telecom company, Optus. At the same time, Singapore Airlines has unsuccessfully attempted to purchase a majority share in Air New Zealand, and it was also involved in the unsuccessful effort to resuscitate Australia's failed airline Ansett. These, together with Singapore's position in the regional Southeast Asian economy, have helped Singapore to transcend the city-state economy by building an "external economy" or a by "expanding the economic space of Singapore" (*ibid.*: 152) Total direct investment abroad rose from \$16.9 billion in 1990 to \$70.6 billion by the end of 1997, more than half of which was in Asia (*ibid.*: 153).

Unfortunately, just as Singapore was recovering from the Asian meltdown of 1997, the country was affected by the global crisis that followed the attacks on the World Trade Center in New York on 11 September 2001. For Singapore, with its large Muslim minority and its location beside the largely Muslim states of Malaysia and Indonesia, the events were problematic. Singapore itself could be considered a place where Islamic radicals could gather as well as a target for attacks by local extremists. This possibility was made explicit the following year when a group apparently affiliated to Ja'amah Islamia bombed a Bali nightclub full of Australian tourists.

These events were followed in 2003 by the SARS epidemic, which struck with considerable virulence in Singapore, where there were over 200 cases and over thirty deaths. The SARS outbreak in Singapore took a severe toll on the country's economy. The country's tourist industry suffered with a drop in the number of visitors of around 30 percent. This pushed Singapore's unemployment rate close to 5.5 percent, up from the previous 5.25 percent. In 2002, Singapore had 7.57 million visitors, who brought \$5.2 billion into the state and constituted 8 percent of its GDP.

However, Singapore's government has been able to use this series of crises to strengthen its hold on the economy and to further buttress its power base. It has ignored the possibility that the SARS crisis may have been in some way self-inflicted due to indifferent public health standards in Singapore, particularly in regard to recent arrivals from China. Instead, the government propaganda campaign in the wake of the crisis stressed Singaporeans pulling together under government leadership to face the epidemic. However, it was difficult to ignore completely the fact that there had been no cases at all in neighboring Malaysia.

Overseas investments by Singapore's GLCs and its impulse to market itself as a financial center have brought greater scrutiny of the unique organizational features of Singapore Inc. Up to the present, since they have been run by and for the government, the GLCs and their affiliates have avoided regulation and the ordinary regimes of financial scrutiny to which other enterprises are normally subject. With the internationalization of Singapore capital and the heavy involvement of the government in this move, international financial interests are demanding greater transparency and privatization of these enterprises. Rodan argues that this has placed the government in a difficult situation:

> Any serious diminution of the positions of GLCs could have major implications for the political regime. First, because the PAP's paternalistic brand of authoritarianism is largely administered through state control of capital and resources via the GLCs since GLCs provide channels for political reward and retribution. The fortunes of the GLCs will also influence the reformulation of any new social contract between the government and Singapore's citizens.
>
> (Rodan 2004: 480–1)

Typically, the government has been able to use co-optation rather than force to advance its interests among the elite. The government has thus created a powerful class of what Jayasuriya and Rosser have styled "nomenklatura capitalists who exercise immense control over the enterprises they manage but are yet dependent on the PAP for their position" (Jayasuriya and Rosser 2001: 247). They argue that this linkage between the GLCs and the ruling party has ensured the longevity of the PAP and has prevented the emergence of an alternative reform coalition, which might have been fostered by truly private capital.

Privatization and increased transparency would not only expose the government to more scrutiny than it has been used to; it would also mean a real diminution of state control over its elite as well as exposing Singapore's society as a whole to global market forces, and at the same time exposing the PAP to the creation of other power centers in society. Until now, the PAP's control of the economy has been able to prevent the emergence of an autonomous domestic capitalist class. This level of control would no longer be possible in a more open economy.

Until now, only domestic capitalists have found the partnership between the government and the GLCs an obstacle. Singapore's attempts to negotiate free-trade agreements with the United States and other developed countries have brought the system under greater international scrutiny and resulted in international business interests demanding greater transparency in the workings of the GLCs.

Rodan has argued that

> because the political and economic interests of the PAP are systemati-
> cally protected and advanced through a highly politicized state
> integrating the ruling party and the public bureaucracy. Reforms being
> advocated by elements of international capital are meant precisely to
> curtail the influence of some of those relationships.
>
> (Rodan 2004: 480–1)

Garry Rodan has suggested that the concern in the West about Muslim
terrorism provided Singapore's leaders with an opportunity to avoid a
greater liberalization of the economy. The 9–11 crisis and its aftermath have
also given the PAP greater license to cite emergency circumstances to extend
further controls over society and the economy. Thus the current "emergency" situation may provide yet another opportunity for the government to
retain and possibly expand its controls over the economy and society in
general.

Conclusions

The transformation of Singapore's economy under the PAP has freed it, in
some respects, from it prior dependence upon its immediate hinterland. The
expulsion from Malaysia and the rise of economic nationalism in its immediate neighborhood threatened Singapore's old *entrepôt* economy. The
development of its own industrial base gave Singapore economic prosperity
and made it the first of the Southeast Asian NICs.

The EOI pattern of industrialization, backed by foreign investment, was
also a double advantage for the PAP and the state that it had created. FDI
allowed the PAP to form a partnership with international capital. Not only
did this eliminate the need to share power with domestic capitalists, but the
Singapore state could also dictate, to a considerable extent, the terms on
which foreign capital was invested. Thus, for instance, the government was
able to draw 40 percent of the entire industrial wage packet into the CPF.
Each employee put in 35 percent, and each employer was required to
contribute 5 percent.

This gave the government a considerable cash reserve with which to
embark on urban redevelopment, public housing and the upgrading of
infrastructure. Not only was the government able to create new wealth and
much greater prosperity for the population; it was also able to use the
economy as a vehicle to establish a much higher level of control over the
state and society.

Up to the end of the twentieth century, Singapore's political economy has
been based on the prosperity generated by the economic policies of the PAP,
which has used that affluence to legitimize its claim to power. So long as
Singapore can stay ahead of its neighbors, economically, it may be possible

to maintain power on that basis. The problem, of course, is that Malaysia, Thailand and Indonesia are all catching up very quickly. They have larger populations and will work for lower wages than Singaporeans can afford. Singapore's leaders moved to upgrade their manufacturing capability in the 1980s and began to move out of low-wage manufacturing. With attempts to move into the knowledge economy and to develop Singapore as a financial and educational center for the region, the government has managed to stay a few steps ahead of the local competition. However, there are bigger competitors on the horizon, such as Hong Kong and Shanghai, which compete with Singapore not only as global cities but also as Chinese cultural centers. It remains to be seen whether Singapore can maintain the lead it gained in the 1970s and 1980s.

The current international crises, although damaging to Singapore's attempts to recover from the shock of the 1997 recession, may also provide another "emergency" context that will benefit Singapore's managers. One thing that is clear in Singapore's spectacular growth over the past five decades is that the power of the state over society and the economy has also increased, and each crisis, real or manufactured, has provided broader opportunities for the expansion of state power. So great has this power become that it has been necessary in the economic field (as in the creation of an opposition in the political field) to create and manage an area for free enterprise and entrepreneurship.

At the same time, can the Singapore government continue to keep its tight hold on the domestic economy through the structure of GLCs and statutory boards that make up Singapore Inc.? It is doubtful that international capital will allow Singapore to operate in the global economy as a corporate entity while maintaining the major elements of the domestic economy as its closed shop. The calls for greater transparency by international financial interests will ultimately force groups such as Temasek Holdings to open their books to closer scrutiny and to allow a more level playing field in areas where the government has currently no overseer.

Conclusion

A major aim of this study of Singapore's history has been to attempt to tease out strands or themes of continuity between the past and the more recent era of political independence. Lee Kuan Yew, like Thomas Stamford Raffles before him, had assumed he was escaping from history. Each saw his "creation" of a new Singapore as an opportunity to "make the world anew." In many ways, there was a justification for such assertions. Certainly, their actions were major watersheds in Singapore's history.

On the other hand, neither quite made the break with the preceding periods that they thought. Raffles thought he was abolishing slavery, eliminating piracy and establishing a base for free trade and, we should probably assume, the kind of state that would align with the principles of the Enlightenment – a government that, by governing least, would govern best. Moreover, if we are to believe Raffles' biographers, he had no intention of creating an empire. He intended Singapore to be a base where British trade could be protected and where traders of the archipelago could gather.

Some of these things happened, and some did not, but more importantly, there were a number of significant ironies. Trade was free, and it stayed that way. Most of all, however, it was free for the opium trade. Raffles was clearly no opponent of the opium trade, although it is unlikely that he saw it as the primary justification for the foundation and survival of Singapore. He was clearly unhappy with William Farquhar's decision to farm out the revenues and to "compromise" with the native chiefs and Chinese *taukehs* in organizing the finances and management of the state. When Crawfurd took over the government of Singapore, he reaffirmed Farquhar's measures in setting up opium and spirit farms and went even further by authorizing a gambling farm.

If Singapore became a sanctuary for British trade, it flourished as an "Asian port." As an Asian port, it became a sanctuary for Chinese trade and for the economy that the Chinese had been in the process of organizing when they were so rudely interrupted by the Dutch in the 1780s. The Bugis and Chinese traders who had been doing business at Riau moved their operations to Singapore and kept them going. The Baba Chinese of Melaka, Penang and other Dutch ports, who had participated in the junk trade, likewise moved to Singapore. What was new? The innovation, perhaps, was British control. The British eliminated the Malay rulers and deprived them of their traditional sources of income.

The campaigns against Malay piracy and the slave trade and the drive to insure the "freedom" of trade all cut at the heart of the existing political economy of the Malay *negri* of the Straits. If Malay chiefs wanted to survive as rulers, they would have to cooperate with the British and, like the Temenggongs of Johor, ultimately move out of Singapore, form partnerships with the Chinese and attempt to manage the exploitation of the material resources of the Malayan peninsula. As a result, the Malays were pushed out of power in Singapore, and they have never been able to regain a position there.

This is not to say that a measure of Chinese dominance in the region would not have occurred regardless of British actions. Their rise to economic hegemony was already in progress, and the British moves did little more than give them a slight edge. The broader forces of history were already at work when Raffles appeared on the scene, and he did little to alter their fundamental direction, at least in the initial stages. In the long run, however, Raffles did provide a point of entry for global capitalism. In the beginning, this was represented by the opium trade, and for many years that persisted as the sustaining economic force of Singapore. The opium trade is what made Singapore the trading nexus between the global economy and the local economies of Southeast Asia.

Singapore became the center of regional trade because of its control over the opium trade, in the first place, and second because it had become the central exchange point for Chinese labor in the archipelago. This creation of a labor exchange may have been one of the true innovations. It depends how one views it. Traditional Southeast Asian ports seem to have been slave markets. In Singapore, there was no slave market, only a coolie market, and one could argue that the difference is academic. In any case, it was largely the work of Chinese merchants.

The system of tax farms, labor organization and commodity production that came to center on Singapore was also largely the creation of the Chinese *taukehs* who had moved there. Opium, and the debt structure it created, made possible the rise of Singapore as a transshipment center for the trade goods of Southeast Asia. In the first instance, most of these continued to go to China, as they had in the eighteenth century, but by mid-century European markets were claiming increasing shares of the commodities exported from Singapore.

I have shown that the opium trade and the system of labor organization and exploitation that was born in Singapore set up a dynamic of social conflict within Singapore. On the one hand, there was the creation of a partnership between the Singapore government and the European merchants of Singapore with the wealthier Baba merchants. The latter controlled the flow of opium and capital from the Europeans to the smaller Chinese capitalists and their laborers. They also dominated the opium revenue farms, which, in addition to enriching the *taukehs*, also financed the colonial state.

While not all laborers ended up as opium addicts or at least as debt slaves to their respective *kangchu* stores, a great many did. Their indebtedness sustained the economic system of Singapore. This was also the economic system that was expanding, like the shock wave of an explosion, into the Malay states, the island of Sumatra and the territories of Borneo. The "explosion" crossed whatever political boundaries or limits may have existed and bound a large hinterland to the Singapore economic nexus. The surrounding Malay states, Dutch territories and other British possessions came within its ambit.

For a time, the revenue farmers and those Chinese who had allied themselves with the British found themselves challenged by the power of the Chinese *kongsis*, or "secret societies," that formed the basis for Chinese labor organization in the region. The outbreaks of social violence in Singapore, Penang and their surrounding areas that occurred during the years between 1846 and the 1870s, should be seen as expressions of a primitive class conflict between the interests of global capital and the Chinese laborers. While it cannot be denied that ethnicity played a role in these conflicts, sometimes reinforcing class solidarity and at other times undermining it, there was a fundamental conflict of economic ideologies. In the end, however, it was possible to destroy the power of these societies. On the one hand, by stressing ethnic solidarity, *taukehs* were able to destroy working-class solidarity. On the other hand, the free traders and their Baba allies allowed the leaders a share of the revenue farms and recruited the violent elements in the societies as labor crimps and revenue police (Trocki 1990).

The system of revenue farms, labor control and commodity production flourished into the 1880s. It gave a number of Chinese *taukehs* great wealth, and it promoted the trading interests of the larger European merchants. The system also firmly integrated Singapore and the surrounding Southeast Asian territories into the global imperial economy. As this economy grew, the system of revenue-farming syndicates grew with it. In fact, we may argue that the revenue-farming syndicates provided the points of access for the global economy into the local areas.

However, it became clear at a certain point that the colonial state would not long tolerate the growth of these syndicates and the consolidation of Chinese economic power that they represented. The structures of indebtedness, ties of brotherhood and links of language and culture all shut Europeans out of primary production in the Asian world. Moreover, as they grew, the ambitions of Chinese *taukehs* also grew, until we have the example of the coalition of Singapore Hokkien who tried to capture the revenue farms of Saigon and Hong Kong under one management. This was a combination that could have given them control over the entire opium and coolie trade in Southeast Asia, the China coast and the entire Pacific basin (Trocki 2004).

However, these schemes came too late to stop the juggernaut of European imperial expansion. The Industrial Revolution had given Europe new power to extend its reach around the world and to extract and utilize resources on an entirely new scale. The economy of the revenue farmers was eroded from both directions.

On the one hand, European colonial governments sought to end their dependence on revenue farmers to collect colonial revenues. This came at a time when European governments were in the process of banning opium and other "dangerous" drugs in their own countries. While the pressures from these "temperance" interests did not end the exploitation of local populations through opium sales, they did supply the impetus to create government monopolies, to take the place of revenue farms and to put the distribution of opium under state control. Even where they were slow to actually seize the farms, government officials became more aware of the operation of the farms and kept closer controls on the farmers themselves (Trocki 1999: ch. 7).

At the same time, the ability to recruit labor from India[43] (rather than China) and the consequent ability to control it gave European investors a means of overcoming the Chinese monopoly of labor. Thus, as the rubber industry grew in Malaya and surrounding areas, colonial governments were able to use Indians and Javanese rather than Chinese. At the same time, the need for Chinese labor in the tin mines was filled by the employment of steam dredges and other mechanical devices that opened the way for corporate investment in the Malay states. The British takeover of the Malay states in the 1880s also created a more secure investment climate for corporate plantation interests to extend their investments. These developments strengthened both the colonial states and the European mercantile interests that had based themselves at Singapore.

Chinese capital and Chinese labor were not entirely defeated by the growth of European corporate interests. It seems that much of the capital accumulated by the revenue farmers went to finance some of the first Chinese banks in Singapore and maintained the power of the various Hokkien and Teochew syndicates, although by the early twentieth century the leaders of these groups were thoroughly dominated by locally born Chinese, most of whom had become British subjects. At the same time, energetic recently arrived Chinese turned their energies to the creation of economic empires of their own within the British sphere. People such as Lim Nee Soon and Tan Kah Kee became the new generation of Chinese who made fortunes in pineapples and rubber far in excess of those amassed by European traders.

However, the heyday of this extractive economic system was coming to an end. On the one hand, the Chinese masses were beginning to transform themselves from single male laborers to families with children. They were establishing schools and becoming literate. Newspapers were established, and they found themselves under the influence of writers from China who were motivated by sentiments of Chinese nationalism, socialism and communism. Not only were they concerned about events in China, even though many had decided to make their lives in Singapore and Malaya, but they also began to seek economic and political leverage locally. They began to form labor unions to challenge the power of both the *taukehs* and the colonial state.

The other challenge to the system came from the Japanese. The expansion of the Japanese empire in Asia both inflamed the fires of Chinese and other nationalisms and exposed the weaknesses of the European powers. Despite their most drastic measures, Japanese attempts to destroy Chinese nationalism only drove it underground and ultimately aided the growth of the Malayan Communist Party and the Malayan People's Anti-Japanese Army. By the end of the war, the MCP was the best-organized and most vital force in British Malaya.

In some respects, the postwar era may be seen as a continuation of the struggles that characterized the nineteenth century: that is, the power of the Chinese masses pitted against the alliance of the local Chinese elites, in this case the English-educated, and the forces of global Euro-American capital. This seems to be the one constant theme running through the entire history of Singapore. The years between 1945 and 1965 saw the confrontation between these two major forces. Although the lines of battle were often obscure, with hindsight and the perspective of nearly half a century, it is possible to make them out.

The British returned to Malaya and Singapore to find the entire population caught up in a vast social, political and cultural uprising. The MCP, the forces of Malay nationalism and the various English-educated leaders who dared to step forward were fired by a mix of nationalism, socialism and anti-colonialism. Demands for democratic rule and an end to European occupation confronted the British at every turn. The British possessed a number of advantages, however, not the least of which were the divisions that existed between the Malays, the various groups of Chinese, the English-educated and the various economic classes. They also had their own divisions (of troops), and more arms, more money and the advantages of global leverage. Behind them were the Americans, who, by 1947, had taken upon themselves the task of confronting communism throughout the world.

Singapore was virtually aboil with social and political ferment. Labor unions, political groupings, student groups (in middle and high schools as well as the university) and other movements challenged the status quo. The previous agencies of social control, the colonial police forces and the indigenous organizations typified by the SCCC, found it difficult to regain their former positions of power. Business groups were either crippled by the economic shambles that they confronted in the postwar period, or else they were tempted, through sentiments of patriotism, to support the anti-colonial movements of the Left. Others in the Chinese business community who entertained political ambitions proved to be hopelessly conservative and entirely out of touch with the rest of the population.

Although it was possible for the British to bring their monopoly of fire-power to bear to crush political movements, first in 1948 and again in 1956, it was clear that they could at best mount a holding action. The future would belong to the group that could harness the power of the Chinese masses, on the one hand, and that could gain the imprimatur of the colonial power. Britain could not maintain colonial rule against the worldwide anti-colonial tide, but nor could it afford to leave Singapore in the hands of unfriendly, antithetical forces.

This situation provided an opportune entry point for Lee Kuan Yew and the PAP. As English-educated lawyers, bureaucrats and professionals, they could speak to the colonialists in terms that they both understood. At the same time, with a socialist ideology (which at that time had considerable credibility in Britain), they could gain the confidence of the Left in Singapore and form an alliance with the leaders of the Chinese masses. Labor unions, student unions and the MCP placed their support behind the PAP.

Between 1959 and 1965, the PAP carefully played one group against another. It teamed up with the Left to win the elections and dominate the parliament. Then it sought allies with the British and the Malayans to destroy the Left in Operation Cold Store. It courted the SCCC to gain support among the Chinese-educated for merger with Malaysia. At the same time, it destroyed the credibility of English-educated opponents like David Marshall. Next, when it was clear Singapore had no future in Malaysia (if indeed, the party ever really believed it did) it committed itself to policies that would antagonize the leadership in Kuala Lumpur. It promoted social democracy and multiculturalism, and it sought to form a political alliance with progressive groups in Penang and the Borneo states. Goh Keng Swee was thus able to quietly negotiate an exit from Malaysia before the British or the Australians could move to stop it. Singapore was independent, and the PAP was in complete control.

It was necessary over the next several years for the new leadership to accomplish two tasks. One was the elimination of the SCCCI, as a power base for opposition, and the other was to find a way to rebuild the economy and to employ the Chinese masses. The industrialization policy answered both these needs. Industry could provide jobs for the Chinese-educated workers, while foreign investment, as Rodan has pointed out, could offset the need to form an alliance with domestic capital (Rodan 2001).

By the early 1970s, with the expanding manufacturing industries and the rising oil industry, Singapore's leaders found themselves in an enviable posi-tion. All political opposition had been crushed, the economy was flourishing, and society had been brought almost completely under control by the PAP. Lee Kuan Yew had created a system giving the government virtually complete control over the economy and society. The organization of Singapore Inc., only in its early stages at that time, was already providing the government with enough wealth that "corruption" in the traditional sense of the word was not even necessary. Singapore was so small that, given modern technology, it was possible to keep virtually the entire population under surveillance most of the time.

The government controlled jobs, education, health care and housing. The final irony seems that the city that was founded on the ideals of the Enlightenment, on the idea that the government that governs least governs best, has emerged with what seems to be a new form of totalitarianism. At the moment, it appears an almost unbeatable combination of forces. The problem lies in the question of persistence and replication. Capitalism has shown itself to be destructive of most kinds of social order as it ultimately undermines them.

As Rodan has argued, the current system is under pressure from international capital to dismantle the structures of Singapore Inc. that have provided a means of rewarding its elite class (Rodan 2004). Once the state is no longer able to supply the needs and aspirations of its key servants, it risks opposition. Once the state is unable to assure economic prosperity for the masses, it risks opposition. Although it is successful at this point, the system may need a certain combination of local and global conditions in which to to flourish, and it is not clear that that environment will persist in its present form. Beyond that, however, it needs another generation of talented and adventurous leaders who are capable of seizing future opportunities. One must ask whether the system of governance built by the last generation has left room for another creative generation to emerge.

Notes

Chapter 1

1 D.G.E. Hall has cataloged these misadventures, which included ill-fated attempts at Mergui, Poulo Condor, and Balambangan as well as the unprofitable settlement at Benkulu (Hall 1953).

2 Anthony Reid has noted that Southeast Asian rulers did not usually rely on fortifications of their own, since warfare usually depended heavily on elephants and because they feared losing their forts to their enemies. These rulers were also reluctant to allow Europeans to fortify their own dwellings or factories for fear of not being able to control them (Reid 1988).

3 According to the *Tufhat al-Nafis* (Ali Haji ibn Ahmad 1982), five Bugis brothers had left Celebes with their father, and after adventures raiding and trading in the Gulf of Siam and the Straits of Melaka had joined the Johor ruler in his struggle against Raja Kecil around the beginning of the eighteenth century. At the time, Bugis seafarers were among the pre-eminent maritime forces in Southeast Asia, with raiding and trading networks ranging from the coast of Australia to Burma and from Sumatra to Luzon (Andaya 1975).

4 The *Betsy* was actually a country ship that had been chartered by the EIC to ship about 2,000 chests of opium on its own account (Vos 1993). This was not commonly done, but the EIC was facing a cash crunch and was looking for a quick payoff. For some reason, Captain Geddes lingered overly long at Riau before proceeding to China and thus presented an attractive target. The fourth Anglo-Dutch war (1781–84) presented a French privateer, then allied with the Dutch, and forces from Melaka with an opportunity to seize the ship, with the tacit cooperation of Raja Haji, the Riau Yang di-Pertuan Muda. Vos estimates the value of the opium cargo at between $3 million and $5 million.

5 "Farm" in this context meant a monopoly and had nothing to do with agriculture. Opium poppies were not grown in Singapore, and the opium was therefore imported from India. The "farmers" merely processed the raw opium into smokeable *chandu* for local retail sales.

6 The only exception was during the 1820s, when the colony had a gambling farm. This produced greater revenue than did the opium farm at the time, but it was discontinued because interests in England came to believe that it was immoral to gather revenue from gambling.

Chapter 2

7 Generally speaking, shares were more valuable than wages. However, laborers usually had little cash and thus were often required to borrow against their

shares; they often had to sell them at prices below their market value. In mining ventures, which were much riskier than plantations, laborers were sometimes able to choose. If the mine seemed certain to show a profit, then laborers could ask for shares. If, on the other hand, success was questionable, they would ask for wages and thus be sure of payment whether or not the mine succeeded (Pasquel 1896).

8 Oddly enough, the *Xiao Dao Hui* uprising in China was led by Hokkien members and centered in Shanghai and Xiamen. The rift between Hokkien and Teochew in Singapore arose following a dispute over the spoils of the revolt when a group of Hokkien refugees of the movement arrived in Singapore in 1853. This led to the Hokkien–Teochew riots of 1854. The use of pro-Ming, anti-Qing termi-nology among the members of the *Tiandihui* or Singapore *Ghee Hin* seems to date from this incident, but it is clear that by this time the largest faction in the organization were the Hokkien. Chng (1999) quotes an 1860 government report, which noted that 15,000 of the Ghee Hin's membership were Hokkien, while only 3,500 were Teochew. There were also 4,000 Cantonese, 2,500 Hainanese and 1,500 Hakka. However, Chng points out, out of forty-six (from seventy-three) tablets where it has been possible to identify the origins of the individuals, only two were Hokkien. The majority of those that have been identified seem to have been Teochew.

9 It is of interest that the term "Ceylonese" is still used on Singapore identity cards to designate the race of Tamils who came from Sri Lanka.

10 "Bazaar" or Pasar Malay was a "stripped down" version of Malay that was widely used as a *lingua franca* throughout maritime Southeast Asia. It has a restricted vocabulary, and the use of prefixes and suffixes, the principle form of grammatical modification in court or standard Malay, is kept to a minimum. This was the version of Malay spoken by many *peranakan* Chinese and other non-native speakers of the language. It was also the version that supplied the template for Bahasa Indonesia. Among Malaysian Malays, this form of Malay is considered somewhat crude.

Chapter 3

11 Initially, Penang, founded in 1786, had been one of four Indian presidencies, but by 1824, it had been downgraded and the Straits Settlements were placed under Bengal and were ruled from Calcutta. Melaka had been taken under British control in 1795, during the Napoleonic wars, and was returned to the Dutch in 1818. The Anglo-Dutch Treaty of 1824, under which the Dutch recognized British control of Singapore, saw Melaka returned to the British as the two European powers divided the Malay world between themselves through the middle of the Melaka and Singapore Straits.

12 Raffles' initial treaty of 1819 with the Temenggong and the Sultan in fact only gave the East India Company the right to establish a factory within the Temenggong's domain and gave it possession of a strip of land, several miles along the seafront, extending a cannon-shot distance inland. On 7 June 1823, Raffles and the two chiefs signed another treaty placing the entire island under British rule. The chiefs also gave up their rights to collect taxes and port duties and to receive presents from the captains of Asian vessels. It was not until Crawfurd signed yet another treaty on 2 August 1824 that the full cession of the island took place.

13 Raffles actually set up a system for appointing Chinese kapitans and other headmen for Singapore, but it was never really put into practice (Wong 1963).

14 At the time, they also included Asian merchants in their number. The provisional committee set up to manage the group in 1837 contained an Arab, two Chinese and an Armenian (Buckley 1903).

15 The Sumatran state of Siak was a perfect example of this process. Tim Barnard has described the rise and decline of this state under its "pirate" founder, Sayed Ali, in the late eighteenth century. He was a half-Arab son of a former sultan's daughter who spent several years raiding the coasts of Sumatra, the Malayan Peninsula and Borneo before gathering sufficient resources and reputation to oust his uncle and seize the throne (Barnard 2003).

16 Gutta percha is the latex-like sap of the gutta tree, native to Malayan forests. Its elastic properties were discovered when a sample was sent from Singapore to London and it was reported to the Royal Society. In the 1840s, it was found that the substance was effective for shielding trans-oceanic telegraph cables, which were then beginning to be laid across the Atlantic. There was a rush on the substance, and it proved a source of considerable wealth to the Temenggong and his associates, who appear to have controlled the trade in it (Trocki 1979).

17 It seems that their support was not simply altruistic but that they had significant economic interests involved the success of their candidates.

18 His formal title was "Temenggong Sri Maharaja," thus it could be said that he was simply making a minor modification, but since he realized that Europeans recognized the status of the title "Maharaja," it was clear that he was making a bid for greater respect from the West.

19 The Tyersall palace burned down sometime in the 1920s, but the property, adjacent to the Singapore Botanical Gardens, continues to be in the hands of the Johor family; however, because of legal disputes with the Singapore government, it continues to be disused. The disposition of the Kampong Glam palace was similarly in limbo until 2002, when it was taken over by the Singapore government for a Malay cultural center.

20 While researching an earlier book (Trocki 1990), it became clear to me that discovering the names of each and every Singapore revenue farmer was a difficult task. There seems to have been no fixed way of recording these names in the official documents that have survived from the nineteenth century, and one had to search for stray pieces of correspondence and occasional references in the Singapore newspapers for this sort of information. Often, different sources would provide different information. Finding out the names of people who might have been members of the revenue-farming syndicate or *kongsi* was even more difficult.

21 Kiong Kong Tuan was a native of Penang who had married a daughter of Choa Chong Long, the Melaka-born Chinese who had been named by Raffles as the first Kapitan China of Singapore and who had held the opium farms for a considerable period of time during the 1830s.

22 It is of interest that when the societies were classified into "dangerous" and "friendly" that the surname groups were listed in the "friendly" category.

23 In doing so, he took a lesson from his colleague, Governor Hennessy of Hong Kong. Hennessy had done the same thing in 1878 and had received a major increase in the farm rental when a syndicate of Singapore and Saigon Chinese (including Cheang Hong Lim) lodged a successful bid for the Hong Kong opium farm and ousted the local Cantonese syndicate (Trocki 2004).

24 Yeoh cites issues of the *Straits Times* dated 7 June 1887 and 4 May 1888.

Chapter 4

25 The Malayan Union, a scheme conceived while Malaya was under Japanese occupation, would have swept away the old patchwork of British Malaya, eliminating the Straits Settlements, the Federated and Unfederated States, and the Malay rulers. The latter were felt to have collaborated with the Japanese. It would have created a unitary state in which all residents, Malays, Chinese and others,

would have had equal citizenship rights. Since it was assumed that many Malays would object to this scheme, Singapore was excluded partly because its large population of Chinese would have given the Chinese a numerical majority in the new state. Retention of Singapore also seemed a convenient means of keeping control of Britain's substantial economic and strategic interests in the region.

26 These documents are detailed reports on anti-communist activities undertaken by US State Department officials, USIS officials and CIA operatives in Asia. They focus on the anti-communist situation in Singapore and show the coordinated efforts by the USA to isolate the People's Republic and discredit its policies and those of anyone who showed the least sympathy for or interest in China. The reports are organized according to "Course of Action No. 1" etc. with "Action Taken" and "Result" for each one. For example:

> Course of Action No. 1, Action Taken: None. Congen [Consul-General] officers have encountered no instances during the period under review when it was necessary to urge the British to urge the local government leaders to take a course of action considered by the U.S. to be necessary. Direct contact with local leaders, with or without British knowledge, has been found to be the most effective channel for advancing U.S. interests in Singapore.

> Course of Action No. 7, Action Taken: In two conversations with Runme Shaw, Director of Shaw Brothers, a large film company in SEA, COTTRELL [Sterling J. Cottrell, US Consul in Charge] set forth U.S. views toward the communist cultural offensive which includes dissemination of films. Result: Shaw turned down CC [Communist Chinese] invitation to attend and/or enter films in Asian Film Festival scheduled in Peking August 31. He also refused a commie offer to buy his films for exhibit.

27 The term "Middle Road" simply indicates that the offices of most of these unions were located along Singapore's Middle Road, just off Bras Basah Road near the Kampong Glam district.

28 None of the individuals arrested by Lee Kuan Yew in 1963 during "Operation Cold Store" ever admitted being members of the MCP after their release. Admissions while in custody must be considered as having been made under duress and probable torture. The biographical and autobiographical literature on these individuals includes Bloodworth (1986), Lee (1996), Lee (1998), Harper (1999), Said Zahari (2001), and Tan and Jomo (2001).

29 This PAP statement attacking David Marshall was issued during the 1961 Anson by-election campaign. It is typical of the rhetoric of the period:

> The people of Singapore feels [sic] astonished, at the same time, I believe the people of the Federation would also feel astonished, for a person like Marshall, though we know that he is a first class politics juggler, but we all at least had thought that he would support the Malayanisation. Now he turns a somersault and becomes at present in our country the most unruly and trigger-happy-for-danger racial politician.
>
> (DM83.15, undated statement, *c*. June–July 1961)

30 Maria Hertog was a girl of Dutch parentage who had been left with a Malay family when her parents fled from the Japanese. She was thus raised as a Malay and a Muslim. In 1951, she was 15 years old and had been betrothed to a Malay man. Her European parents had won a lawsuit in Singapore and had forced her return. The case drew considerable public attention in Singapore, and

when the decision was handed down, a riot erupted and a number of people, including Europeans, were killed.

31 In his diary, Marshall described meeting Nicoll after publishing his "I believe" statement. He noted the tense atmosphere and commented that Nicoll was afraid that Marshall would frighten away the expatriates. Nicoll gave him "a lecture on Singapore's role as a vendor of services – efficiency essential, dissatisfied expatriates will leave in disturbing numbers – no adequate domiciled replacements – insists on a need for further recruitment of expatriate cadets though accepts the need 'for faster Malayanisation, as you call it, of the public service.' Does not accept the principle that a competent domiciled officer should receive a post if there is a more competent expatriate available. Chinese only interested in money" (DM7 p.9; 54/10/22).

32 Han Suyin was then married to the British police official Leon Comber and was working as a doctor in the hospital in Johor Bahru (Chan 1984).

33 *Ibid.*, 14 November 1960.

34 Singh appears to have been a victim of his own generosity and sloppy accounting practices, since the money he used was often first taken out of his own pocket and spent on the welfare of indigenous members. The conviction was largely on technicalities.

35 (DM326.9 23rd March 1963 – Report on P.P.S.O. detainees and detention conditions). After searching the law books, Marshall discovered an obscure ordinance that permitted members of the Assembly to visit and inspect prison conditions:

> The men are detained in individual cells, 11 ft. long × 5ft. wide × 11ft. high, with a 1 [and] ½ ft. high barred window at the very top of one side, and a 12" barred window on the other, very thick walls and a 2 [and] ½ inch thick steel door painted white; an iron bed cemented to the floor, with springs, a thin grass mattress, two blankets, one aluminium chamber-pot with cover, one aluminium beaker for water, one electric bulb (40 watts) right against the ceiling. Those were the only prison articles in each cell.
>
> The heat in each cell was oppressive, and I understand that this is particularly so when the cell door is locked and remains locked for 23 hours and 15 minutes in every day. The detainees are not allowed to receive any newspapers whatsoever "not even the Straits Times or Sin Chew." They are not allowed to receive any books from outside, not even dictionaries and engineering or medical books, whether from their own homes or reputable stores.
>
> A few copies of the Bible and some paper-backs and tattered infantile reading matter from the prison stores are available to the detainees.
>
> The detainees are not allowed any writing materials, not even a pencil, but recently they have been allowed once a fortnight to have pen and paper to write one letter.
>
> All meals must be taken in the cells. All calls of nature must take place in the chamber-pot in the cell because the detainee is not allowed to leave his cell except for a period of 45 minutes a day (originally 20 minutes) when seven detainees at a time (originally two) are allowed to file out to the showers and to run about the cement courtyard by way of exercise under supervision to prevent any conversation.

36 DM478.8. Committee of Seventeen, Speeches before UN Committee on Colonialism. 30/7/62, audio cassette.

37   Ah. There you've got a different kettle of fish. Rajaratnam, quite unique, he's dispassionate, cold intellect with an eagle's eye view of international relations. And the exquisite courtesy of a truly civilized human being even if he doesn't like you. His sense of courtesy smooths many a ruffled feeling. He is the true gloved hand. You don't know that there's an iron fist till it hits you. He's a very unusual man, I call him the man with seven league boots because his understanding of foreign relations, his capacity to go to the quintessence of an issue, the very core and to find the simple solution, and to build patiently and quietly.

(DM512, 24 September 1984: 62)

38 The SCCC became the Singapore Chinese Chamber of Commerce and Industry (SCCCI) in the 1960s.

Chapter 5

39 By 2004 there were still only three universities in Singapore. In addition to NUS, there was Nanyang Technological University (actually, the resurrected ghost of Nanyang) and Singapore Management University. There were also five polytechnics and the National Institute of Education. Aside from a few junior colleges, that was the full extent of post-secondary education in Singapore.
40 A Singaporean colleague who is English-educated but who had studied Chinese in Taiwan and considered herself quite proficient in Chinese told me that she struggled to read Hong Kong and Taiwan comic books, while 17- and 18-year-olds had no trouble whatsoever.
41 Ironically, birth control pills and IUDs, methods that would give women control over their own fertility, have been discouraged by the government on the grounds that they would lead to sexual promiscuity.

Chapter 6

42 Garry Rodan has defined Singapore Inc. as "that set of relationships bringing GLCs and statutory bodies under the coordinated control of Singapore's political and bureaucratic elites" (Rodan 2004).

Chapter 7

43 Since India was already a British colony, British administrators and British merchants could control the system at both ends, and the entire process was regulated under British law.

References

Abdullah, b. A.K. (1970). *The Hikayat Abdullah*. Kuala Lumpur: Oxford University Press.

Ali Haji ibn Ahmad, R. (1982). *The Precious Gift (Tufhat al-Nafis)*. Kuala Lumpur: Oxford University Press.

Allen, G.C. and Donnithorne, A.G. (1957). *Western Enterprise in Indonesia and Malaya: A Study in Economic Development*. London: George Allen & Unwin.

Andaya, L.Y. (1975). *The Kingdom of Johor*. Kuala Lumpur: Oxford University Press.

Anderson, B.R.O.G. (1990). "The languages of Indonesian politics." *Language and Power: Exploring Political Cultures in Indonesia*. Ithaca, NY: Cornell University Press, 123–51.

Ban, K.C. (2001). *Absent History: The Untold Story of Special Branch Operations in Singapore, 1915–1942*. Singapore: Raffles Imprint of SNP Media.

Barnard, T. (2003). *Multiple Centers of Authority: Society and Environment in Siak and Eastern Sumatra, 1674–1827*. Leiden: KITLV Press.

Barr, M.D. (2000). *Lee Kuan Yew: The Beliefs Behind the Man*. Richmond, Surrey: Curzon Press.

Barr, M.D. and Low, J. (2005). "Assimilation as multiracialism: the case of Singapore's Malays." *Asian Ethnicity* 6(3).

Bellows, T.J. (1968). "The Singapore party system: the first two decades." PhD thesis, Yale University, New Haven, Conn.

Bloodworth, D. (1986). *The Tiger and the Trojan Horse*. Singapore: Times Books International.

Blythe, W. (1969). *The Impact of Chinese Secret Societies in Malaya: A Historical Study*. London: Oxford University Press.

Braddell, R. (1934). *The Lights of Singapore*. London: Methuen.

Buckley, C.B. (1903). *An Anecdotal History of Old Times in Singapore*. Singapore: University of Malaya Press.

Bulley, A. (2000). *The Bombay Country Ships, 1790–1833*. Richmond, Surrey: Curzon Press.

Butcher, J.G. (1979). *The British in Malaya, 1880–1941: the Social History of a European Community in Colonial South-East Asia*. Kuala Lumpur and New York: Oxford University Press.

Cameron, J. (1865). *Our Tropical Possessions in Malayan India: Being a Descriptive Account of Singapore, Penang, Province Wellesley, and Malacca; Their Peoples, Products, Commerce and Government*. London: Smith, Elder and Co.

Chai, W., Clark, C. *et al.* (1991). *Political Stability and Economic Growth: Case Studies of Taiwan, South Korea, Hong Kong and Singapore.* Chicago: Third World Institute for Policy Research.

Chan, H.C. (1976). *The Role of Intellectuals in Singapore Politics.* Department of Political Science, University of Singapore.

—— (1984). *A Sensation of Independence: A Political Biography of David Marshall.* Singapore: Oxford University Press.

Cheah, B.K. (1983). *Red Star Over Malaya: Resistance and Social Conflict During and After the Japanese Occupation of Malaya, 1941–1946.* Singapore: Singapore University Press.

Chia, L.S. (1989). "The port of Singapore." In K.S. Sandhu and P. Wheatley (eds), *Management of Success: The Moulding of Modern Singapore.* Singapore: Institute of Southeast Asian Studies, 314–36.

Chia, S.Y. (1989). "The character and progress of industrialization." In K.S. Sandhu and P. Wheatley (eds), *Management of Success: The Moulding of Modern Singapore.* Singapore: Institute of Southeast Asian Studies, 250–79.

Chng, D.K.Y. (1999). *Heroic Images of Ming Loyalists: A Study of the Spirit Tablets of the Ghee Hin Kongsi Leaders in Singapore.* Singapore: Singapore Society of Asian Studies.

Chua, A.L. (2001). "Negotiating national identity: the English-speaking domiciled communities in Singapore, 1930–1941." *History.* Singapore: National University of Singapore, 184.

Chua, B.H. (1995). "Culture, multiracialism and national identity in Singapore." Department of Sociology, National University of Singapore, 125.

—— (2003). *Life Is Not Complete without Shopping: Consumer Culture in Singapore.* Singapore: Singapore University Press.

Chua, B.H. and Tan, J.E. (1999). "Singapore: where the new middle class sets the standard." In M. Pinches (ed.), *Culture and Privilege in Capitalist Asia.* London: Routledge, 137–58.

Chui, K.-C. (1991). "Political attitudes and organizations *c.*1900–1941." In E. Lee and E.C.T. Chew (eds), *A History of Singapore.* Singapore: Oxford University Press, 66–91.

Chui, K.-C. and Hara, F. (1991). *Emergence, Development and Dissolution of the Pro-China Organisation in Singapore.* Tokyo: Institute of Developing Economies.

Clammer, J. (1985). *Singapore: Ideology, Society, Culture.* Singapore: Chopmen.

Comber, L. (1959). *Chinese Secret Societies in Malaya: A Survey of the Triad Society from 1800 to 1900.* Locust Valley, NY: J.J. Augustin.

Cooke, N. and Li, T. (eds) (2004). *Water Frontier: Commerce and the Chinese in the Lower Mekong Region 1750–1880.* World Social Change Series. Singapore: Rowman & Littlefield and Singapore University Press.

Cortesão, A. (ed.) (1944). *The Suma Oriental of Tomé Pires.* London: Hakluyt Society.

Crawfurd, J. (1971). *Descriptive Dictionary of the Indian Islands and Adjacent Countries.* Kuala Lumpur: Oxford University Press.

—— (1987). *Journal of an Embassy from the Governor-General of India to the Courts of Siam and Cochin China; Exhibiting a View of the Actual State of Those Kingdoms.* Singapore: Oxford University Press.

Department of Social Welfare (1947). *A Social Survey of Singapore: A Preliminary Study of Some Aspects of Social Conditions in the Municipal Area of Singapore.* Singapore: Department of Social Welfare.

—— (1958). *Urban Incomes and Housing: A Report on the Social Survey of Singapore, 1953–54*. Singapore: Government Printing Office.

Dhanabalan, S. (1989). "Social integration must be maintained." *Speeches*. Ministry for National Development, Singapore. B (1): 3–7.

Doshi, T. (1989). *Houston of Asia: The Singapore Petroleum Industry*. Singapore: Institute of Southeast Asian Studies and East West Institute.

Federal Research Division (1989). *Singapore: A Country Study*. Washington: Library of Congress.

Firmstone, H.W. (1905). "Chinese names of streets and places in Singapore and the Malay peninsula." *Journal of the Straits Branch of the Royal Asiatic Society* 42: 53–208.

Furber, H. (1951). *John Company at Work: A Study of European Expansion in India in the Late Eighteenth Century*. Cambridge, Mass.: Harvard University Press.

Furnivall, J.S. (1948). *Colonial Policy and Practice: A Comparative Study of Burma and Netherlands India*. New York: New York University Press.

Goh, K.S. (1978). Report on the Ministry of Education. Singapore: Ministry of Education.

Gunesekera, M. (1989). "Discourse genres in English newspapers of Singapore, South India and Sri Lanka." PhD thesis, University of Michigan, Ann Arbor.

Hall, D.G.E. (1953). "From Mergui to Singapore, 1686–1819." *Journal of the Siam Society* XLI(1): 1–18.

Han, S. (1964). "An Outline of Malayan Chinese Literature." *Eastern Horizon* 3(6): 6–16.

Harper, T.N.T. (1999). *The End of Empire and the Making of Malaya*. Cambridge: Cambridge University Press.

Jackson, J.C. (1968). *Planters and Speculators: Chinese and European Agricultural Enterprise in Malaya, 1786–1921*. Kuala Lumpur, University of Malaya Press.

Jayasuriya, K. and Rosser, A. (2001). "Economic crisis and the political economy of economic liberalisation in South-East Asia." In G. Rodan, K. Hewison and R. Robison (eds), *The Political Economy of South-East Asia: Conflicts, Crises, and Change*. Melbourne, Oxford and New York: Oxford University Press: 233–58.

Kaye, B. (1960). *Upper Nankin Street Singapore: A Sociological Study of Chinese Households Living in a Densely Populated Area*. Singapore: University of Malaya Press.

Keith, A.N. (1949). *Land Below the Wind: The Author's Life in North Borneo*. London: Michael Joseph.

Kwa, C.G. (1998). "Studying Singapore before Raffles." In S.H. Alatas (ed.), *Malay/Muslims and the History of Singapore*. Singapore: Centre for Research on Islamic and Malay Affairs, 12–37.

Lau, A. (1998). *A Moment of Anguish: Singapore in Malaysia and the Politics of Disengagement*. Singapore: Times Academic Press.

Lee, K.Y. (1998). *The Singapore Story: Memoirs of Lee Kuan Yew*. Singapore, New York and London: Prentice Hall.

Lee, P.P. (1978). *Chinese Society in Nineteenth Century Singapore: A Socioeconomic Analysis*. Kuala Lumpur: Oxford University Press.

Lee, T.H. (1996). *The Open United Front: The Communist Struggle in Singapore, 1954–1966*. Singapore: South Seas Society.

Leung, Y.S. (1988). "The economic life of the Chinese in late nineteenth-century Singapore." In L.T. Lee (ed.), *Early Chinese Immigrant Societies: Case Studies from North American and British Southeast Asia.* Singapore: Heinemann Asia,126–58.

Lewis, D. (1995). *Jan Compagnie in the Straits of Malacca, 1641–1795.* Athens, Ohio: Ohio University Center for International Studies.

Liew, K.K. (2003). "Raised voices and dropped tools; labour disputes at the harbour and naval base in Singapore (1952–1972)." *History.* Singapore: National University of Singapore.

Lim, C. (1994a). "One government, two styles." *Straits Times,* Singapore: 12–14.

—— (1994b). "The PAP and the people – a great affective divide. *Straits Times,* Singapore: 24 and 26.

Lim, P.P.H. (2002). *Wong Ah Fook: Immigrant, Builder and Entrepreneur.* Singapore: Times Editions. Issued under the auspices of the Institute of Southeast Asian Studies, Singapore, and the Institute Sultan Iskandar, Universiti Teknologi Malaysia.

Little, R.E.S. (1848). "On the habitual use of opium in Singapore." *Journal of the Indian Archipelago and Eastern Asi*a *(JIAEA)* II(1): 1–79.

Low, L. (2001). "The Singapore developmental state in the new economy and polity." *Pacific Review 14(3): 411–41.*

Marcuse, H. (1964). *One Dimensional Man.* London: Sphere Books.

Miksic, J.N. (1985). *Archaeological Research on the Forbidden Hill of Singapore: Excavations at Fort Canning, 1984.* Singapore: National Museum.

Mills, L.A. (1925). "British Malaya: 1824–1867." *Journal of the Malayan Branch of the Royal Asiatic Society* 3(2).

Minchin, J. (1990). *No Man Is an Island: A Portrait of Singapore's Lee Kuan Yew.* North Sydney: Allen & Unwin.

Mulliner, K. (1991). *Historical Dictionary of Singapore.* Metuchen, NJ: Scarecrow Press.

Nankoe, H., J.-C. Gerlus, and M.J. Murray (1993). "The origins of the opium trade and the opium régies in colonial Indochina." In J. Butcher and H. Dick (eds), *The Rise and Fall of Revenue Farming: Business Elites and the Emergence of the Modern State in Southeast Asia.* London: St Martin's Press, 182–95.

Pang, K.F. (1983). "The Malay royals of Singapore." *Sociology.* Singapore: National University of Singapore.

Pasquel, J.C. (1896). "Chinese tin mining in Selangor." *The Selangor Journal: Jottings Past and Present* IV(No. 2, 4 Oct., 25–9; No. 3, 18 Oct., 43–7; No. 6, 29 Nov., 99–103; No. 8, 27 Dec., 136–40; No. 10, 24 Jan., 168–73).

Philips, C.H. (1961). *The East India Company 1784–1834.* Manchester: Manchester University Press.

Purcell, V. (1965). *The Chinese in Southeast Asia.* London: Oxford University Press.

Rahim, L.Z. (1998). *The Singapore Dilemma: The Political and Educational Marginality of the Malay Community.* New York: Oxford University Press.

Reid, A. (1988). *Southeast Asia in the Age of Commerce, 1450–1680,* Volume 1, *The Lands Below the Winds.* New Haven, Conn., and London: Yale University Press.

Roberts, E. (1837). *Embassy to the Eastern Courts of Cochin China, Siam, and Muscat; in the Sloop-of-War Peacock, David Geisinger, Commander, During the Years 1832–3–4.* New York: Harper & Brothers.

Rodan, G. (1993). "Preserving the one-party state in contemporary Singapore." In K. Hewison, R. Robison and G. Rodan (eds), *Southeast Asia in the 1990s: Authoritarianism, Democracy and Capitalism.* St Leonards, NSW: Allen & Unwin, 75–108.

—— (2001). "Singapore: globalisation and the politics of economic restructuring." In G. Rodan, K. Hewison and R. Robison (eds), *Political Economy of Southeast Asia: Conflicts, Crises, and Change*. Melbourne: Oxford University Press, 138–77.

—— (2004). "International capital, Singapore's state companies, and security." *Critical Asian Studies* 36(3): 479–99.

Roff, W.R. (1967). *The Origins of Malay Nationalism*. Kuala Lumpur and Singapore: University of Malaya Press.

Rudolph, J. (1998). *Reconstructing Identities: A Social History of the Babas in Singapore*. Singapore, Aldershot, Brookfield (USA) and Sydney: Ashgate.

Rush, J.R. (1990). *Opium to Java: Revenue Farming and Chinese Enterprise in Colonial Indonesia, 1800–1910*. Ithaca, NY: Cornell University Press.

Said Zahari (2001). *Dark Clouds at Dawn: A Political Memoir*. Kuala Lumpur: Insan.

Saw, S.H. (1991). "Population growth and control." In E.C.T. Chew and E. Lee (eds), *A History of Singapore*. Singapore: Oxford University Press, 219–41.

Siah, U.C. (1847). "The Chinese in Singapore, general sketch of the numbers, tribes and avocations of the Chinese in Singapore." *Journal of the Indian Archipelago and Eastern Asia* II: 283–90.

Siddique, S. (1990). *Singapore's Little India: Past Present and Future*. Singapore: Institute of Southeast Asian Studies.

Sidhu, J.S. (1980). *Administration in the Federated Malay States, 1896–1920*. Kuala Lumpur: Oxford University Press.

Singapore (1918). *Proceedings and report of the commission appointed to inquire into the causes of the present housing difficulties in Singapore, and the steps which should be taken to remedy such difficulties*. Singapore: Government Printing Office.

Singapore Legislative Assembly (1956). *Singapore Chinese Middle Schools Students' Union*. Singapore: Government Printing Office.

Song, O.S. (1923). *One Hundred Years' History of the Chinese in Singapore*. Singapore: University of Malaya Press.

Stoler, A.L. (1985). *Capitalism and Confrontation in Sumatra's Plantation Belt, 1870–1979*. New Haven, Conn., and London: Yale University Press.

—— (1989). "Making empire respectable the politics of race and sexual morality in 20th-Century colonial cultures." *American Ethnologist* 16(4): 634–60.

Tai, C.L. and Chen, P.S.J. (1977). *Life and Living Environment in Kampongs and HDB Public Housing Estates in Singapore*. Singapore: Institute of Humanities and Social Sciences, College of Graduate Studies, Nanyang University.

Tan, J.Q. and Jomo, K.S. (eds) (2001). *Comet in Our Sky*. Kuala Lumpur: Insan.

Tarling, N. (1963). *Piracy and Politics in the Malay World: A Study of British Imperialism in Nineteenth-Century South-East Asia*. Singapore: Donald Moore Gallery.

Tay, K.S. (1989). "The architecture of rapid transformation." In K.S. Sandhu and P. Wheatley (eds), *Management of Success: The Moulding of Modern Singapore*. Singapore: Institute of Southeast Asian Studies, 860–78.

Taylor, J.G. (1983). *The Social World of Batavia: European and Eurasian in Dutch Asia*. Madison: University of Wisconsin Press.

Trocki, C.A. (1979). *Prince of Pirates: The Temenggongs and the Development of Johor and Singapore, 1784–1885*. Singapore: Singapore University Press.

—— (1990). *Opium and Empire: Chinese Society in Colonial Singapore 1800–1910*. Ithaca, NY: Cornell University Press.

—— (1993). "The collapse of Singapore's great syndicate." In J. Butcher and H. Dick (ed.), *The Rise and Fall of Revenue Farming: Business Elites and the Emergence of the Modern State in Southeast Asia*. New York and London: St Martin's Press, 166–81.

—— (1999). *Opium, Empire and the Global Political Economy: A Study of the Asian Opium Trade*. New York and London: Routledge.

—— (2001). "Development of labour organisation in Singapore, 1800–1960." *Australian Journal of Politics and History* 47(1): 115–29.

—— (2004). "The internationalization of Chinese revenue farming networks: In N. Cooke and L. Tana (eds), *Water Frontier: Commerce and the Chinese in the Lower Mekong Region, 1750–1880*. Singapore: Rowman & Littlefield and Singapore University Press, 159–73.

Turnbull, C.M. (1972). *The Straits Settlements 1826-67: Indian Presidency to Crown Colony*. London: The Athlone Press, University of London.

—— (1977). *A History of Singapore*. Kuala Lumpur: Oxford University Press.

—— (1989). *A History of Singapore 1819–1988*. Kuala Lumpur: Oxford University Press.

Varma, R. and N. N. Sasiry (1969). *Habitat Asia: Issues and Responses: Volume II, Japan and Singapore*. New Delhi: Concept Publishing Company.

Vaughan, J.D. (1971). *The Manners and Customs of the Chinese of the Straits Settlements*. Kuala Lumpur: Oxford University Press.

Visscher, S. (2002). "The Singapore Chinese Chamber of Commerce." *History*. Amsterdam: 550.

Vos, R. (1993). *Gentle Janus, Merchant Prince: The VOC and the Tightrope of Diplomacy in the Malay World, 1740–1800*. Leiden: KITLV Press.

Wake, C.H. (1975). "Raffles and the rajas: the founding of Singapore in Malayan and British colonial history." *Journal of the Malaysian Branch of the royal Asiatic Society (JMBRAS)* 48(1): 47–73.

Wang, T.P. (1995). *The Origins of Chinese Kongsi*. Selangor Darul Ehsan, Malaysia: Pelanduk Publications.

Warren, J.F. (1984). "Living on the razor's edge: the rickshawmen of Singapore between the two wars, 1919–1939." *Bulletin of Concerned Asian Scholars* 16(4): 38–51.

—— (1986). *Rickshaw Coolie: A .People's History of Singapore, 1880–1940*. Singapore: Oxford University Press.

—— (1993). *Ah Ku and Karayuki-San: Prostitution in Singapore, 1870–1940*. Singapore and New York: Oxford University Press.

Wong, C.S. (1963). *A Gallery of Chinese Kapitans*. Singapore: Ministry of Culture, Dewan Bahasa dan Kebudayaan Kebangsaan.

Wong, L.K. (1960). "The trade of Singapore, 1819–1869." *JMBRAS* 33(4) (December 1860): 1–135.

—— (1965). *The Malayan Tin Industry*. Tucson, Ariz.: Association of Asian Studies.

—— (1991). "Commercial growth before the Second World War." In E.C.T. Chew and E. Lee (eds), *A History of Singapore*. Singapore: Southeast Asian Studies Program and the Institute of Southeast Asian Studies, 41–65.

Wynne, M.L. (1941). *Triad and Tabut: A Survey of the Origins and Diffusion of Chinese and Mohammedan Secret Societies in the Malay Peninsula 1800–1935*. Singapore: Government Printing Office.

Yen, C.-H. (1986). *A Social History of the Chinese in Singapore and Malaya, 1800–1911*. Singapore: Oxford University Press.

Yeo, K.W. and Lau, A. (1991). "From colonialism to independence, 1945–1965." In E.C.T. Chew and E. Lee (eds), *A History of Singapore*. Singapore: Oxford University Press, 117–53.

Yeoh, B.S.A. (1996). *Contesting Space: Power Relations and the Urban Built Environment in Colonial Singapore*. Kuala Lumpur: Oxford University Press.

Yeoh, B.S.A., Huang, S. *et al.* (1999). "Migrant female domestic workers: debating the economic, social and political impacts in Singapore." *The International Migration Review* 33(1): 114.

Yong, C.F. (1992). *Chinese Leadership and Power in Colonial Singapore*. Singapore: Singapore Times Academic Press.

Index